BRITAIN AND THE LABOR TRADE IN THE SOUTHWEST PACIFIC

BRITAIN AND THE LABOR TRADE
IN THE SOUTHWEST PACIFIC

O. W. PARNABY

DUKE UNIVERSITY PRESS

DURHAM, N. C.   1964

Library of Congress Catalogue Card number 64-13987
Cambridge University Press, London N.W.1, England

The publication of this book
was assisted by a grant from the
University of Auckland

Printed in the United States of America
by the Seeman Printery, Inc., Durham, N.C.

PREFACE

This book is an attempt to set the recruiting and use of Pacific island labor into the context of plantation labor in the Empire in the nineteenth century. It is in this context that the British government made its policy decisions concerning the Pacific island labor trade. There were, of course, other influences unconnected with labor questions, which affected policy in this and other matters. One of the most significant of these was Treasury control of expenditure. This is illustrated in some detail in Chapter I.

However, the more immediate field of reference for Pacific island labor questions was the British government's previous experience with the slave trade and Indian indentured labor. In the first instance the government referred problems of recruiting control to slave trade legislation and only slowly realized that recruiting abuses in the Pacific were a new and different problem requiring new remedies. It approved proposals for the employment of Pacific islanders if these conformed to those acceptable to the government of India for the employment of Indian indentured labor, thus overlooking the differences in the circumstances of Indians and Pacific islanders. Nor did the British government appreciate that the values theoretically expressed in the Indian indentured labor regulations—individual rights and freedom of contract—were not of much concern or interest to the government of Queensland, where most of the Pacific islanders were employed. The purpose of the colony of Queensland's labor legislation was to protect the European worker from the competition of cheap colored labor. As the colony enjoyed responsible government, the views of the government of Britain had little practical effect.

My thanks are due to the editors of *Historical Studies* and *The Journal of the Polynesian Society* for permission to publish material that appeared in those journals. I thank Professor W. P. Morrell and the late Professor Paul Knaplund for reading the manuscript and offering helpful advice. From the late Professor V. T. Harlow I learned not only much concerning the technique of historical research, but also to admire his own exacting standards of scholarship.

I am indebted for financial assistance to the University of Melbourne, for it was under one of its traveling research scholarships that I first began work on Pacific history; to the University of Oxford who elected me Beit Senior Research scholar; and to the research committee of the University of New Zealand, and the University of Auckland.

Last, but most of all, my thanks are due to my wife, an historian in her own right, whose advice and criticism has been invaluable, and who has made enjoyable those tasks which would be tedious if done alone.

O. W. P.

University of Auckland
May, 1964

CONTENTS

MAPS

FIGURES

TABLES

INTRODUCTION

There have been two periods in British imperial history when the interest in the native peoples of the Empire has been particularly marked. The first of these periods stretches from the late eighteenth century to the thirties and forties of the nineteenth century, and embraces the movement for the abolition of the slave trade and the anti-slavery agitation. It is also within this period—the last decade of the eighteenth century—that most of the modern missionary societies were founded, and they brought before the public and the government the interests of the aborigines within, and on the borders of, the Empire.

The second period belongs to our own time. It had its beginnings in the last decade of the nineteenth century, and derives less from humanitarianism and evangelicalism with its assumption of the superiority of Christian civilization, and more from an informed appreciation and recognition of the indigenous cultures for their own sake. This period has seen former colonial territories with predominantly non-Western populations achieve full autonomy, and, where they chose to remain within the Commonwealth, equality with other members.

The concern of the imperial government with the recruiting and employment of Pacific island labor falls between these two periods. An opportunity is thus provided to gauge the strength of its interest in one aspect at least of the welfare of natives during the middle period, and to see how much this derived from the evangelicalism and humanitarianism so characteristic of the earlier nineteenth century, and whether there is any evidence of the more informed understanding of the later years.

The Pacific island labor trade also challenged the vitality of the imperial interest in native peoples. Neither the machinery evolved for the suppression of the slave trade, nor that for the administration of Indian indentured labor could be applied in the Pacific, as the island labor trade had certain unique characteristics; it called for an original solution that no merely conventional interest was likely to provide. Some of these differences were associated with the nature of the native peoples and their island communities; others with the fact that they were indented for service in a colony possessing responsible government, a condition which did not occur in respect to Indian coolies until Natal received responsible government in 1893.

I

The sense of obligation toward the native people of the Empire developed from the idea of "the natural equality of mankind at large,"[1] one of the basic concepts of both the eighteenth-century Enlightenment and the Evangelical Movement. Such an idea could be reconciled with the exercise of authoritarian rule over native people only by the doctrine that such power was held in trust, for which those who exercised it were accountable. This principle of trusteeship was first publicly propounded by Burke in respect to India.[2] In 1787 it was given institutional expression in the formation of the Committee for the Abolition of the Slave Trade. When the Committee achieved its object, the African Institute was formed in 1807 to press for the abolition of the foreign slave trade, and in the early twenties the Anti-Slavery Society began its work. These institutions and the missionary societies sought to influence the policy of the imperial government toward native people, and one can see this process at work most characteristically and successfully, perhaps, in the campaign of the Anti-Slavery Society in the twenties.

The Anti-Slavery Society was formed in 1823 with a nephew of George III as president, and Henry Brougham and Thomas Fowell Buxton among its vice-presidents. It had

1. Burke on Fox's India Bill, 1 Dec. 1783, quoted in G. R. Mellor, *British Imperial Trusteeship* (London, 1951), p. 22.
2. *Ibid.*

spectacular success in arousing public opinion, and in bringing this to bear on Parliament. The methods of disseminating
propaganda have been described by Henry Taylor.[3] The
half-yearly reports from the Protectors of Slaves in the colonies detailed "every outrage and enormity perpetrated on
the slaves."[4] Taylor and James Stephen,[5] both at the Colonial
Office, laid these before Parliament, and Zachary Macaulay
"forthwith transferred them to the pages of the monthly
Anti-Slavery Reporter by which they were circulated far and
wide throughout the country."[6] So effective was this propaganda that in a circular despatch to the sugar colonies on
15 September 1828 the Secretary of State for the Colonies,
Sir George Murray, stated that public opinion in England
was so strong that, unless the provisions of the amelioration
plan were adopted by them, it would be impossible to prevent direct interference in their affairs by the imperial government.[7] Such was the vitality and influence of the anti-
slavery movement in its early days.

The missionaries exercised, perhaps, most influence on
policy when Lord Glenelg was Secretary of State for the
Colonies between 1835 and 1839. Glenelg, the son of one of
the original members of the Clapham Sect,[8] was a vice-presi-
dent of the Church Missionary Society; his Under-Secretary,
Sir George Grey, Bart., was a committee member as was also
James Stephen, who became Permanent Under-Secretary of
State for the Colonies in 1836.

In the controversy whether the interests of the natives on
the fringe of the Empire would be best served by leaving

3. Henry Taylor, 1800-1886, author; clerk, Colonial Office, 1824-1872;
K.C.M.G., 1869.
4. Quoted in R. N. Bell and W. P. Morrell, eds., *Select Documents of
British Colonial Policy* (Oxford, 1928), p. xxiii. See also Mellor, *op. cit.*, p. 97
for propaganda work in the country districts.
5. James Stephen, 1789-1859, Counsel to Colonial Office, 1813; Permanent
Under-Secretary of State for Colonies, 1836-1847, K.C.B., 1847.
6. Bell and Morrell, *op. cit.*, p. xxiii.
7. Quoted Mellor, *op. cit.*, p. 97. See also Glenelg to Governors of West
Indian colonies, Mauritius, and Cape of Good Hope, 2 April 1838. Bell and
Morrell, *op. cit.*, p. 401.
8. Charles Grant, 1746-1823.

them to the care of the missionaries or by bringing them under British rule by annexation, Glenelg sided with the missionaries, as is illustrated by his repudiation in 1835 of Sir Benjamin D'Urban's annexation of the territory between the Keiskamma and the Kei on the eastern border of the Cape. D'Urban complained that in this matter Glenelg had preferred information sent from London Missionary Society sources rather than from him.[9]

This period—the thirties—with the success of the anti-slavery campaign, the ending of apprenticeship, and the temporary triumph of the missionary's annexation policy, marked the peak of the influence of missionary and anti-slavery societies on colonial policy.

From the forties, however, there was a perceptible weakening of this influence. The societies were still as active in disseminating information among their members and in placing their views before the Secretary of State; but these were not heeded as they were formerly. Part of the reason for this was in the character of the societies themselves; the emotionalism of Exeter Hall tended to distort and exaggerate facts, and so provided the Colonial Office with good reason for putting them aside. Another reason was that the personnel of the Colonial Office itself were less interested. When Stephen retired in 1847 the main link with the humanitarians was broken, though his successors, Herman Merivale[10] and Sir Frederic Rogers,[11] were men of high principle and had the welfare of the natives at heart. There was a definite bias against the missionary viewpoint when, in 1871, Rogers was succeeded by R. G. W. Herbert,[12] to whose urbanity the missionary enthusiasm was positively distasteful.

9. D'Urban to Glenelg, 9 June 1836, quoted in Mellor, op. cit., p. 252.
10. Herman Merivale, 1806-1874, Professor of Political Economy, Oxford 1837-1842; published Lectures on Colonisation, 1841; Permanent Under-Secretary of State for Colonies, 1848-1859.
11. Frederic Rogers, Baron Blachford, 1811-1889, Permanent Under-Secretary of State for Colonies, 1860-1871; succeeded to father's baronetcy, 1851; Baron Blachford, 1871.
12. R. G. W. Herbert, 1831-1905, Premier of Queensland, 1859-1867; Assistant Secretary, Board of Trade, 1868; Assistant Under-Secretary, Colonial Office,

INTRODUCTION

One can see the weakening of the humanitarian influence
in two questions: the suppression of the slave trade and the
regulation of coolie emigration. In the forties the humanitarians were divided on the question of the use of force for
the suppression of the slave trade off the west coast of Africa.
The Manchester School was able to exploit this breach in
the ranks by joining forces with the pacifist group among
the humanitarians, and opposing not so much the use of
force as the expense involved in keeping a squadron off the
west coast of Africa for the purpose of suppressing the slave
trade. This combination of parties was all but successful in
having the squadron withdrawn.[13]

With respect to coolie labor there was a definite tendency
for the condition of the laborer to become more servile. The
engagement of Indian coolie labor for work in Mauritius
had begun in 1834, and by 1837 had grown to some size.
Brougham and Buxton called the attention of Parliament
to the abuses likely to develop under this system, and secured
the appointment of a Committee of Inquiry and a temporary
ban on the engagement of coolies. When Parliament in 1839
considered an alteration in the Passenger Act to allow the
indenture of coolies to be resumed, the British and Foreign
Anti-Slavery Society—founded in that year, the old Anti-
Slavery Society having disbanded after achieving its object—
petitioned against it. The Society also gave a full criticism
of the provisions of 1842 for the resumption of Indian indentured labor, and with the Aborigines Protection Society,
formed by Buxton in 1837, continued to watch the conduct
of the system; but it was unable to move the Colonial Office
to check the tendency for the condition of the coolie to become more servile.

Again the opposing pressure on the Colonial Office came
from the Manchester School; a secure labor supply for the

1870; Permanent Under-Secretary of State for Colonies, 1871-1892; K.C.B.,
1882; G.C.B., 1902.
    13. Christopher Lloyd, *The Navy and the Slave Trade* (London, 1949),
chap. viii.

sugar colonies was a *quid pro quo* for the abolition of the sugar duties. But in order to ensure that free labor introduced from India would work on the sugar plantations of Mauritius and the West Indies, those colonies introduced penal clauses into their labor legislation. Against these the Anti-Slavery Society protested and the ordinances were disallowed,[14] but the same end was attained by substituting for the penalty of prison, the penalty of taxation. Other restrictions crept in and were not checked until representations made to the Secretary of State in 1869 by G. W. Des Voeux, a stipendiary magistrate in British Guiana, led to the appointment of a Royal Commission in that colony. Its findings,[15] together with those of a similar commission[16] in Mauritius appointed in 1871 on the recommendation of the governor, Sir Arthur Gordon, though not supporting all the charges made about the condition of the coolie, revealed the extent that practice had departed from the principles of free indenture laid down in 1838.

The tendency of free labor to sink toward slavery is even more noticeable in the case of "free" African labor introduced into the West Indian colonies. Although in 1841 Negro slaves freed at the West Indian Mixed Commission Court were allowed to emigrate to the West Indies, the imperial government had resisted any suggestion that slaves should be bought and freed in Africa, and then engaged as laborers for the West Indies. Such a suggestion had been made by the Kingston Chamber of Commerce.[17] But in 1842 the imperial government adopted the resolutions of the Select Committee on West Africa and assumed responsibility for supervising emigration from Sierra Leone to the West Indies.[18]

In the late forties neither Earl Grey, the Secretary of State for the Colonies, nor Merivale, at the Colonial Office, pre-

14. Mellor, *op. cit.*, p. 199.
15. *P.P.* 1871, XX, 483 ff.
16. *P.P.* 1875, LIII, 201 ff.
17. W. L. Matheson, *Great Britain and the Slave Trade 1839-65* (London, 1929), p. 148.
18. Mellor, *op. cit.*, p. 210.

tended that African labor was free, and both justified restrictions on this labor which they admitted would be "highly improper if applied to persons in a more advanced stage of civilisation."[19] Such an admission would not have been possible in the thirties. It has some special significance for Pacific island labor which had more in common with the "free" African system than with any other. But Grey and Merivale stopped short of the recognition of "any regulations which involve the principle of slavery"[20] and the feeling against the latter was strong enough to protest against the French system of "free emigration."

From 1843 the French had bought slaves from the Arabs on the east coast of Africa, set them free and engaged them as immigrant laborers for Réunion.[21] When in 1854 they induced the Portuguese to allow this system to be extended to Mozambique, the British government protested; but the French replied that it would continue until Britain allowed France to engage "free" labor in India.[22] It was on the west coast of Africa that French methods aroused most opposition. In March 1857 the French government made a contract with the Marseilles firm of Regis for the supply of 5,000 Negroes to Guadaloupe and Martinique. In July Brougham raised the matter in Parliament and Lord Palmerston, the Prime Minister, protested to the French government.[23] Later in the year the Anti-Slavery Society led a deputation to Lord Clarendon, the Foreign Secretary, against the French system;[24] and two incidents in 1858, the *Regina Coeli* case, when Negroes rose and murdered the white crew,[25] and the *Charles and Georges* case, when a French ship was seized by the Portuguese as a prize,[26] brought the system to an end.

19. *Ibid.*, p. 217.
20. *Ibid.*
21. Reginald Coupland, *Exploitation of East Africa 1856-90* (London, 1938), chap. vii.
22. *Ibid.*
23. *Anti-Slavery Reporter*, Aug. 1857.
24. *Ibid.*, Dec. 1857.
25. *Ibid.*, Oct. 1858.
26. *Ibid.*, Nov. 1858.

By 1860 therefore, when the attention of the imperial government was directed to the recruiting of Pacific island labor, both the imperial government and the voluntary societies were aware of the problems of administering colored indentured labor. But neither at the Colonial Office nor among the voluntary societies was there quite the same jealous regard for the rights of the colored laborer as there had been in the thirties.

II

A new factor in imperial affairs since the heyday of humanitarian influence was the gradual assumption by certain colonies of responsible government. Until the forties the imperial government's interest in and concern for native affairs had not been complicated by the full jurisdiction of local legislatures in these matters. However, in some of the West Indian colonies the power of the imperial Parliament was restricted by the rights enjoyed by the colonial Assemblies.

The amelioration policy in respect to these colonies provides an opportunity to see the methods used by the imperial government to get this policy adopted by the Assemblies. As Canning observed in 1824, there were three methods which the imperial government might adopt: direct force, fiscal sanctions, or admonition.[27] The third course was tried first. The Order-in-Council of 1824, passed for the crown colonies, was sent as a model for legislation by the Assemblies. In 1831, after repeated failure by the method of admonition, fiscal concessions were offered as an inducement to adopt the provisions of another Order-in-Council. No stronger methods were used—Jamaica passed her own abolition act in conformity with the imperial act—until the Abolition Act Amendment Act in 1838,[28] when the imperial government legislated for Jamaica, authorizing the governor to regulate

27. *Hansard*, n.s. 1824, X, 1105-1106, 16 March 1824, quoted in Mellor, *op. cit.*, p. 92.
28. 1 and 2 Vict., c. 19.

apprenticeship by proclamation. The Jamaican Assembly protested most strongly against such legislative interference, and threatened that "if the British Parliament is to make laws for Jamaica, it must exercise that prerogative without a partner."[29]

Such interference by the imperial government was hardly possible after the grant of responsible government. It had been recognized in the *Report of the Commons Committee on Aborigines in British Settlements* in 1837 that "the protection of the Aborigines should be considered as a duty peculiarly belonging and appropriate to the Executive Government, as administered either in this country, or by the Governors of the respective Colonies."[30]

Yet within ten years of this *Report*, the principle of responsible government had been conceded in Canada. How were the two principles of imperial responsibility for native affairs and colonial self-government to be reconciled, if at all? In Canada there was an interval during which the imperial government continued to act as protector of the Indians, but after 1860 the Canadian Parliament assumed responsibility, and no attempt was made to reserve Indian affairs in the British North America Act of 1867.

This was the general pattern in other colonies to which responsible government was extended. In New Zealand the Treaty of Waitangi in 1840 secured for the Maoris the enjoyment of their lands, and this was confirmed in the Constitution Act of 1852.[31] Also by this constitution a sum of money was provided for Maori affairs which could not be altered by the legislature except by a reserved bill. By his reserve powers the governor could, though in fact no governor did, declare certain areas Maori districts in which Maori law and customs would be recognized. Control over Maori affairs was retained by the imperial government after the

29. "Protest of the Assembly of Jamaica," June 1838, quoted in Bell and Morrell, *op. cit.*, p. 405.
30. Quoted in Bell and Morrell, *op. cit.*, p. 547.
31. 15 and 16 Vict., c. 72.

assumption of responsible government in 1856, but New Zealand made representations to bring native affairs within its own jurisdiction.[32] These representations were met sympathetically by Merivale, who, although recognizing that justice to the natives would be more secure if their affairs remained under imperial control, nevertheless thought that it was "impracticable to suggest the establishment in the same colony of responsible government for the settlers and a separate administration for native affairs under the Home authorities."[33]

Rogers, however, was in favor of "keeping the matter for the present in the hands of people responsible to the Crown."[34] New Zealand did in fact take over control of native affairs from 1861. From this time Rogers felt that New Zealand could be forced to a mild and just policy toward the natives, if the imperial troops were withdrawn and settlers were obliged to rely on conciliation rather than force.[35]

This expectation was not fulfilled. There followed the Maori Wars and the confiscation of the land of rebel Maoris. A proclamation exempting the land of loyal Maoris led to disputes culminating in the Parihaka crisis between 1878 and 1882 when the action of the New Zealand government implied the repudiation of her obligations under the Treaty of Waitangi. Though the imperial government was undoubtedly critical of these aspects of New Zealand's native policy, there was no attempt to infringe the colony's autonomy in local matters.

In 1872 the imperial government again placed the welfare of native people under the control of another colonial parliament when the Cape Colony assumed responsible government with no greater restrictions than the repetition of a clause of the earlier constitution that native people should enjoy the same political rights as Europeans.

32. Memorandum of Richmond, 29 Sept. 1858. Bell and Morrell, *op. cit.*, p. 588.
33. Bell and Morrell, *op. cit.*, p. xxvi.
34. G. E. Marindin, ed., *Letters of Lord Blachford* (London, 1896), p. 223.
35. Bell and Morrell, *op. cit.*, p. xxvi.

In the light of these developments between 1847 and 1872, it is not surprising that when the new colony of Queensland was given responsible government in 1859, no special provision was made for native affairs. The native inhabitants were comparatively few and very primitive, and they provided no problems on the scale of those elsewhere. It was to be the immigrant, and not the indigenous native, that was to claim the Queensland government's attention. But this was not foreseen at the time Queensland was granted her constitution; she was therefore free to follow her own native policy, and short of retracting the constitution granted, the imperial government could use only persuasion if that policy was thought to be unsatisfactory.

The advent of responsible government did not necessarily mean that less interest was taken in imperial affairs by people in England, but it did mean that the imperial government could not directly interfere when voluntary societies drew its attention to the unsatisfactory treatment of native people by colonial governments. It also meant that the imperial government looked to the self-governing colonies to join with it in policing the relations of British subjects with native people in areas outside British territory, but in the spheres of influence of the colonies concerned. The difficulty of getting such co-operation was a further hindrance to effective action. For these two reasons the imperial government appears less responsive after 1850 than it had been earlier to the welfare of native people.

Another factor inhibiting action, which had been present since the end of the seventeenth century, but which became almost a fetish in the nineteenth century, was Treasury control of expenditure. Economy in public expenditure was rigidly enforced; every proposal involving increased expenditure required Treasury approval, and without it the proposals could not be carried out.

It is not surprising therefore, that when the recruiting and employment of Pacific island labor began in the late forties, the imperial government took little action. It felt obliged to put down kidnaping and violence, but it thought of controlling this by the methods it had used for decades to suppress the slave trade. Only slowly did it realize these were inadequate, and then the Treasury refused to meet the expenses of new measures.

The employment of Pacific islanders was thought of by the imperial government in terms of the indenture of Indian coolies. This system had general approval for it was assumed that, since the system was based on a free contract, the interests of all parties were well served. Coolie emigration relieved the redundancy of population in India, it gave the coolie a chance of economic advancement, it helped to develop the resources of the colonies, and it was to the advantage of the employer. The same was hoped for from the indenture of Pacific islanders; but the Colonial Office, in particular, was slow to see that these conditions did not hold. The lack of previous contact with Europeans, the great variety of dialect and language, the absence of any recognized government supervision—all these removed the possibility of the native's understanding the labor contract. He had little or no notion of the character of a labor contract, or what, if anything, he might gain from it. Nor was there any redundancy of population in the islands; on the contrary the emigration of young males disrupted the island communities. Those who did leave, did so more out of naïve curiosity about the world beyond their horizons than from any desire to improve their economic status.

The failure to appreciate these differences is the measure of the failure of the imperial policy toward the recruiting and use of Pacific island labor. It was the islanders' misfortune that this labor trade should occur at a time when, for the reasons stated, the imperial government was not as active in the interests of native peoples as it had been early in the nineteenth century or as it was to be in our own time.

BRITAIN AND THE LABOR TRADE IN THE SOUTHWEST PACIFIC

CHAPTER I. EARLY ATTEMPTS AT REGULATION

As trade and settlement spread through the Pacific islands during the nineteenth century, Europeans used the native inhabitants to meet their labor needs. Natives were employed on vessels engaged in trade and *bêche-de-mer* fishing; they worked for sandalwood traders; and they provided labor for plantations when these became a regular part of the economy of the settled islands and the continental fringe after 1860.

To meet these needs a class of trader arose who specialized in recruiting and shipping natives to places where they were wanted. Violence and deceit practiced by such people against natives first drew the attention of the British government to what became known as the labor trade.

The ultimate solution of this problem was annexation, but the British government sought to postpone this as long as possible by seeking alternative remedies, such as imperial legislation. However no effective legislation was passed until 1872, although cases of kidnaping had been regularly reported from as early as 1842. But this does not mean, as Ward suggests,[1] that no attempt was made before 1872 to control the labor trade. The act was drafted at least ten years earlier, and what is of interest is why it was delayed.

Before kidnaping became a problem, there was in existence legislation for dealing with certain crimes committed in the Pacific.[2] This, together with the slave trade acts and

1. J. M. Ward, *British Policy in the South Pacific, 1786-1893* (Sydney, 1948), p. 231.
2. 57 Geo. III, c. 53 (1817). "For more effectual punishment of murders and manslaughters..." committed in the "South Pacific Ocean as well on the High Seas as on land in the Islands of N.Z. and Otaheite and in other islands and ... places not within H.M. Dominions...." These offenses could be tried by Commissions issued under 46 Geo. III, c. 54, but the nearest colonial courts possessing such authority were in Ceylon. 4 Geo. IV, c. 96, and 9 Geo. IV, c. 83, gave the Supreme Courts of N.S.W. and Van Diemen's Land power to "enquire of, hear, and determine all treasons, piracies, felonies, robberies, murders, conspiracies and other offences" committed within Ad-

treaties, was thought adequate to deal with the offense. When, however, cases of kidnaping were brought to the courts, deficiencies in this legislation were revealed. As early as 1861 the Colonial Office drafted a bill to meet these inadequacies. This was the basis of the 1872 act, although it was not until 1869 that the Colonial Office abandoned the illusion that the slave trade acts could be invoked against kidnaping, and added to the draft bill new clauses making kidnaping itself an offense.

This last consideration helps to explain why a bill drafted in 1861 was not brought before Parliament until 1872. A more important factor was the attitude of the Treasury. Beginning with Godolphin and Lowndes, and hardening into established convention by the nineteenth century, every departmental proposal involving increased expenditure needed Treasury approval. In the mid-nineteenth century, when current political theory ruled that the state should interfere as little as possible in the getting and spending of wealth, the watchword of the Treasury was economy. When the draft bill was submitted for their approval, they refused to make available the increased grant that its operation would make necessary. In such ways as this, the Treasury came to exercise a dominant influence on the policy of other departments— a trend which the respective permanent heads bitterly resented.[3] It was only the shock of the murder of Bishop Patteson, which broke through this Treasury opposition, and brought the bill before Parliament in 1872.

I

One of the first occasions on which Pacific islanders were recruited for regular work occurred in 1847, when some were

---

miralty jurisdiction or in the islands of the Indian or Pacific Oceans not subject to H.M. or any European states, by masters or crews of any British vessel, or by any British subject.

    3. See Sir Thomas Farrer (Permanent Secretary to Board of Trade) to Sir Ralph Lingen (Permanent Secretary to Treasury), 1872, quoted by Sir John Wood, Treasury Control, in *Political Quarterly*, XXV, No. 4 (Oct. 1954), 375-376.

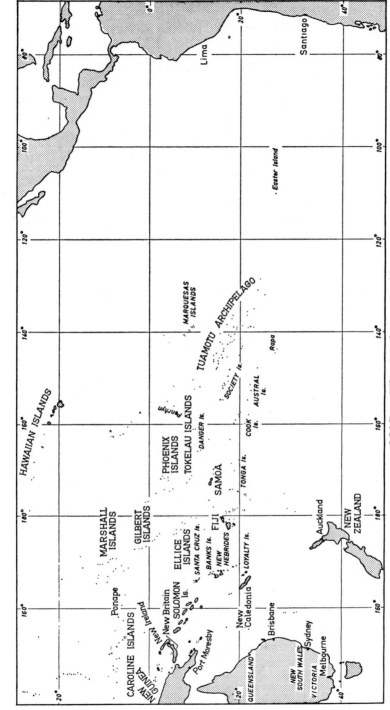

MAP 1. The Southwest Pacific

taken to work as shepherds in New South Wales. Here, since its foundation, settlers had been able to draw on a supply of convict laborers, but the 1837 Committee on Transportation foreshadowed the end of this system. It is not surprising therefore, that squatters, accustomed to cheap and servile labor, should at this time look for an alternative source. The New South Wales squatter without convict labor imagined his predicament to be similar to that of the West Indian or Mauritius planter whose slaves had been freed. It was in fact a Mauritius correspondent who suggested in a letter to a Sydney resident in April 1836 that New South Wales should emulate Mauritius and introduce coolies from Bengal.[4] Some coolies were in fact introduced[5] following a report of a committee of the New South Wales Legislative Council in 1837, but public opposition, particularly from the working class, was so strong that no systematic scheme was ever established.[6]

In 1838 the *Sydney Morning Herald* had suggested that laborers might be obtained from the neighboring Pacific islands much more cheaply than from India.[7] In 1847, with the final failure of plans for coolies from India, Ben Boyd, New South Wales squatter and trader, sent out two ships to recruit Pacific islanders and these returned to Twofold Bay in southern New South Wales with sixty-five natives on board. But rumors had spread through Sydney that the natives had been taken against their will. Although an enquiry by the New South Wales attorney-general dismissed these rumors as unfounded,[8] information supplied to the governor of New Zealand by a Wesleyan missionary, the Reverend Walter Lawry, caused the former to ask the naval officer in command on the Australian station to make an investigation.

4. *P.P.* 1837-1838, XXII, 669, Appendix, p. 174.
5. Messrs. T. Blythe and Sons to Messrs. T. Bettington and Co., 22 April 1836, *P.P.* 1841, XVI, [45].
6. See Paul Knaplund, "Sir James Stephen on a White Australia," *The Victorian Historical Magazine*, XII (June 1928), 240-242.
7. See article on "Immigration Restriction," *Australian Encyclopaedia* (1925).
8. Sir Charles Fitzroy to Earl Grey, 24 Dec. 1847, *H.R.A.* Series I, XXVI, 119.

The results of the enquiry supported the missionary's account that natives taken by Boyd at Uvea in the Loyalties had sought the protection of the native chief when the vessel called at Rotumah, and that shots had been fired by the crew of the vessel in seeking to recapture the fugitive natives.[9]

On receiving this information from the governor of New Zealand, the Secretary of State for the Colonies wrote to the governor of New South Wales stating that it was "the anxious desire of Her Majesty's Government to do all in their power to prevent the ill treatment of the natives of the islands of the Pacific by British subjects."[10] The only practical suggestion made by the Secretary of State was that if the government prevented the condition of natives employed in New South Wales from sinking into one of slavery, employers would not hope for such advantages as to procure these natives by improper means. It is an overstatement to say that at this time the case against the labor traffic had been carefully examined in Great Britain and that from this moment British policy was on record.[11] Nothing more had been said than that Her Majesty's Government desired to prevent the ill treatment of natives by British subjects. How this was to be done was a problem whose difficulty the Secretary of State had hinted at; further experience was to show the full extent of the problem.

II

By 1859 the system of acquiring native labor was extensively practiced among the islands. Toward the end of that year the British consul at Apia informed the New South Wales governor that the Sydney ship *Two Brothers* had kidnaped four natives from Lifu in the Loyalties and taken them to the New Hebrides, where they had worked for twelve

9. See enclosure in Grey to Earl Grey, 10 March 1848, *P.P.* 1847-1848, XLIII, [1002, pp. 82-86].
10. Earl Grey to Sir Charles Fitzroy, 29 July 1848, *H.R.A.* Series I, XXVI, 524.
11. Ward, *op. cit.*, p. 219.

months cutting sandalwood without remuneration; they had then been sold for pigs, yams, and firewood at Ascension Island. The attorney-general advised action in the New South Wales Supreme Court against the guilty parties.[12]

This was possible under 12 and 13 Vict., c. 96, by which crimes committed within the jurisdiction of the Admiralty could be tried in any colony as if they had been committed within the waters of the colony. It was deemed an offense had been committed by the master of the *Two Brothers* under the Slave Trade Consolidation Act, 5 Geo. IV, c. 113 S. 9: conveying persons across the sea in order to sell them into slavery. But the attorney-general recommended that as the colonial court had no authority to subpoena witnesses outside colonial territory, the imperial government should be consulted on the best method of meeting this difficulty. The Colonial Office referred the attorney-general's memorandum to the Law Officers,[13] who found this difficulty insuperable. It was a cardinal rule of British criminal procedure, they said, that the accused should be confronted by witnesses for the prosecution whose evidence must therefore be adduced *viva voce*. The colonial courts could no more be relieved of this necessity than could the courts of England.[14] Rogers, the Permanent Under-Secretary of State for the Colonies, had suggested earlier[15] that those who felt the practical inconvenience of the existing law—the Law Officers of the Australasian colonies—should be consulted; and this course was followed after the negative reply of the imperial Law Officers.[16] Of the replies received from the Australasian governors, those from New Zealand and New South Wales were the most useful. The attorney-general of New South Wales suggested that the consuls in the Pacific should be

12. Enclosure, Denison to Newcastle, 8 Feb. 1860, Colonial Office 201/513.
13. Colonial Office to Law Officers, 20 June, 1860, C.O. 201/513. (Colonial Office and Law Officers hereinafter will be referred to as C.O. and L.O.)
14. L.O. to C.O., 18 July 1860, C.O., 201/514.
15. Minute in Denison to Newcastle, 8 Feb. 1860, C.O. 201/513.
16. Circular despatch to governors of Australasian colonies, 27 Aug. 1860, C.O. 201/513.

invested with authority to endorse and serve subpoenas issued by imperial or colonial courts. The acting chief justice of New South Wales made a similar suggestion, and added a recommendation which for a dozen years wrecked each attempt at imperial legislation on this matter: that the expense of bringing such witnesses before the colonial courts should be met by the imperial Treasury.[17] The New Zealand attorney-general recommended that the governors of the Australasian colonies should have power to issue special commissions for the trial of offenders on the high seas. He also broached the subject of native evidence and suggested the extension of 6 Vict., c. 22, relating to unsworn testimony in the Pacific.[18]

The Secretary of State for the Colonies, the Duke of Newcastle, submitted these despatches to the Law Officers with a request that a bill be drafted to give every "facility which the genius of the English criminal law would allow for the prosecution and conviction of British subjects committing crimes in places where no civilized jurisdiction exists, and more specially of persons who are guilty of outrages on natives of uncivilized or semi-civilized countries beyond Her Majesty's dominions," considering how the remedies suggested by the colonial governments could be applied without risking greater evils than those they were designed to check.[19]

In the succeeding months a bill was drafted and finally printed in February 1862.[20] The second clause of the bill sought to remedy the difficulty of the power of colonial courts to subpoena witnesses outside colonial territory, by granting the courts power to "award and issue a Commission ... directed to a Special commissioner ... who is ... required and authorised to repair with all convenient speed to the

17. Enclosure in Denison to Newcastle, 20 Nov. 1860, C.O. 201/513.
18. Governor of New Zealand to C.O., 23 Nov. 1860, C.O. 209/156.
19. C.O. to L.O., 4 April 1861, C.O. 201/513 (bound with Denison to Newcastle, 8 Feb. 1860).
20. For MS copy of draft bill, see enclosure, C.O. to Foreign Office, 7 Feb. 1870, Foreign Office 58/127. (Foreign Office hereinafter will be referred to as F.O.)

place where such proof as aforesaid is to be obtained and there to examine witnesses and receive proof concerning the matters charged. . . ." The court had power to rule the exact mode of taking such depositions which were to be allowed and read "as if the witness so deposing had been present, sworn and examined, *viva voce*. . . ." This clause was practically a transcript of article 4 of 6 and 7 Vict., c. 98 (Slave Trade Consolidation Act).[21]

While the main purpose of the bill was provided for in the second clause, the fourth clause attempted to meet another difficulty that had been outstanding since the New South Wales courts had been empowered to try offenses committed in the Pacific: the inadmissibility of the evidence of natives precluded from taking the oath in the ordinary way.[22] So often natives were the only witnesses of crimes, and no legal remedy was therefore possible without providing some means by which their evidence could be accepted by the court. By the fourth clause of this draft bill, the supreme courts of the colonies could declare in "what manner the evidence shall be taken of witnesses or deponents who are ignorant of the nature of an oath, and the evidence . . . taken in any such form and manner as aforesaid shall be as valid as if an oath had been administered in the form and with the ceremonies commonly adopted."

These two clauses, if passed, would have gone far toward making the body of legislation since 1824 effective for preventing and punishing crimes associated with the recruiting of native labor. But the bill did not intend to create any new offense. The offenses under the bill were set out in the first clause; they were limited to offenses under the slave trade acts and any offense accompanied by violence which, if committed in England, would be deemed a felony. The *Two Brothers* case which gave rise to this draft bill was thought

21. For the report of the Legal Adviser to the Treasury, Mr. Rothery, on this bill, see enclosure in Treasury to C.O., 6 Sept. 1870, C.O. 201/560.
22. *H.R.A.* Series IV, I, 555. Attorney-General of N.S.W. commentary on 4 Geo. IV, c. 96.

to be an offense against the slave trade acts, but it was not typical of the evils associated with the recruiting of native labor which had occurred in the past and were to recur with increasing frequency in the future. If there was any time limit to a laborer's engagement, or if he was paid anything at all, or taken to work where the institution of slavery was not recognized, then there was no offense against the slave trade acts. And if there was no violence associated with his recruiting, then there was no indictable offense under the acts. Yet, though none of these offenses may have been committed, the native was often taken against his will, and this was bound to lead to retaliation by natives and interference with legitimate trade. From the experience of the next decade the imperial government came slowly to realize that even the minimum regulation of recruiting could not be effective without providing for new offenses at law.[23]

It was the third clause of the draft bill which provoked Treasury opposition, so that its submission to Parliament was delayed for more than ten years. This clause embodied the suggestion of the New South Wales acting chief justice that the expenses of bringing witnesses to appear before the court should be met by the imperial Treasury. The answer to the question who should pay rested on the answer to a further question: which government, the colonial or the imperial, was responsible for the crimes and their suppression? Newcastle, at the Colonial Office, took the view that "the object of the whole act is an Imperial and not a Colonial one."[24] He was not satisfied with the original clause of the draft bill by which the imperial government was to meet only the expenses of such witnesses as were brought from the islands to appear before the court, and he had amended the clause to include all other expenses of prosecution. The Foreign Office suggested that the expenses should be met by the

23. As early as 1832 Goderich realized that there were crimes peculiar to the Pacific area which were not provided for under English law. *H.R.A.* Series I, XVI, 513. Goderich to Bourke, 31 Jan. 1832.
24. C.O. to Treasury, 14 March 1862, C.O. 201/513.

colony in which the offender was domiciled.[25] Newcastle opposed this view[26] as providing a loophole for shifting or repudiating responsibility. He wanted the responsibility to rest definitely with one government, and he preferred that the imperial government should assume it, for if the colonial governments were asked to pay, they might not show sufficient concern in the matter to prosecute at all.[27]

The colonies had no opportunity to take part in this discussion, but the acting chief justice of New South Wales, who happened to be in England early in 1862, told one of the legal advisers to the Colonial Office that the colonies regarded the suppression of crime outside their territory as an imperial matter, and if the colonies were asked to pay the expenses, they would regard this as an attempt by the imperial government to tax them for imperial purposes.[28]

The Treasury took no part in this debate. It pigeonholed the correspondence from the Colonial Office until the following year when atrocities associated with the recruiting of natives for work in Peru reminded both the Foreign Office and the Colonial Office that nothing had yet been done to regulate recruiting by British subjects in the Pacific.

III

When the Peruvian government abolished slavery in 1855, Chinese coolies supplied immediate labor needs. A decree of January 1861 provided for the introduction of "natives of the South Western Islands of the Pacific" for agricultural work and domestic service. Under this decree in April 1862, J. C. Byrne applied for and received a license for six years to introduce such labor. Byrne was an Irishman who since

25. Enclosure in C.O. to Treasury, 4 April 1862, C.O. 201/524.
26. C.O. to Treasury, 4 April 1862, C.O. 201/524.
27. C.O. to Treasury, 14 March 1862, C.O. 201/513. In 1870 the Treasury used precisely the same argument for refusing to pay: if Her Majesty's Government offered to meet the expenses of the act this would weaken the resolve of the colonial governments to put down the traffic (Treasury to C.O., 29 Dec. 1870, C.O. 201/560).
28. Memorandum by Legal Adviser (Bennet), 3 March 1862, C.O. 201/513.

1857 had been a French citizen. He already had introduced 3,000 Pacific island laborers into New Caledonia. In Peru he formed a company to carry out his plan, and by June 1862 had fitted out a ship to carry 170 natives. Natives of both sexes were to be engaged for five years and to be returned at the end of that period, if they so desired, at the expense of the purchaser of the contract.[29]

Other recruiters received licenses, and by the end of 1862 eighteen or twenty vessels were engaged in bringing laborers to Peru. A traffic on such a scale was fraught with danger for the native, and in November 1862 Lord Russell, the Foreign Secretary, asked the British consul at Lima "to watch carefully the proceedings of these vessels."[30]

The need of such a warning was borne out by events. One Peruvian vessel, partly owned by a British merchant, was reported to have kidnaped natives at Penrhyn and Niue islands;[31] two were seized by the French and their masters charged with illegally carrying natives from islands under the protection of France.[32] At Rapa, in the Austral group, the natives themselves seized a recruiting vessel.[33] It was at this island that a Peruvian vessel put ashore three hundred natives suffering from smallpox. Many of them were too weak to move out of reach of the tide, and all but nine either drowned or died from the disease, but not before they had infected many of the natives of the island.[34] Reports such as these led the British consul at Lima to protest to the Peruvian government, which agreed to stop the traffic.[35]

The missionary societies had organized meetings of protest in the Australian colonies,[36] and the Anti-Slavery Society

29. Barton to Russell, 29 May 1862, *P.P.* 1864, LXVI.
30. Russell to Jerningham, 26 Nov. 1862, *P.P.* 1864, LXVI.
31. Enclosure in Young to Newcastle, 16 March 1863, C.O. 201/526.
32. Miller to Jerningham, 3 March 1863, *P.P.* 1864, LXVI.
33. Young to Newcastle, 21 May 1863, C.O. 201/526.
34. Saville to Mullens, 14 Sept. 1871, London Missionary Society, South Seas Correspondence 33/1/B. (London Missionary Society hereinafter referred to as L.M.S.)
35. Ribeyro to Jerningham, 1 May 1863, *P.P.* 1864, LXVI.
36. Young to Newcastle, 20 and 22 June 1863, C.O. 201/526.

had petitioned the Foreign Secretary,[37] who was able to reply that the Peruvian government had ceased to issue licenses to recruit, and that the natives already in Peru would be returned to their islands.[38] Yet more than two years later, the London Missionary Society in Samoa protested that 370 natives taken from the Ellice Islands, and 530 from Niue, Puka Puka, and Tokelau, had not been returned. The Aborigines Protection Society forwarded this information to the Foreign Secretary, Stanley, who on enquiry, found that of 1,200 islanders taken to Peru less than one hundred had arrived back in the islands. An attempt had been made to send back about 871 natives in three vessels. Of 360 sent in the *Barbara Gorner* only 40 arrived alive at the Gambier Islands. Two hundred of the 482 sent in the *Adelante* died of smallpox and were thrown overboard, while the remainder were abandoned on a small isolated island. Of those that remained in Peru, two-thirds had died of smallpox, but one hundred were reported to be living contentedly.[39]

The matters arising out of the Peruvian labor trade had been handled by the Foreign Office. The Colonial Office had no wish to become involved. Rogers, the Permanent Under-Secretary, was on his guard against any suggestion that the most effective action open to the British government was to annex the islands where the labor trade was carried on—a suggestion which he read into the correspondence received from the Foreign Office on the Peruvian labor trade.[40]

But this correspondence, together with that from the governor of New South Wales on the same subject,[41] reminded the Colonial Office that it had received no reply from the Treasury to the despatches of the previous year about the expenses clause in the draft bill. In its long-delayed reply[42] the Treasury refused to meet any expenses under

37. 4 Sept. 1863.
38. F.O. to Anti-Slavery Society, 8 Sept. 1863, Anti-Slavery Society Archives.
39. *Colonial Intelligencer*, Jan.-Dec. 1866, p. 534.
40. F.O. to C.O., 3 Jan. 1863, minute by Rogers, C.O. 201/528.
41. Young to Newcastle, 16 March 1863, 20 June 1863, C.O. 201/526.
42. Treasury to C.O., 27 June 1863, C.O. 201/529.

this clause except those connected with bringing witnesses from the islands. These would be met only if the prosecution had been instituted by the order of the governor of the colony; but as a check on the amount to be spent, and as the Treasury considered the suppression of crime in the Pacific to be the responsibility of the Australasian colonies, it thought the local government should share the expenses equally with the imperial government.

Rogers deplored this "haggling spirit." He believed the imperial government was responsible for the actions of British subjects in the Pacific islands, and to throw even part of the cost of prosecution on the colonial government was for the imperial government to abandon its duties. If the imperial government would not meet the full cost, he would prefer to let the bill lapse.[43]

One other matter had passed between the Colonial Office and the Foreign Office at this time. The Colonial Office— still laboring under the illusion that slave trade remedies could be applied—had suggested that the commanders of Her Majesty's ships despatched to put down the Peruvian labor trade should be furnished with slave trade warrants. In answer to this the Foreign Office had pointed out that "Great Britain has no power by Treaty to interfere with any but the African slave trade."[44]

Because of the attitude of the Treasury, the bill was once again put aside. Though the introduction of Pacific islanders to Queensland was brought to the notice of the imperial government from time to time after 1863, it was not until 1869 that the question of imperial legislation was raised again. In that year the same problems that the government had been considering since 1860 cropped up in connection with three cases which aroused and outraged public opinion and made some action an urgent necessity. These were the *Lyttona,* the *Daphne,* and the *Young Australian* cases.

43. Rogers' minute, Treasury to C.O., 27 June 1863, C.O. 201/529.
44. F.O. to C.O., 25 Aug. 1863, C.O. 201/528.

IV

The *Lyttona* was a vessel licensed under the Queensland act[45] to recruit labor for work in Queensland. In July 1868 it called at Erromanga in the New Hebrides, where a resident Presbyterian missionary, James McNair, accused the master of taking on board nine Erromangans against their will. According to the missionary the information that the natives had been kidnaped was given to him by other natives from the ship. McNair wrote to the master of the vessel, who came ashore, denied the charge, but signed an agreement to land the natives in question. When he returned to his ship he failed to keep his agreement and sailed away.

McNair's account of the incident was the first version to reach the Colonial Office. It followed an established line of communication between the Presbyterian missionaries in the New Hebrides and Whitehall. McNair wrote to the Secretary of the Foreign Missionary Committee of the Reformed Church of Scotland, who forwarded the letter to the Hon. Arthur Kinnaird.

Kinnaird, a Liberal, was the member for Perth. He was a committee member of the Church Missionary Society, the treasurer of the London Missionary Society, and a close friend of Gladstone, who often conferred with him on ecclesiastical matters. Kinnaird began his career in the Foreign Office, and though he left the service to become a banker on his marriage to the daughter of the Quaker banker, W. H. Hoare, he seems to have retained some personal connections at the Foreign Office, for he was always able to get prompt attention there to any matter he forwarded from the missionary societies.

The Colonial Office thus received McNair's account from the Foreign Office[46] a fortnight before the despatch from the

45. 31 Vict., No. 47.
46. F.O. to C.O., 5 June 1869, C.O. 234/23.

governor of Queensland[47] enclosing the report of an enquiry[48] into the affair made in consequence of a letter from Commodore Lambert, the officer commanding the naval force on the Australian station to whom McNair had also written. As the Colonial Office knew the matter was to be raised in the House of Commons,[49] it gave prompt attention to it. Dealtry, the principal clerk, pointed out that there was no legal remedy for a mere act of kidnaping unless it was accompanied by an act of violence.[50] This was the first occasion that the Colonial Office had acknowledged that new offenses needed to be created at law if action was to be taken against kidnaping. Rogers asked that the draft bill of 1862 be resurrected and sent to the Law Officers to see how it could be improved to meet this difficulty.[51]

The Law Officers suggested adding clauses to the draft bill to make it a felony to decoy any native; to receive any native on board without his consent; and to hire, despatch, or fit out a vessel for this purpose.[52] On the basis of these recommendations, Holland, the legal adviser to the Colonial Office, and Rothery, the legal adviser to the Treasury on slave trade matters, drew up clauses which subsequently became law as clauses 9 and 16 of the 1872 act.[53]

47. Blackall to Granville, 16 April 1869, received 19 June, *P.P.* 1868-1869, XLIII, 408.

48. This enquiry by the Queensland immigration agent revealed inaccuracies in the missionary's statement. The natives concerned were examined by the immigration agent, who was satisfied they came willingly. Smith, the master of the vessel, said he had asked the islanders, when he received McNair's complaint, whether they wanted to go ashore, and had received a negative answer. He had invited McNair to come on board and question the natives himself, but McNair had refused. Rogers accepted the findings of this enquiry, though he regretted that no evidence from the natives had been forwarded to the Colonial Office (minute on Blackall to Granville, 16 April 1869, C.O. 234/22). However, McNair's purpose of stirring the Colonial Office to take action against kidnaping had been accomplished before the inaccuracy of his report was known.

49. Dealtry's minute (2 June) on Blackall to Granville, 16 April 1869, C.O. 234/22.

50. Dealtry's minute on F.O. to C.O., 5 June 1869, C.O. 234/23.

51. Rogers' minute on F.O. to C.O., 5 June 1869, C.O. 234/23. Dealtry's minute on Emigration Commission to C.O., 27 July 1869, C.O. 234/23.

52 L.O. to C.O., 11 Jan. 1870, C.O. 201/560.

53. 35 and 36 Vict., c. 19.

The second case, that of the *Daphne*, underlined this new awareness of the need for legislation creating additional offenses by finally removing the illusion that the slave trade laws could be used to control kidnaping in the Pacific. Early in 1869 the *Daphne* received a license under the 1868 Queensland act to recruit fifty-eight natives from the Pacific islands for work in Queensland. Instead it recruited a hundred natives and took them to Fiji, where the vessel was seized and the master and crew arrested by Commander Palmer of H.M.S. *Rosario* and charged with slave dealing under 5 Geo. III, c. 113.

This charge, brought against the master of the *Daphne* in Sydney Water Police Court, was dismissed on the grounds that there was no proof that the natives were brought on board by illegal means, or that they were deported to any place with a view to being dealt with as slaves, as the place to which they were to be taken was not one recognizing the institution of slavery.[54] In the opinion of the New South Wales chief justice, Sir Alfred Stephen, if there was any agreement limiting the time of service or providing for payment there could be no offense under the slave trade acts; in fact there was nothing at all illegal about recruiting labor in the Pacific, unless some act of violence against the natives concerned could be proved.[55] When brought before the Vice-Admiralty Court some weeks later, the *Daphne* was not condemned as a slaver, but Palmer was protected from a claim for damages by a ruling of the court that he had just cause for seizure.[56]

54. Enclosure 15 in Blackall to Granville, 11 July 1869, *P.P.* 1871, XLVIII, 468.

55. Stephen to Belmore, 10 July 1869, subsequent enclosure 2 in Admiralty to Lambert, 1 Oct. 1869, *P.P.* 1871, XLVIII, 79. There were at least two instances before the passing of the 1872 act in which recruiters were proceeded against under the common law felony for kidnaping: *Challenge*—the master was sentenced at Central Criminal Court, Sydney, to two years' imprisonment for kidnaping (see *Sydney Morning Herald* report of trial, 8 Aug. 1871); *Jason*—master sentenced to five years' imprisonment for kidnaping (see Normanby to Kimberley, 26 Dec. 1871, *P.P.* 1873, L, 244).

56. Lambert to Secretary to Admiralty, 6 Oct. 1869, enclosure 1 in No. 30, *P.P.* 1871, XLVIII, c. 399.

It was the view of Palmer's more easy-going superior officer, Lambert, that he should not have seized the *Daphne*.[57] This view was at first accepted by the Admiralty, but the Foreign Office felt that morally, if not legally, the Pacific island labor trade was becoming a kind of slave trade and that pending further legal remedies, the action taken by Palmer should be approved.[58] The Admiralty subsequently showed its approval by the definite act of promoting Palmer to captain and paying the legal expenses he had incurred in the *Daphne* case.[59] Nevertheless, Palmer's action may have done more to encourage than deter labor recruiters. It demonstrated that they had nothing to fear from the existing law; the slave trade acts were not applicable, and the Queensland law applied only to vessels licensed in that colony.

While the *Lyttona* case first impressed on the Colonial Office the fact that kidnaping could not be put down without legislation creating new offenses at law and the *Daphne* case exploded the myth that the slave trade acts could be applied, the *Young Australian* case emphasized once again how useless any law was that did not enable the courts to accept the evidence of natives who could not take the oath in the ordinary way.

The *Young Australian* was a Sydney vessel recruiting labor for Fiji. In October 1868 it had taken on board three natives of Api in the New Hebrides. Placed in the hold, they had adopted such a belligerent attitude that other natives there had fled in terror. The crew had quelled the disturbance by firing into the hold until the three natives were silenced. For this the master, Hovell, and a native member of the crew were charged in the New South Wales Supreme Court under 9 Geo. IV, c. 83, with murder on the high seas. The evidence leading to the coroner's inquest had been

---

57. Lambert to Secretary to Admiralty, 1 July 1869, *P.P.* 1871, XLVIII, c. 399.

58. F.O. to Admiralty, 2 Sept. 1869, *P.P.* 1871, XLVIII, c. 399; minute by Vivian, F.O., on Admiralty to F.O., 8 Sept. 1869, F.O. 58/126.

59. Childers' reply to Kinnaird, *Hansard*, 3rd Series, CC, 1427.

supplied to Thurston, the consul at Fiji, by natives who were on board the ship.[60] Before the trial, the governor of New South Wales asked Thurston to supply further evidence for use at the trial from natives "sensible of the obligations of an oath from religious sentiment and belief."[61] Thurston arranged for two natives from Rotumah to go to Sydney, and one of them did give evidence. He took the oath on the English Bible, stating that he was a Christian and could read the Rotumah Book which was a translation of the English Bible.

It was on the evidence of this native that the court decided that the murdered natives had been taken on board by force—a decisive point which established the guilt of the accused, for if the natives had not been taken by force then the defense of justifiable homicide while resisting attack might have been accepted. On the evidence the judgment was that the natives were murdered while attempting to escape from illegal restraint, and the accused were sentenced to penal servitude for life.

After the trial, the counsel for the defense, Sir James Martin, wrote to the governor,[62] protesting that the Rotumah native was falsely sworn. The Rotumah Book was a translation of the New Testament only, and therefore the native did not understand the full significance of the oath taken on the English Bible. This was a legal quibble; but supported by a petition signed by 1,746 "respectable" citizens of Sydney, and a charge that the case had been prejudiced beforehand by a letter in the Sydney Morning Herald from the secretary of the Presbyterian Missionary Society, it secured the remission of the sentences.[63]

Some such objections might continue to be made to native evidence until the authority it was to have in the

60. Thurston to Clarendon, 23 March 1869, P.P. 1868-1869, XLIII, 438.
61. Belmore to Thurston, 10 March 1869, enclosure 1 in Belmore to Granville, 20 March 1869, P.P. 1868-1869, XLIII, 408.
62. Martin to Governor of N.S.W., 2 July 1869, N.S.W. Legislative Assembly Papers, 1869, I, 330.
63. Belmore-Kimberley, 6 Oct. 1871, P.P. 1872, XLIII, c. 479.

courts was clearly defined. Provision had been made in the draft bill of 1861 for the supreme courts of the Australasian colonies to declare in what manner evidence should be taken from witnesses ignorant of the nature of an oath. As the Treasury had refused to meet the expenses of this proposed legislation, the clause had not become law, and in the *Young Australian* case it was possible for the prisoners' sentences to be remitted largely because of doubt about the court's authority to accept native evidence.

Impressed by the need for legislation and the great publicity given to the *Young Australian* case by the opponents of the labor trade, the Colonial Office once again approached the Treasury[64] with the draft bill amended to include the clauses relating to the new offenses which the *Lyttona* and *Daphne* cases had revealed to be so necessary. In this move the Colonial Office had the support of the Foreign Office, for in January 1869 the Foreign Office had reached an impasse with the Treasury over plans for extending the jurisdiction of the consul in Fiji.[65] The *Young Australian* case had raised again the question of the legal powers of the consul in respect to the arrest of members of the crew still remaining in Fiji[66] who were concerned in the murder of the natives, and the power of the consul to send witnesses to the Supreme Court at Sydney. When these matters were referred to the Law Officers, they had suggested a clause might be included in the draft bill extending the consul's power in respect to the arrest of persons and the taking of evidence.[67] Since 1863 the Foreign Office had been attempting to extend the jurisdiction of the consul, and in view of

64. C.O. to Treasury, 5 April 1870. I could not find this despatch, but reference is made to it in a minute by Holland in Treasury to C.O., 6 Sept. 1870, C.O. 201/560, and in Rothery's report on the draft bill in Treasury to C.O., 6 Sept. 1870, C.O. 201/560.
65. Treasury to F.O., 26 Jan. 1869, F.O. 58/124.
66. The attorney-general of N.S.W. held that warrants could not be issued in that colony for the arrest of persons still remaining in the islands. (Belmore to Granville, 5 Nov. 1869, enclosed in Rogers to Spring Rice, 7 Feb. 1870, *P.P.* 1871, XLVIII, c. 399.)
67. L.O. to C.O., 11 Jan. 1870, C.O. 201/560.

the impasse with the Treasury it welcomed this suggestion from the Law Officers, and gave the Colonial Office full support.[68]

V

With the support of the Foreign Office, the Colonial Office approached the Treasury in April 1870.[69] On this occasion the Treasury refused to allow any imperial funds to be used, although in 1863 it had agreed to share the expenses equally with the colonies concerned. This decision was made in spite of the recommendation of Rothery, its legal adviser on slave trade matters, that the imperial government should meet expenses where crimes were committed by British subjects not domiciled in the colonies. Not only was the Treasury reply negative but it was delayed for eight months. In September it had forwarded without comment Rothery's report made in June,[70] but a definite answer was not given until December,[71] and then only after repeated requests from the Colonial Office. This financial stringency was immediately made clear and definite on a practical issue. At the end of 1869 "Bully" Hayes, one of the most notorious kidnapers in the South Seas, had been detained by the British consul at Apia on a charge of kidnaping.[72] The consul had no means of holding Hayes a prisoner, and as a request to Commodore Lambert for support had not been granted, Hayes had no difficulty in making off. When the Foreign Office received the consul's reports it consulted the Board of Trade and the Treasury on what action could be taken.[73] Rothery reported to the Treasury that Hayes was guilty of slave dealing and could be proceeded against under 5 Geo. IV, c. 113.[74]

68. F.O. to C.O., 18 Feb. 1870, F.O. 58/127.
69. See n. 64, above.
70. Treasury to C.O., 6 Sept. 1870, C.O. 201/560.
71. Treasury to C.O., 8 Dec. 1870, ibid.
72. Williams (consul at Samoa) to F.O., 7 March 1870, C.O. 234/25.
73. F.O. to Treasury, 19 Sept. 1870, F.O. 58/128.
74. P.P. 1871, XLVIII, c. 399, no. 89.

The Foreign Office proposed to send copies of Rothery's report to the consuls in the Pacific, and a set of special instructions to the consul at Samoa advising him to have Hayes brought to justice if the opportunity offered. The Colonial Office was asked to send a similar circular to the governors of the Australasian colonies. When this proposed action was made known to the Treasury, it replied promptly, drawing the Foreign Office's attention to its despatch of 8 December to the Colonial Office refusing to meet any expenses for the trial in Australasian courts of offenses committed in the Pacific, and concluding:

My Lords feel assured that on a representation to the several colonial governments in Australia and New Zealand, those governments will not fail to perceive that both for their own and for the interests of the general public it will be their duty to make every effort to put down this traffic, and an undertaking on the part of Her Majesty's Government to defray any expenditure connected with this service, would only tend to weaken if not put a stop to the proceedings of the colonial governments.[75]

This confirms the view expressed about this time in the withdrawal of imperial troops from the colonies, that with the growth of responsible government the imperial government's burden of financial responsibility for those colonies would be diminished until with separation it would cease. It was Rogers' view that separation was inevitable,[76] but at the same time he believed that the Imperial government had certain responsibilities that might involve expense and that could not be left to the colonies. In a revealing minute on the Treasury despatch he wrote:

This is the kind of letter which makes me think that England is ceasing to deserve the title of a first class power and had better abandon it. Here is a great duty attaching to her, if it attaches to anybody, as the great maritime power of the world, and as the country from whom these obnoxious proceedings directly or indirectly proceed and the Treasury refuse to aid in putting down all these abuses for fear of risking a few hundred or thousand

75. Treasury to F.O., 29 Dec. 1870, C.O. 201/560. Cf. Newcastle's opinion, p. 11 above.
76. G. E. Marindin, Letters of . . . Lord Blachford (London, 1896), p. 299.

pounds. . . . This seems to me governing an Empire in the spirit of a subordinate department of the Inland Revenue Office.[77]

As a result the Colonial Office and Foreign Office turned from the Treasury to the Australasian colonies. A circular despatch to the governors outlined the proposed legislation and asked whether the colonial governments would be prepared to meet the full expenses of any cases tried in their courts under the proposed legislation.[78] Granville also sent a circular despatch to the consuls in the Pacific asking them not to incur any expenses in apprehending persons guilty of kidnaping until they were informed whether the Australasian colonies would bear the expenses involved.[79]

The answers received from the colonial governments were encouraging. As Tasmania and Western Australia did not feel sufficiently involved they refused to meet any expenses; Victoria deferred a decision; but the other colonies expressed degrees of willingness. New Zealand and South Australia were prepared to meet expenses where their citizens were involved; New South Wales offered no objection; Queensland, sensitive to criticism of her own labor trade, professed ignorance of any acts of violence which had escaped punishment, for which the proposed bill was intended to provide, but as a proof of her readiness to prevent any outrages, agreed to meet the expenses of any actions taken in her courts under the bill, provided they were connected with the introduction of Pacific islanders into Queensland.[80]

These replies were received by the Colonial Office in August and September of 1871. In the latter month Bishop Patteson was murdered in the islands. This news made such a vivid impact on official circles in England that Treasury

77. Minute on Treasury to C.O., 30 Dec. 1870, C.O. 201/560.
78. The circular despatch was sent to the Foreign Office on 11 March 1871 for approval (*P.P.* 1871, XLVIII, c. 399, no. 104) and forwarded to the governors of the Australasian colonies on 20 April 1871 (*P.P.* 1872, XLIII, c. 496, no. 1).
79. Enclosure in circular despatch from Kimberley to Belmore, 29 April 1871, *P.P.* 1872, XLIII, c. 496, no. 2.
80. Appendix D, Cabinet Confidential Print, Gladstone Papers, 44618.

opposition to legislation was withdrawn and no recourse to the Australasian colonies was necessary.

Patteson, educated at Eton and a fellow of Merton College, Oxford, had gone to New Zealand in 1855 at the invitation of Selwyn, the Bishop of New Zealand. He was to be responsible for missionary work in the islands and in 1861 he was appointed Bishop of Melanesia. It was he who moved the mission headquarters to Norfolk Island and began the training of native teachers there. He was trusted and respected by all the natives who knew him. Patteson himself had complained that unscrupulous labor recruiters had made use of his good name to persuade natives to come on board their vessels.[81] Some natives from the island of Nukapu in the Santa Cruz group had been kidnaped in this way.[82] When the bishop next visited this island on 20 September 1871, he and a companion who went ashore alone were clubbed to death by a relative of a kidnaped native.

When the news reached the Australian colonies, public meetings were convened in most of the capitals.[83] In Sydney, the Governor himself took the chair and the meeting was addressed by the chief justice as well as representatives of the missionary societies. These and other public meetings in the country districts, and resolutions of the various churches, assemblies, and conferences urged the passage of imperial legislation, stricter supervision by the Queensland government and British consuls in the Pacific, and talks with France on the control of the labor trade to New Caledonia. However, the Colonial Office had anticipated this volume of pressure and moved as soon as it received the details of the tragedy.[84] Kimberley, the Secretary of State for the Colonies, ordered

81. See (extract from *Southern Cross,* 6 Nov. 1869) enclosure in Granville to Blackall, 18 Feb. 1870, *P.P.* 1871, XLVIII, 468, 76.
82. Belmore to Kimberley, 28 Dec. 1871, *P.P.* 1873, L, 244.
83. Belmore to Kimberley, 23 Nov. 1871; Canterbury to Kimberley, 28 Dec. 1871; Du Cane to Kimberley, 29 Dec. 1871; Ferguson to Kimberley, 27 Dec. 1871, *P.P.* 1873, L, 244.
84. Belmore to Kimberley, 22 Nov. 1871, received to 19 Jan. 1872, *P.P.* 1872, XLII, 496.

all other printing to be stopped until the papers relating to Patteson's death were printed. Within a few days he had brought the matter before the cabinet,[85] Treasury opposition was waived, and the draft bill was introduced into the House of Commons.[86]

Knatchbull-Hugesson, the Under-Secretary of State for the Colonies, explained the bill to the Commons.[87] It arose out of the atrocities which culminated in the murder of Bishop Patteson. It was not intended to suppress the labor trade as some of the missionary societies and the Anti-Slavery Society desired[88] but to rid of abuse an essentially useful and good system of labor. Here he quoted Bishop Patteson as saying, "I advocate the regulation and not the suppression of the traffic." The bill was essentially the same as the draft bill of 1862 with the omission of some minor clauses and the addition of the clauses drawn up in 1870 to make kidnaping an offense and to provide for the seizure of vessels engaged in it. In the Lords some additional clauses were added requiring all vessels engaged in recruiting to be licensed and from the masters of such vessels a bond of £500 against kidnaping.[89]

The bill finally received the Royal Assent on 27 June 1872,[90] almost exactly twelve years after the Law Officers had been asked to consider legislation. The act covered the problems which had been raised by recruiting abuses throughout this period: it created new offenses to meet the deficiencies of the slave trade acts; the courts were empowered to compel the attendance of witnesses from outside British territory, and to exercise discretion in accepting native evidence.

In all this the imperial government had been concerned

85. Cabinet meetings, 22 Jan. and 30 Jan. 1872. Gladstone Papers, 44640.
86. 15 Feb. 1872, *Hansard*, 3rd Series, CCIX, 522.
87. *Ibid.*
88. Admiral Erskine moved an amendment to this end and was supported by other members of the Aborigines Protection Society: R. N. Fowler, Sir Charles Wingfield, Thomas Hughes. (Aborigines Protection Society hereinafter referred to as A.P.S.)
89. *Hansard*, 3rd Series, CCXI, 184.
90. 35 and 36 Vict., c. 19.

only with putting down kidnaping. The act had nothing to say about the contract to work, wages, hours, length of service, or the return of the native to his own island. It was a piece of preventive legislation—a substitute for the slave trade acts. While in some ways the imperial government thought of the Pacific island labor trade in terms of the slave trade, in one way it saw a difference—the slave trade was an evil to be suppressed; the Pacific island labor trade, like Indian coolie migration, it was thought, could be of great benefit if properly regulated. But the slave trade acts were supported by international treaties; the 1872 act was limited in its operation to British subjects and British vessels. To be fully effective it required similar legislation by other powers whose subjects were engaged in the labor trade.

Assessed within these limits—the agreed purpose of preventing British subjects from kidnaping natives of the Pacific—the efforts of the imperial government had been strenuous and sincere.[91] The long delay in passing legislation was due mainly to the Treasury policy of economy, although the Foreign Office and Colonial Office were rather slow to appreciate the inadequacy of the existing legislation. The Pacific, like the territory beyond the boundaries of the colonies in South Africa, was one of the many areas where, in that age of economy, the imperial government was attempting through experience to evolve a technique of maintaining order and justice which could be an alternative to annexation.

91. Ward, *op. cit.*, chap. xxi, "The Kidnapping Problem," has nothing at all to say of the attempts of the imperial government to legislate in this matter before 1871. Writing of 1869 he says, "At no time did the Imperial Government hint at the possibility of imperial legislation to control the labour trade" (p. 227).

CHAPTER II. THE LABOR TRADE AND THE ANNEXATION OF FIJI

The main purpose of the 1872 act was to prevent acts of violence by British subjects against natives in the course of recruiting. The imperial government had assumed no more responsibility for the labor trade than that; it had not pronounced on the principle of recruiting and employing Pacific islanders, nor attempted to interfere with or regulate the conditions under which the laborers worked.

In Fiji, however, the imperial government could not avoid coming to grips not only with recruiting abuses but with the administration and supervision of the conditions under which Pacific islanders worked, for in that group of islands Pacific islanders were imported and employed by British subjects. It was not just the labor problem which demanded the attention of the imperial government. It was the problem of administering a settlement in which the majority of settlers were British and looked to Britain to provide the order and good government they so much needed. The problem of regulating the introduction and employment of native laborers was inseparably bound up with the problem of government.

In these circumstances a number of courses were open to the imperial government. The most obvious, but the least attractive, was annexation. This was finally adopted, but only when forced upon the imperial government by the failure of more attractive alternatives: the granting of jurisdiction to the consul, and the setting up of a government by the settlers themselves.

The problem of government was present, and the first offer of cession was made, before the labor trade began. But with the rapid growth of settlement and the development of plantations the introduction and employment of laborers made the problem of government more acute, and was one of the more important motives for action by the imperial government.

I

Native laborers were first imported into Fiji toward the end of 1864. When Manchester's supply of raw cotton was threatened by the American Civil War, Fiji was among those areas considered as potential new sources. Successful cotton production in the sixties confirmed the favorable report made by Dr. Seeman, who accompanied J. B. Smythe, the special commissioner sent in 1860 to enquire into the offer of cession made the previous year. In 1865 cotton exports were £9,000; in 1871 they had risen to £88,920.[1] The white population of the island group which was 400 in 1866,[2] had increased to 1,700 in 1873, of whom 1,400 were British subjects.[3] The estimated native population of the two hundred islands which comprised the group was 160,000.[4] This, one might think, would provide ample labor for the plantations of the white settlers. But the Fijian showed little inclination to leave his own social group and his customary way of life and work continuously for the white man. For this reason, from 1864, natives in steadily increasing numbers were brought from other island groups to work on the plantations of the European settlers.

For a number of years this labor trade was supervised, unofficially, by the British consul. Apart from a few exceptions[5] only British ships were employed, and to these the consul issued a certificate to recruit for each voyage. When the first ship left Fiji in October 1864, Consul Jones wrote to

1. McArthur, *Hansard*, 3rd Series, CCXII, 192.
2. Thurston's report on naval trade and social conditions of Fiji, 1866, *P.P.* 1871, XLVII, 435, Appendix.
3. March's memorandum on Fijian affairs, 7 May 1873, *P.P.* 1874, XLV, c. 983. The figure given by Erskine, 2,040 (*Hansard*, 3rd Series, CCXII, 192 ff.) is probably excessive.
4. Carnarvon, *Hansard*, 3rd Series, CCXXI, 179.
5. March to Clarendon, 17 Dec. 1869, *P.P.* 1871, XLVIII, c. 399.

the Presbyterian missionaries in the New Hebrides, where the recruiting was to be done, asking to be informed how the natives were engaged as he had no interpreter.[6] Later the Wesleyan Mission in Fiji sought the co-operation of the Presbyterian missionaries in the interests of the New Hebridean laborer who migrated to Fiji, but the Presbyterians were uncomprisingly opposed to the labor trade and refused to do anything which might imply acquiescence in it.

It was usual for the master of a recruiting vessel on his return to Fiji to give the consul a list of natives aboard and the islands from which they came. The consul examined the natives, but without the help of interpreters competent in the many dialects spoken in the New Hebrides, it was hardly possible for him to determine whether they came voluntarily.[7] The only guarantee of a fair engagement for labor service was the good character of the master and crew of the recruiting vessels; and nothing better could be said of them than that they "do not appear to be below the class employed generally in the mercantile marine of Great Britain."[8] Some financers of recruiting voyages paid a bonus to the master and crew for each native recruited and thus provided an incentive for unscrupulous recruiting methods.[9]

The agreement between the laborer and the planter was also drawn up or ratified in the presence of the consul. Sometimes the master of a recruiting vessel acted as agent for the planter, engaging laborers on terms agreed beforehand. But other masters acted independently, bringing natives to Fiji to be engaged after arrival. By the agreement the planter paid the passage money, which, though it varied with the

6. Enclosure 5 in No. 9 Admiralty to Murray, F.O., 9 Dec. 1868, *P.P.* 1868-1869, XLIII, 438.

7. For the missionaries' views on this question see answers to a questionnaire sent out by the Anti-Slavery Society in 1871. Printed in the Reverend J. Kay, *Slave Trade in the New Hebrides* (Edinburgh, 1872), p. 48.

8. Draft memorandum, 7 April 1870, prepared for Kinnaird from March's despatches, F.O. 58/127.

9. Evidence of Fred Truman to Committee on Polynesian Labor appointed by Cakobau Government, 1871, C.O. Confidential Print No. 40, July 1874, C.O. 808/2.

demand,[10] was usually from £3 to £5 from the New Hebrides and £8 to £10 from the Gilbert Islands, the second and less important recruiting ground.[11] The laborer was usually engaged for a period of three to five years at a wage of £2 to £3 per annum paid in kind at the end of the engagement and usually in the presence of the consul. The employer agreed to provide food and clothing similar to that of the Fijian native, and to pay the return passage of the laborer at the end of his engagement.

The consul had no legal authority to compel the planters to observe these agreements. Their fulfilment depended on the willingness of the planter to recognize them as binding. And on the whole, until the end of 1868 the consuls seemed to be satisfied with the way the system worked. They believed the native had improved his condition by migrating to Fiji; he was well-fed and housed and not overworked, and was daily brought into contact with a superior race. The health of the natives was reasonably good and the death rate not excessively high. They worked in groups, those from the same village and clan being kept together. Those from the New Hebrides were said to be good workers, but the Gilbertese were considered idle and ill-tempered. But whether any abuse was brought to the notice of the consul depended very much on whether the native was able to make his grievance known. And until he became familiar with his surroundings and the language, this was very doubtful. One feels that the consuls were satisfied only because they had no adequate means of knowing if the system was free of abuse. They supposed the natives were engaged fairly because the crews of recruiting vessels were not molested when they returned to the same areas to recruit. Because some of the natives engaged for a second or third time, they assumed the natives must be well-treated on the plantations.[12]

10. In 1874 it was as high as £10 or £15 for natives from New Hebrides; enclosure, F.O. to C.O., 3 Sept. 1874, C.O. 83/5.
11. March to Clarendon, 17 Dec. 1869, *P.P.* 1871, XLVIII, c. 399.
12. Thurston to Stanley, 1 Dec. 1868, in reply to a despatch enclosing a

But the illusion was shattered early in 1869, and as a result the acting consul, John B. Thurston, refused to issue certificates for the recruiting of labor and thus ended the period of unofficial supervision of the labor trade. The *Young Australian*[13] case was the principal cause of Thurston's decision. The information that disclosed this atrocity came to Thurston almost by chance from certain Tanna natives. He might easily have heard nothing about it. But before the case had been disposed of, it had raised the question of the consul's powers, not only for supervision of the trade, but of his jurisdiction over both British and foreign subjects, as some of the latter were among the accused in this case. There were other secondary causes for Thurston's action—instances of recruiting vessels that brought laborers to Fiji and left without reporting to him, and of fictitious sales of British vessels to avoid British regulations.[14] In view of the failure of his unofficial measures, Thurston asked for an early reconsideration of the consul's position.[15] Other requests that the consul be given full authority to supervise the labor trade came from a meeting of Fijian planters held at Levuka on 20 April,[16] and from a meeting of Sydney merchants with interests in Fiji held on 1 October 1869.[17]

II

Shortly before these requests were received, the imperial government had found insuperable obstacles in the way of

memorandum from the New Hebrides Mission giving instances of abuses, *P.P.* 1868-1869, XLIII, 438.

For conditions of laborers in Fiji, see also Jones to Foreign Office, 18 July 1867, F.O. 58/124; Thurston to Belmore, 30 March 1869, enclosure 2 in No. 4, *P.P.* 1868-1869, XLIII, 408; March to Clarendon, 17 Dec. 1869, *P.P.* 1871, XLVIII, c. 399.

13. See pp. 19 ff., above.

14. Enclosure in Belmore to Granville, 18 May 1869, *P.P.* 1868-1869, XLIII, 408.

15. Thurston to Belmore, 30 March 1869, enclosure in above.

16. Enclosure 3 in No. 8, *P.P.* 1871, XLVIII, c. 399.

17. Enclosure in Belmore to Granville, 27 Oct. 1869; see C.O. to F.O., 7 Feb. 1870, F.O. 58/127.

extending the consul's authority. The question had been
raised in 1859, though not, as in this instance, in relation to
the labor trade. Then W. T. Pritchard, the British consul,
had concluded an agreement with Cakobau,[18] a principal
chief, to set up a court. This action had never been approved
by the imperial government; therefore, in their view, Cakobau had no authority to make a treaty that could be recognized under the Foreign Jurisdiction Act, upon which all
British jurisdiction in foreign countries rested.[19]

After Pritchard was superseded as consul, the Foreign
Office instructed his successor, Captain H. M. Jones, V.C.,
to enquire into both the desirability and possibility of granting the consul jurisdiction in Fiji and Tonga. At the same
time he was warned against action inconsistent with the laws
of his own country or of international usage.[20] Jones drew
the attention of the Foreign Office to United States legislation
giving limited jurisdiction to United States consuls in the
Pacific in lands not under any civilized power.[21] He later
forwarded an agreement between himself and the Confedera-
tion of Bau formed in May 1865 with Cakobau as president.
He thought this government of Fiji had authority to make a
treaty that could be recognized under the Foreign Jurisdiction Act.[22] The Foreign Office sought the opinion of the
Law Officers, who agreed that there was sufficient authority
in this agreement to justify the issue of an Order-in-Council
under the Foreign Jurisdiction Act.[23]

But when the matter was referred to the Treasury,[24] nothing more was heard of it until, on receipt of another despatch

18. The spelling is that used locally in Fiji in which b is pronounced
like mb in timber, c is pronounced like th in thy. The name is sometimes
spelled phonetically, i.e., Thakombau.
19. Pritchard to Russell, 31 Dec. 1859, P.P. 1862, XXXVI. Russell to
Pritchard, 20 Aug. 1860, P.P. 1871, XLVII, 435, 38.
20. Russell to Jones, 14 Sept. 1863, F.O. 58/124.
21. Jones to Russell, 15 Dec. 1864, F.O. 58/124.
22. Jones to Clarendon, 24 Nov. 1865, F.O. 58/124.
23. F.O. to L.O., 18 Oct. 1866; L.O. to F.O., 30 Oct. 1866; see draft from
F.O. to Treasury, 6 Nov. 1866, F.O. 58/124.
24. F.O. to Treasury, 6 Nov. 1866, F.O. 58/124.

from Jones,[25] the Foreign Office reminded the Treasury that over twelve months had passed and no answer had been received. Prodded to action, the Treasury asked the government draftsman to draw up an Order-in-Council,[26] which the Foreign Office later submitted to the Law Officers. On this occasion the Law Officers took a different view. There seemed to be, they said, no treaty within the meaning of the Foreign Jurisdiction Act, and only by straining the act could jurisdiction by "sufferance" be assumed. They advised the passing of a new Foreign Jurisdiction Act, assimilated to the United States legislation mentioned by Jones, to give Her Majesty jurisdiction in territory where there was no government capable of making a treaty with Her Majesty's Government.[27]

The Treasury was informed of this opinion, and agreed to have the suggested bill drafted. But the bill, when forwarded to the Foreign Office, was accompanied by a despatch full of captious objections to it. In all probability, the concluding paragraph contained the real objection of the Treasury:

If a jurisdiction is created . . . courts must be established. . . . These cannot exist without a Government to protect them, nor a Government without taxes, nor taxes without some form of police—and all these being created under British law must . . . in the too probable case of default, be supported from Imperial sources. . . .[28]

When this correspondence was referred to the Colonial Office,[29] Holland, the legal adviser, wrote a long minute disagreeing with the Treasury's legal objections to the bill, and at the same time substituting a new draft bill based on an Act for the Prevention and Punishment of Offences committed by Her Majesty's subjects in South Africa,[30] to which there should be no legal objection. But Holland's minute

25. Jones to Clarendon, 18 July 1867, F.O. 58/124.
26. For copy of draft Order-in-Council, see F.O. 58/124.
27. See minute by Holland on F.O. to C.O., 2 Feb. 1869, C.O. 201/554.
28. Treasury to F.O., 26 Jan. 1869, F.O. 58/124.
29. F.O. to C.O., 2 Feb. 1869, C.O. 201/554.
30. 26 and 27 Vict., c. 35; cf. 6 and 7 Wm. IV, c. 57.

found no place in the reply of Granville, the Secretary of
State for the Colonies,[31] who agreed with the Foreign Office
that Fiji should not be made a British colony, suggesting first,
that British subjects be informed that Her Majesty's Government would not guarantee them against dangers they incurred by settling among savages, and second, that voluntary
co-operation between settler and consul to maintain order
should continue.

His first suggestion was adopted by the Foreign Office.
Clarendon, the Secretary of State for Foreign Affairs, instructed March, the newly appointed consul to Fiji, not to
compromise his neutrality in any way,[32] and asked the Admiralty to request naval officers on the Australian station
to confine themselves to matters which concerned the legitimate interests of British subjects, and to refrain from doing
anything that would give color to the erroneous notions current in regard to territorial acquisition in these islands.[33] The
Colonial Office was asked to write similarly to the governors
of the Australasian colonies.

With regard to the second suggestion, Clarendon replied
that such a course had been tried but had failed.[34] No alternative course was suggested by the Foreign Office, and all
thought of amending the Foreign Jurisdiction Act was abandoned when Sir Edward Thornton, the British ambassador
in Washington, informed the Foreign Office that the United
States act conferring jurisdiction on consuls in countries
without a civilized government was inoperative.[35]

Shortly after this the Foreign Office received full details
of the *Young Australian* case, together with Thurston's appeal to Lord Belmore, the governor of New South Wales, for
extension of his authority, and a similar request forwarded

31. C.O. to F.O., 26 Feb. 1869, C.O. 201/554.
32. Clarendon to March, 19 March 1869, enclosure in F.O. to C.O., 19
March 1869, C.O. 201/554.
33. F.O. to Admiralty, 19 March 1869, *P.P.* 1868-1869, XLIII, 438.
34. F.O. to C.O., 19 March 1869, C.O. 201/554.
35. Thornton to Clarendon, 10 April 1869, F.O. 58/124.

by the planters of Fiji.[36] As an immediate reaction, the Foreign Office deplored the condition of affairs that had developed in Fiji; it wrote asking the consul for full details of the labor trade,[37] and hinted at legislation.[38] However, a month later, the Foreign Office suggested that Belmore, in reply to the planters' petition, might advise the European planters to co-operate with the consul to regulate the labor trade.[39] These new requests did not move the Foreign Office to change its mind and renew its attempt to find a means of extending government to Fiji.

The question of consular jurisdiction now merged with the renewed effort of the Colonial Office following the *Young Australian* and *Daphne* cases to get the draft bill on kidnaping brought before Parliament.[40] The Colonial Office referred the matter to the Law Officers, who had suggested that the consuls, who seemed debarred under the Foreign Jurisdiction Act from exercising magisterial authority over British subjects generally, might be given powers under the bill to issue warrants for the arrest of persons accused of kidnaping, and to send them to the Australasian colonies for trial.[41] This report was referred by the Colonial Office to the Foreign Office. Clarendon, in reply, thought these were very necessary powers, together with some sort of authority to the consul to regulate the labor trade, and stated that he proposed to consult the Law Officers again on the matter.[42] The Law Officers advised the Foreign Office to consult the governments of France and United States to see whether they would allow the British consul authority over their subjects in respect to the labor trade. Clarendon informed the Colonial Office that he thought this neither necessary nor de-

36. No. 28, C.O. to F.O., 8 June 1869, *P.P.* 1868-1869, XLIII, 438. No. 37, C.O. to F.O., 29 July 1869, *P.P.* 1868-1869, XLIII, 438. No. 8, C.O. to F.O., 13 Aug. 1869, *P.P.* 1871, XLVIII, c. 399.
37. Clarendon to March, 3 Aug. 1869, No. 40, *P.P.* 1868-1869, XLIII, 438.
38. F.O. to C.O., 3 Aug. 1869, C.O. 201/554.
39. F.O. to C.O., 2 Sept. 1869, C.O. 201/554.
40. See chap. i.
41. L.O. to C.O., 11 Jan. 1870, C.O. 201/560.
42. F.O. to C.O., 18 Feb. 1870, F.O. 58/127.

sirable, and that he did not intend to proceed any further in the matter.[43] Early in 1871, in response to further requests from Consul March, the Foreign Office revived the attempts to get a bill passed to give the consul jurisdiction, but again this was checked by the Treasury policy of financial restriction.[44]

III

There were two principal reasons—legal and financial—why the Foreign Office did not extend the jurisdiction of the consul so that, among other things, he might effectively control the labor trade. There was no recognized government in Fiji capable of concluding a treaty with the imperial government for the extension of the consul's powers under the Foreign Jurisdiction Acts. Nevertheless, both the Foreign Office and the Colonial Office were prepared on the experience of powers granted to magistrates beyond British territory in South Africa,[45] and on an act of the United States Congress, to pass legislation giving jurisdiction to Her Majesty's Government in islands of the Pacific where no treaty-making government existed. But these efforts were not sufficiently purposeful to withstand the specious legal objections of the Treasury, which wished to avoid any financial commitments. As the Foreign Office and Colonial Office had both agreed that Fiji should not be made a British colony, the new consul, March, who arrived in Fiji at the end of 1869, had no alternative but to follow the policy which his predecessor, Thurston, had discarded as ineffective—the issuance of regulations without the force of law and depending for their effectiveness on the good will of the planters.

March's regulations, issued early in 1870,[46] were an unmodified adaptation of the Queensland act and regulations of

43. F.O. to C.O., 19 March 1870, C.O. 201/561.
44. F.O. to C.O., 2 Feb. 1871; F.O. to Treasury, 29 March 1871; Treasury to F.O., 6 May 1871; F.O. 58/124.
45. 26 and 27 Vict., c. 35; cf. 6 and 7 Wm. IV, c. 57, 15 Aug. 1836.
46. March to Clarendon, 7 Feb. 1870, P.P. 1871, XLVIII, c. 399.

1868.[47] They were far more comprehensive than any previous regulations, but they lacked the first essential—that they should be acceptable to the planters. To the latter they were unnecessarily cumbersome, and they passed resolutions of protest at a meeting held in Levuka on 5 June 1870.[48]

One must question the wisdom of the Foreign Office in appointing March when it had rejected all methods of maintaining order except that which rested on the co-operation of settlers and consul. March was tactless and officious—a man who inspired opposition rather than confidence. While in Fiji he acquired no great knowledge of the islands nor understanding of the natives,[49] but his opposition to the planters endeared him to the Anti-Slavery Society, whose members in the House of Commons spoke up boldly for him.[50]

The Foreign Office approved the regulations promulgated by March.[51] In respect of the protests from the planters, the Foreign Office advised no alterations of the regulations that would lessen the protection offered to the native laborer.[52] But this approval meant very little indeed. By refusing to annex Fiji or to extend the consul's jurisdiction, the Foreign Office might have been charged with complete indifference to the labor trade carried on there. This action saved it from that charge; yet at the same time it feared it might be taken in some places to imply official sanction of the labor trade,[53] and such responsibility it was not prepared to accept. By approving March's regulations without officially recognizing them, the Foreign Office agreed both that something ought to be done and that someone else ought to do it.

For a short time March issued licenses under the regulations until this became pointless because of the general disregard of them. Early in 1871, after the failure of the

47. See chaps. iii, iv, and v.
48. March to Clarendon, 14 June 1870, *P.P.* 1871, XLVIII, c. 399.
49. See Goodenough and Layard Report, 1874, XLV, c. 1011, 3.
50. *Hansard*, 3rd Series, CCXVI, 934 ff.
51. Granville to March, 8 Sept. 1870, F.O. 58/128.
52. Granville to March, 10 Oct. 1870, F.O. 58/128.
53. See enclosure, C.O. to F.O., 24 Oct. 1871, *P.P.* 1872, XLIII, c. 496.

renewed effort of the Foreign Office to get a bill before Parliament to extend the consul's jurisdiction, the Foreign Office directed March to enforce the regulations.[54] But any chance of their being observed declined as the relations between the consul and the settlers deteriorated. The breach between them became complete with the formation in June 1871 of a ministry of five Europeans and two natives under the 1867 constitution by which Cakobau had been proclaimed King of Fiji.

This government assumed responsibility for the labor trade, and the Foreign Office hoped that here it had found someone to act for it. The first actions of the Cakobau government promised well. A committee was appointed to enquire into the labor trade, and this was followed by an act. The committee collected much evidence from those engaged in recruiting labor.[55] Its report hinted that the Fijian abuses were no worse and often not as bad as those of the Queensland trade. This was one instance of a general practice—the deliberate confusion of the Queensland and Fiji labor trades in order to shift the responsibility one way or the other. The provisions of the 1871 act[56] were no less comprehensive than the Queensland legislation, and the amending act[57] passed in the following year was an advance on the contemporary Queensland act in limiting the hours of work of the laborer. But the question at issue was not so much the content of the legislation as the capacity of the government to enforce it.

By the end of 1871 the imperial government had decided to recognize the Fiji government, and had advised the Australian colonies to do the same,[58] although the latter, at their Inter-colonial Conference in 1870, were more in favor of annexation than recognition of the Fiji government. But the imperial government made the recognition dependent

54. Evidence of Towson to Cakobau Committee on Polynesian Labor, C.O. Confidential Print No. 40, July 1874, C.O. 808/2.
55. C.O. Confidential Print No. 40, July 1874, C.O. 808/2.
56. Cakobau Rex. 8, 14 Dec. 1871.
57. Cakobau Rex. 34, 23 July 1872.
58. Kimberley to Belmore, 3 Nov. 1871, P.P. 1872, XLIII, c. 509.

on the making and enforcing by the *de facto* government of satisfactory regulations for the import and employment of laborers.[59]

The two labor laws Cakobau Rex 8 of 1871 and Cakobau Rex 34 of 1872 were forwarded to the Colonial Office,[60] where R. G. W. Herbert, who had succeeded Rogers as Permanent Under-Secretary of State for the Colonies, regarded the first as "just about as good as that of this country or of any other colony," and a "complete answer to those who have urged that we neglect a high duty in hesitating to make Fiji a colony."[61] But a few months later Kimberley, who agreed with Herbert, acknowledged that "a law may look very plausible on paper but everything depends on the mode of its enforcement."[62] It soon became evident that the condition of immigrant laborers was no better and probably worse than it had been before the legislation of the Cakobau government.

Early in 1872 the *Carl* case occurred.[63] It was an even more atrocious case of the murder of kidnaped natives than the *Young Australian* case. There were numerous instances of violent treatment of natives on plantations.[64] The condition of the laborers was made worse by a financial crisis in

59. Minute by Kimberley on Stephen to Kimberley, 19 April 1872, C.O. 201/569; also minute by Kimberley on No. 2067, C.O. 234/31.

60. Thurston to Kimberley, 24 June 1872; Thurston to Kimberley, 11 Sept. 1872, C.O. 83/2.

61. Minute by Herbert on Thurston to Kimberley, 24 June 1872, C.O. 83/2.

62. Minute by Kimberley on Thurston to Kimberley, 11 Sept. 1872, C.O. 83/2.

63. Enclosures in F.O. to C.O., 22 Oct. 1872, *P.P.* 1873, L, 244. The accused were tried in Melbourne and found guilty of manslaughter and sentenced to fifteen years' imprisonment under the Imperial Act 12 and 13 Vict., c. 96. They were sent to prison, not remanded, while enquiries were made on the right of the colonial court to carry out the sentence. On appeal to the Supreme Court the prisoners were discharged as illegally detained. The case was taken to the Privy Council, which ruled that the Victorian Supreme Court had power to carry out the sentence, but if it had any doubts it should have remanded the prisoners until application had been made to the Home Secretary. The Privy Council advised that the order of discharge should be reserved as improperly made. However, the prisoners were not recaptured.

64. See *Anti-Slavery Reporter*, July 1872, Oct. 1872, April 1873. Some of these accounts are based on official reports.

1873 and 1874 in which many of the planters were unable either to pay the wages of the natives at the end of their agreement or to return them to their native islands. In these circumstances the imperial government was forced to reconsider its earlier decision that Fiji should not be made a British colony.

IV

The need to control the labor trade was only one of the reasons why the imperial government annexed Fiji, but one which increased in importance between the first offer of cession in 1859 and the eventual annexation in 1874. The arguments advanced in 1859 were almost exclusively economic or strategic; native affairs were quite secondary, and had not been complicated by the introduction of laborers from other island groups. From time to time in the succeeding years the Colonial Office rejected proposals for annexation made as one means of curbing the disorders in the islands. In 1870 another offer of cession came from the British residents and principal chiefs, but to this the imperial government did not reply.[65] However, the question was raised again when the Australian Intercolonial Conference of 1870 asked the imperial government to declare Fiji a British protectorate. This request was refused.[66] At this time the imperial government had alternative plans for meeting the problem of government in Fiji. It was considering how the consul's jurisdiction might be extended, and it hoped the European settlers in Fiji would set up their own government.

Early in 1871 Belmore, the governor of New South Wales, forwarded to Kimberley a suggestion from the government of Fiji that it should be placed under the protection of the independent Kingdom of Hawaii.[67] Although Kimberley

65. Enclosure in Robinson to Carnarvon, 3 Oct. 1874, *P.P.* 1875, LII, c. 1114; *Hansard*, 3rd Series, CCXVI, 934 ff.
66. Kimberley to Canterbury, 16 March 1871, *P.P.* 1871, XLVII, 435.
67. Belmore to Kimberley, 28 April 1871, C.O. 201/563.

dismissed the idea of a Hawaiian protectorate, he proposed that Fiji might be offered to New South Wales if both houses of the New South Wales Parliament were willing to accept it.[68] It was Lowe, chancellor of the exchequer and a former member of the New South Wales Legislative Council, and Cowper, the New South Wales agent general in London, who had made this suggestion to Kimberley.[69] Kimberley had no objection to it, although some might question the wisdom of placing a native community under the control of a colony with responsible government. But, Kimberley pointed out, the imperial government had done that in Canada, and it was about to grant responsible government and withdraw its troops from the Cape, so why not allow New South Wales to govern Fiji?

This statement has significance for the labor trade to Queensland. For some three or four years the imperial government had been pressing the responsible government of that colony to give adequate protection to the immigrant Pacific islanders. If the imperial government regretted that it could not interfere more directly for the protection of the laborers, Kimberley would hardly counsel the creation of a similar situation in Fiji, unless he was prepared to subordinate the welfare of the natives to expediency of policy.

New South Wales had no desire to assume responsibility for Fiji,[70] and was very reluctant to acknowledge the *de facto* government, a course which the imperial government advised in the event of New South Wales' refusing to annex Fiji.[71]

The failure to reach any satisfactory solution to the problem of government in Fiji brought together in England various interested groups who for the next two years pressed the imperial government either to annex Fiji or declare a pro-

68. *Ibid.* Minute by Kimberley.
69. Kimberley to Gladstone, 26 July 1871, Gladstone Papers CXXXIX, f. 187-194.
70. Belmore to Kimberley, 9 Aug. 1871, *P.P.* 1872, XLIII, c. 509.
71. Kimberley to Belmore, 3 Nov. 1871, *P.P.* 1872, XLIII, c. 509.

tectorate over it. The author of this movement was William McArthur. McArthur was a curious blend of all the different interests that gave him support. He was a committee member of the Aborigines Protection Society. As a Wesleyan who had achieved high office—he was M.P. for Lambeth and was later Lord Mayor of London—he received many letters from the Wesleyan missionaries about the state of affairs in Fiji. He was also a banker and head of a trading firm with interests in Samoa, on behalf of which he later applied for a license to recruit Pacific island labor.[72] As he had business interests in Australia and New Zealand, McArthur appreciated the motives that had led the Australasian colonies to press the imperial government to annex Fiji.

All these interests—humanitarian, missionary, economic, and strategic—McArthur brought together by the formation of the Fiji Committee, of which he was chairman, and F. W. Chesson, of the Aborigines Protection Society, secretary.[73] The humanitarian and missionary representation in this movement was perhaps stronger than any one of the other interests, and it placed prominently in the foreground, as a reason for annexation, the need to control or abolish the labor trade. These various interests worked through deputations to the Secretary of State and debates in Parliament.

In June 1872 McArthur introduced a motion in the House of Commons[74] that Britain should establish a protectorate in Fiji. He pointed out how wrong time had proved the report of Smythe, following the 1859 offer of cession, that annexation was neither economically nor strategically desirable. To this he added that Britain, as a Christian nation that had spared no expense to suppress the African slave trade, was bound to proclaim a protectorate over Fiji as the only effective means of dealing with the labor trade. In this debate McArthur received support from Admiral Erskine, E. H. Eastwick, and Sir Charles Wingfield, all members of

72. Minute on Loftus to Derby, 9 June 1884, C.O. 201/601.
73. Fiji Committee to C.O., 3 July 1874, C.O. 83/5.
74. *Hansard*, 3rd Series, CCXII, 192 ff.

the Aborigines Protection Society, and from the Hon. Arthur Kinnaird, a member of the Church Missionary Society and the London Missionary Society.

Hugessen, the Under-Secretary of State for the Colonies, and Gladstone replied to the motion. Hugessen personally favored annexation, but here he joined Gladstone in opposition, first because no clear wish had been expressed by the inhabitants themselves, and second because the government was not prepared to accept the expense of creating a new colony.

In the course of the debate Eastwick questioned whether annexation would be any more expensive than the additional measures that would be necessary without it for enforcing the 1872 kidnaping act. The same view was expressed by Hugessen[75] at the Colonial Office early the following year when Sir Hercules Robinson, who had succeeded Belmore as governor of New South Wales, enquired whether the imperial government was prepared to assume responsibility for Fiji in view of a warning he had received of the imminent collapse of the Fiji government. And on the same matter Kimberley wrote to Gladstone:

I have been for some time inclining to the opinion that we ought to accept the sovereignty of Fiji. We are and shall be at great expense in attempting to put down kidnapping in the South Sea Islands. If Fiji were under British rule we should cut away the root of the evil....[76]

Early in 1873 it was therefore clear that Kimberley and Hugessen were in favor of annexing Fiji and that the need for controlling the labor trade was a prominent motive with them. With Herbert, the Permanent Under-Secretary of State for the Colonies, on the other hand, it seemed to count little. He opposed annexation.[77] He thought it would be of little

75. Minute on Robinson to Kimberley (telegram), 20 Feb. 1873, C.O. 201/573.
76. Kimberley to Gladstone, 24 Feb. 1873, Gladstone Papers, 44225.
77. Minute on Robinson to Kimberley (telegram), 20 Feb. 1873, C.O. 201/573.

help in controlling the labor trade, which would move to other unannexed islands, the imperial government then being urged to annex these.[78]

Gladstone wished to defer the matter.[79] The Liberal party was seriously divided at this time and he was considering a dissolution. However, he reluctantly agreed that the question should come before the cabinet,[80] where it was decided to appoint James Goodenough, the Commodore of the Australian naval station, and E. L. Layard, the consul in Fiji, to report on which of the various alternatives—consular jurisdiction, the recognition of the *de facto* government, a protectorate, or annexation—the imperial government should adopt.[81]

Just before this cabinet meeting a deputation from the Aborigines Protection Society and the Royal Colonial Institute had urged upon Kimberley the annexation of Fiji,[82] and a few days after the cabinet meeting McArthur moved in the House[83] for the declaration of a protectorate or annexation. He advanced the same arguments as he had used twelve months earlier, adding that he thought the passage of time had strengthened them. They were dismissed by Gladstone, who professed more faith than McArthur in the ability of the *de facto* government to carry on satisfactorily. But Gladstone announced the proposed enquiry of Goodenough and Layard.

Goodenough joined Layard in Fiji in November 1873. They were criticized by Herbert for exceeding their instructions by inviting the king and principal chiefs of Fiji to give an expression of opinion in favor of annexation.[84] They

78. Minute on F.O. to C.O., 5 May 1873, C.O. 83/4.
79. Gladstone to Kimberley, 25 Feb. 1873, Kimberley Papers.
80. 7 June 1873, Cabinet minute, Gladstone Papers, 44641.
81. Instructions to Goodenough and Layard, *P.P.* 1874, XLV, c. 983.
82. *Australian & New South Wales Gazette*, London, 17 May 1873, quoted by Jean I. Brookes, *International Rivalry in the Pacific* (Berkeley, 1941), pp. 365 ff.
83. *Hansard*, 3rd Series, CCXVI, 934.
84. Minute by Herbert on Secretary to Government of Fiji to C.O., 12 Jan. 1874, C.O. 83/5.

eventually received this from Cakobau and the chiefs,[85] and in their report advised its acceptance.[86]

Of the alternatives upon which they were to report Goodenough and Layard chose annexation unequivocally. They held out no hope of the restoration of order and stability under the *de facto* government, and they thought the principle of government by a body of men set up to guard the interests of the white community quite wrong; it had inevitably led to the neglect of the interests of the natives except as taxpayers and laborers, and there were instances in which the "Spirit of the Imperial Kidnapping Act has been violated."[87] They recommended the extension of the consul's jurisdiction, but they hoped their recommendation to annex would be preferred to it.

When their report reached England, Disraeli had succeeded Gladstone as Prime Minister, and Carnarvon was Secretary of State for the Colonies. To him, the Fiji Committee sent a deputation to press for annexation.[88] Carnarvon had probably already made up his mind, for shortly afterward he made a speech in the Lords[89] accepting in principle the idea of annexation, and giving similar reasons to those consistently canvassed by McArthur since 1872—economic, strategic, and the need to control the labor trade. Carnarvon later telegraphed the governor of New South Wales, Sir Hercules Robinson, that the imperial government would accept an offer of cession if the conditions attached to that made to Goodenough and Layard were omitted.[90]

There is nothing to support the contention that Carnarvon and the Disraeli administration were more impressed with these reasons for annexing Fiji than were their predecessors. Kimberley had written to Gladstone in February 1873 that he thought Fiji should be annexed, as that was the

85. 21 March 1874, *P.P.* 1874, XLV, c. 1011, Appendix I.
86. *P.P.* 1874, XLV, c. 1011.
87. *Ibid.*, Sec. 15.
88. 3 July 1874, C.O. 83/5.
89. *Hansard,* 3rd Series, CCXXI (17 July 1874), 179.
90. Carnarvon to Robinson, 25 Aug. 1874, *P.P.* 1875, LII, c. 1114.

only way to end the abuses of the labor trade,[91] and Hugessen had always been in favor of making it a crown colony. Gladstone ostensibly objected to annexation because there had been no clear statement of such a desire from the Fijians themselves, but his real objection was to the expense involved, though Kimberley had begun to see that the expense of trying to control the labor trade without annexing Fiji might be more than the cost of annexation. But Disraeli was just as evasive as Gladstone and might have postponed the annexation indefinitely had not Carnarvon precipitated a crisis by making his statement in the Lords without the authority of the cabinet. For three weeks before he made this statement, Carnarvon had been pressing Disraeli for a cabinet on Fiji to come to a decision on the Goodenough and Layard report.[92] Disraeli repeatedly deferred the matter, but when Carnarvon made his statement in the Lords, Disraeli showed his displeasure in a curt note to Carnarvon that no cabinet would be held.[93] Disraeli had been as reluctant as Gladstone to advance money for this project and was quick to accept the opportunity offered by Carnarvon's independent action to dismiss the project. Carnarvon protested vigorously; he asked for the question to be left in his hands, stating that he had no desire to spend a shilling of imperial funds. If his plans turned out as he expected "it will perhaps be admitted that no colony of modern times was ever established under circumstances of so much difficulty at so little cost to this country."[94]

By his plan Carnarvon hoped to get £4,000 each from New Zealand, Victoria, New South Wales, and Queensland, as they would benefit by the imperial government's adoption of a course which they had continually urged upon it. One can understand Carnarvon's indignation when Queensland

91. See p. 44, above.

92. Carnarvon to Disraeli, 30 June 1874, Carnarvon to Corry, 6 July 1874, Disraeli Papers, Box XII.

93. Sir A. H. Hardinge, *The Fourth Earl of Carnarvon* (London, 1925), II, 133.

94. Carnarvon to Disraeli, 7 Aug. 1874, Disraeli Papers, Box XII.

refused to contribute because, as the governor said, unlike the other colonies "her interest in Fiji is positively nil."[95] To this Carnarvon replied:

> I feel bound ... to observe ... that as Queensland has been largely concerned in the labour traffic, the regulation of which was a principal object of the annexation of Fiji, the colony could not be considered to be uninterested, if indeed it was not under a special obligation to assist in such a case as this.

Another step in Carnarvon's plan was completed when Robinson, who arrived in Fiji in October 1874, received the desired offer of cession, which was signed on 10 October. Annexation by itself would not correct the abuses of the labor trade; it had to be followed by legislation. There was now an executive government in Fiji which could face the problem bequeathed to it by the *de facto* government and work out an efficient system of regulation for the future. To bridge the gap between annexation and the drafting of its own legislation, the Queensland Polynesian Labour Act of 1868 was declared to be in force, and for the first time Fiji had regulations for the introduction and employment of Polynesians that had the full authority of Her Majesty's Government.

95. Normanby to Carnarvon (private), 30 Oct. 1874, Carnarvon Papers, P.R.O. 30/6, 25. Because of disagreements among the Australasian colonies this part of Carnarvon's plan was abandoned, and the annexation financed by a loan of £100,000. Carnarvon regarded the plan as a trial of the "principle of joint action among different members of the Empire"—the principle behind his plan for Federation in South Africa—and much regretted its failure. (Carnarvon, circular despatch to the Australasian Colonies, 9 July 1875, C.O. Confidential Print No. 49, C.O. 808/12.)

CHAPTER III. INDENTURE FOR QUEENSLAND: IMPERIAL APPROVAL

In the discussions that led up to the 1872 act, and in the deliberations on the labor trade in Fiji before annexation, the imperial government had not made any decision on the principle of employing Pacific islanders in British colonies or spheres of influence. That decision was made, however, when assent was given to the Queensland act of 1868 to regulate and control the introduction of Polynesian laborers.

In all matters relating to migration the Colonial Office, and Rogers in particular, relied very much on the opinion of the Emigration Commissioners. The Emigration Commissioners in turn took as their standard of reference the Indian coolie emigration to the West Indies and to Mauritius, which appeared to them a splendid example of the harmony of interests: the resources of the colony were developed, the planters enriched, and the laborers' prospects improved by emigration from a country with a redundant population. Each group pursuing its self-interest served the good of all.

When the new colony of Queensland reported that its resources could not be developed without colored labor, it was natural that it should turn, with the approval of the Colonial Office, to India. But plans for the introduction of Indian coolies broke down, and private interests brought in Pacific islanders as a substitute labor force. The Emigration Commissioners and the Colonial Office approved the principle of the introduction of Pacific islanders on the assumption that it could be regulated as well, and would prove as beneficial to the colony, the employer, and the laborers, as Indian coolie labor had elsewhere. That assumption overlooked very significant differences affecting the ability of the Queensland and imperial governments to supervise recruiting effectively, and the capacity of the islander to make a fair contract.

The recruitment of coolies was done under the careful supervision of the government of India, but the Pacific islander had no government capable of protecting him from unscrupulous recruiters. This was one important difference of which the Colonial Office seemed to be unaware. The Colonial Office also overestimated the capacity of the Pacific islander to further his interest by a contract to work on foreign plantations. The faith in the completely free contract as the best means of promoting the interests of both parties had weakened sufficiently to allow for some sort of government supervision to ensure fair conditions; but what may have been fair conditions for Indian coolies were not necessarily so for Pacific islanders belonging to primitive communities unacquainted with Western economic notions.

On the basis of the experience of its naval commanders in the Pacific, the Admiralty rejected the idea implicit in the proposed Queensland legislation that the Pacific islander was able to make a fair contract; but this view was not accepted by the Colonial Office. In deference to the Foreign Office, however, the Colonial Office agreed to delay the decision on the act until enquiries had been made into allegations by missionary societies; but the Colonial Office view finally prevailed and subsequent events were to test its wisdom.

I

By Letters Patent, issued 6 June 1859, Her Majesty created, under powers given her by Section 46 of 18 and 19 Vict., c. 54, a separate colony in Northern New South Wales, and by an Order-in-Council of the same date gave to it the same privilege of self-government as New South Wales enjoyed. The area of the new colony of Queensland was about 660,000 square miles; most of its 2,250 miles of coast were fringed with tropical forest, while a great part of the interior was semi-arid. Many of its 20,000 inhabitants lived in the towns of Brisbane and Ipswich near the southern border and were described by the first governor, Sir George Bowen,[1] as a "hard headed set of English and Scotch merchants and mechanics."[2] The southern areas of the colony were occupied by pastoralists; the northern tropical regions were as yet unsettled.

By 1859, however, the cotton-growing potential of the new colony had been recognized and welcomed by Manchester cotton merchants, who wanted new and regular sources of raw material because of the uncertainties of the American supply. Before he left for Queensland, Sir George Bowen had discussed the production of cotton in the new colony with Mr. Bazley, M.P. for Manchester,[3] who in September 1860 had been one of the founders of a Manchester company that proposed to spend one-tenth of its capital of £100,000 on cotton cultivation in Queensland; the remainder was to be spent for a similar purpose in the East Indies.[4]

On his arrival, the governor himself was enthusiastic about the possibilities, and in an early despatch stressed the fact that the eastern seaboard of Queensland could make Britain independent of American slave-grown cotton. Imagine, he wrote, "the discouragement of slavery which would accrue from the successful cultivation of that plant by free labour,"[5] and he went on to express the hope that, in the north, cotton would be grown with Asian labor, which, he thought, would do for Queensland what machinery had done for England.

In December 1860, the Secretary of State for the Colonies, the Duke of Newcastle, was petitioned simultaneously by

1. George Fergus Bowen, 1821-1899, K.C.M.G. 1856; G.C.M.G. 1860; P.C. 1886; Chief Secretary, Ionian Islands, 1854-1859; Governor of Queensland, 1859-1868, New Zealand, 1868-1873, Victoria, 1873-1879, Mauritius, 1879-1882, Hong Kong, 1882-1886.
2. Sir George Bowen, *Thirty Years of Colonial Government* (London, 1889), I, 116.
3. *Ibid.*, pp. 195-196.
4. Report of formation of the company at a public meeting in Manchester Town Hall, *Times*, 18 Sept. 1860.
5. Bowen to Newcastle, 6 Jan. 1860, C.O. 234/1.

"land proprietors, stock holders, and others having vested interests in and being resident in Queensland,"[6] and by people in Great Britain with interests in Queensland, that Queensland should have the same privileges in respect to coolie labor as were enjoyed by Mauritius and the West Indian colonies. The central and northern districts, stated the Queensland petition, were unsuitable for European labor; but given coolie labor, Queensland would be able to compete successfully with other sugar-growing colonies and eventually with United States in cotton. The governor entirely concurred with these views, but stated that public funds would not be used to promote the immigration, nor would it be allowed to interfere with the immigration of Europeans.[7]

Although the India Office was prepared to allow emigration to Queensland, provided the same arrangements were made for the protection of the Indian laborers as were in operation in Mauritius and the West Indies, it pointed out that

as the colony of Queensland differs from those to which emigration had hitherto been carried on in the circumstance that the local government and legislature are practically less under the control of the Home authorities, the proposed emigration ... must be regarded as experimental and provisional.[8]

In his reply to the governor, the Duke of Newcastle gave a full summary of the conditions under which the Indian government allowed its subjects to emigrate, and he enclosed a copy of the Mauritius ordinance, No. 30, 1858, as a model for Queensland legislation.

The Queensland government, under R. G. W. Herbert,[9] was so anxious not to lose the advantage of the favorable market created by the world cotton shortage that it would not brook the delay involved in passing an act to regulate

6. Bowen to Newcastle, 18 Dec. 1860, *P.P.* 1861, XL, 2890.
7. *Ibid.*
8. India Office to C.O., 12 Feb. 1861, C.O. 234/5.
9. Later Permanent Under-Secretary of State for the Colonies and, 1859-1866, premier of Queensland, to which colony he had gone as private secretary to the first governor, Sir George Bowen.

coolie immigration; and so, by resolution of both Houses, it empowered the governor to make regulations for that purpose. The government not only submitted these for approval to the Secretary of State,[10] but proposed directly to the government of India that coolies be permitted to proceed to the colony "in anticipation of the formal approval"[11] of these regulations.

The Colonial Office disapproved strongly both of the method by which the regulations were issued and of their substances. Rogers, the Permanent Under-Secretary, considered the method illegal and thought Herbert could not have had the concurrence of his attorney-general. The Emigration Commissioners pointed out that the regulations, though modeled on the Mauritius ordinance, lacked the complicated body of law that the latter implied. Consequently some curious contradictions were present—industrial residence, though mentioned in the sixth article, was nowhere defined; allotment of coolies was referred to in clause eleven, but nothing more was said as to whose responsibility this was, or how it was to be done; and there were other similar defects. These criticisms were incorporated in Newcastle's reply, together with Rogers' minute:

I have read with very great and painful interest the accounts of the Colonists' dealings with the Aborigines. . . . I am confident that the Indian government will not permit those for whose welfare they hold themselves responsible . . . to leave India with the intention of locating themselves in districts where they are exposed to casualties of this kind.[12]

Following this rebuke, the government of Queensland passed the necessary act,[13] and new regulations supplying the deficiencies pointed out by the Secretary of State were drawn up. In October 1862, after some minor amendments, these

10. Bowen to Newcastle, 27 Sept. 1861, C.O. 234/4.
11. India Office minute, Public Despatch to India, No. 4, 1861, India Office Library.
12. Newcastle to Bowen, 2 Feb. 1862. *Selections from Despatches to India,* 5th Series (1862), 368, India Office Library.
13. 26 Vict., No. 5, 2 July 1862.

were approved by both the Secretary of State for the Colonies and the Secretary of State for India.[14] In certain respects these regulations were more generous to the coolie than those in force in Mauritius or the West Indies. If the employer who contracted for the coolie defaulted, the coolie could choose either to enforce the contract or accept an immediate free return passage. The coolie was entitled to a free return passage after five years' service instead of eight, as in Mauritius and West Indies. The rates at which he could redeem the last two years of his service were the same as those in force in the West Indies, but higher than those ruling in Mauritius.[15]

But no coolies were brought to Queensland under these regulations. The Queensland government was prepared to assist cotton growing by free land grants and premiums on export; but in the face of public opposition to Asian immigration[16] the government agreed to reserve public money spent on immigration for the assistance of Europeans only. As the Manchester Company and private planters were not prepared to bear the full cost of indenting coolies, the matter lapsed.[17]

Nevertheless, there were local men determined to produce cotton in Queensland, and to find labor from other sources if Asians were not available. One of these was Robert Towns, a member of the New South Wales Legislative Council, a merchant and shipowner, and a partner in large plantations in New Caledonia. In May 1863 he sent a vessel to recruit Pacific islanders, giving the master an open letter to the missionaries in which he stated his needs:

14. Under-Secretary of State for India to Under-Secretary of State for the Colonies, 27 Oct. 1862, *Ibid.,* 408.

15. *23rd General Report of Emigration Commissioners,* p. 17, *P.P.* 1863, XV.

16. C.O. 234/6. Petitions were forwarded to the governor from the Mechanics Institutes of Brisbane and Ipswich. This marks the beginning of an urban and working-class opposition that was to become increasingly significant.

17. C.O. 234/8. Bowen to Newcastle, 4 Oct. 1863.

I have embarked considerable capital in Queensland in the cultivation of cotton, and as so much depends on the rate of labour
in the ultimate success of this important enterprise, I am en-
deavouring to try out natives from the immediate adjacent
islands.[18]

Towns did not show the tact one would expect when, seeking
to recommend his proposal to the missionaries, he said, "I
with my cotton emigration . . . will do more towards civilis-
ing the natives in one year than you can possibly in ten. . . ."[19]
However, he did ask that the missionaries should, if possible,
send a native teacher or reader with the laborers.

The terms of employment were set out in a form given
to the master of the recruiting vessel; contracts were to be for
six or twelve months, and at the end of the latter period,
Towns promised to return the native "should he require
such." He would pay wages in kind to the value of ten
shillings per month and provide food and housing. Laborers
were to be engaged in "field labour of a light and easy description." Towns appointed Ross Lewin as his recruiting
agent. Lewin had been a seaman in the Royal Navy during
the first China War, after which he had been cashiered. He
went to Australia, from whence he settled in Tanna in the
New Hebrides, where he had a large plantation.[20] He came
to have a reputation for cruel treatment of the Pacific islanders, as bad as that of "Bully" Hayes. He was hardly the
man to carry out Towns's instructions that the natives were
to be treated "with the greatest kindness." The vessel returned with sixty laborers; and so began an immigration of
Pacific islanders to Queensland that was to continue, with
one short interruption, until 1904.

II

The attention of the Queensland government was soon drawn
to what Towns had done. Since no law covered the introduc-

18. Enclosure in Bowen to Newcastle, 16 Sept. 1863, *P.P.* 1867-1868, XLVIII,
391.
19. *Ibid.*
20. Sir A. H. Markham, *Cruise of the Rosario* (London, 1873), p. 89.

tion of Pacific islanders into Queensland, the government saw no need to take any action beyond reporting the circumstances to the imperial government.[21]

The first employers were eminently respectable persons: Towns had as his first partner, Brooks, M.P. for Weymouth in the House of Commons, and later, Cowper, who had been premier of New South Wales and was later agent general for that colony. Another employer, Captain Whish, a member of the Queensland Legislative Council, had been an officer on General Jacobs' staff in Persia in 1856-1857, and his niece had married General Napier, later Lord Napier of Magdala.

The Queensland government was very much in sympathy with the aims of these men—the development of the resources of the colony and the production of cotton for the British market. Although the government had refused to spend any public money on the introduction of colored labor, many of its influential members and the governor himself thought that the resources of the colony could not be developed without it. They therefore welcomed the action of these men who at their own expense had brought laborers from the Pacific islands. It was not surprising therefore that the government should leave these employers free to manage their labor as they desired.

On the plantations of Towns and Whish, the natives did all manner of field work, even tending, under European direction, mechanical instruments such as the steam plow. They worked from dawn to dusk with breaks of one hour for breakfast and lunch—two hours for the latter in summer. For rations they were given one and a half pounds of rice and one and a half pounds of beef a day. As they were not accustomed to working long regular hours in the islands, and as neither of the two items supplied as rations were part of their island diet, it is remarkable that they proved as efficient workers as their employers stated them to be.[22]

21. Bowen to Newcastle, 16 Sept. 1863, *P.P.* 1867-1868, XLVIII, 391.
22. Enclosure in Bowen to Carnarvon, 16 Nov. 1866, *P.P.* 1867-1868, XLVIII, 391.

Towns and Whish had proved that Pacific islanders were worth the cost of importing them. From a variety of sources the demand for them increased rapidly. By 1864 the Hon. Louis Hope had successfully cultivated sugar for commercial purposes, and as an incentive to its production, the government allowed concessions on the purchase of land to be used for that purpose. The new sugar planters joined the cotton planters in seeking Pacific island labor. Others too sought this relatively cheap labor: pastoralists for shepherds, and town residents for domestic servants. This increased demand was reflected in the number introduced in 1867, almost ten times the average for the preceding three years.[23] Of the number in Queensland early in 1868, half were employed in agriculture—mainly on sugar and cotton plantations—while most of the rest were employed by pastoralists in the interior, with about 5 per cent of the total in urban occupations.[24]

Pacific islanders were no longer employed by just a few eminent citizens on well-conducted plantations. The character and standing of the employers was very diverse, and there was now a group of middlemen[25]—agents who undertook to supply islanders to prospective employers—to increase the risk of abuse.

The only legal protection the Pacific islander had in Queensland was the Masters and Servants Act,[26] and then only if he had a written agreement with his employer. Many natives had no agreements; they were quite defenseless. The protection given under the Masters and Servants Act to those with agreements was slight. The agreements varied from employer to employer; there was no set form, and many of them gave to the Pacific islander few rights worth going to

23. Enclosure 1 in Blackall to Granville, 16 April 1869, *P.P.* 1868-1869, XLIII, 408.
24. *Ibid.*
25. See advertisement in Queensland newspaper, 29 April 1867, reprinted in *Colonial Intelligencer*, May 1870: "Henry Ross Lewin ... begs to inform his friends and the public that he intends immediately visiting the South Sea Islands and will be happy to receive orders for the importation of natives to work on cotton and sugar plantations.... Terms £7 each man."
26. 25 Vict., No. 11.

law about. Most of the clauses of the Masters and Servants Act concerned the rights of the master. The one substantial right of the servant was his claim to wages, for which he could sue in case of default. Whether the native laborer exercised this right depended on whether he had the initiative and knowledge to bring his case before a magistrate; and once this was done, unless he could take the oath on the English Bible, he could not give evidence. This meant that the Pacific islanders had practically no protection at law.

During 1867 there were murmurings of protest from some sections of the white community. The motives for these were mixed: partly humanitarian and partly fear that the Pacific islander would compete unfairly with the white laborer. It was widely accepted even among the working class that field work in tropical agriculture could not be done by white labor. So long as the Pacific islander was confined to this there was no great opposition to his employment; but he had been taken into occupations normally filled by white workers —shepherds on sheep runs and urban occupations.

But this opposition had scarcely made itself heard before the question of government intervention was raised by reports that natives brought to Queensland had been kidnaped and British sailors murdered in revenge. The number of vessels engaged in recruiting for Queensland doubled in 1867, and recruiting being as unregulated as employment, the risk of abuses increased proportionately. The first of these reports was made in April 1867 by the officer-in-command on the Australian naval station who had been informed that the crews of three vessels had been murdered in the New Hebrides in revenge for murders and cruelties perpetrated by labor recruiters.[27] Although there was no proof that Queensland vessels were implicated, Bowen brought this report before his Executive Council, which ordered the appropriate minister to report on Pacific islanders brought

27. Bowen to Buckingham and Chandos, 13 July 1867, *P.P.* 1867-1868, XLVIII, 391.

to Queensland, and police magistrates to inspect regularly their places of employment.[28]

Bowen, who had visited some of the plantations where Pacific islanders were employed, was confident there were no abuses, but he informed the imperial government that Queensland was ready to pass any legislation the imperial government thought necessary.[29] At the Colonial Office, the Chief Clerk, Dealtry, and the Parliamentary Under-Secretary, Adderley, were prepared to accept Bowen's assurance and let the matter rest; but on the advice of the Permanent Under-Secretary, Rogers, the Secretary of State, Lord Buckingham, consulted the Emigration Commissioners.[30] In their opinion "it would not be safe to trust altogether to the justice and good faith of the settlers for the protection of people of this class." They advised the issuance of regulations; perhaps not as detailed or elaborate as those already issued for the introduction of coolies, but at least incorporating the principal safeguards.[31]

This was a very significant opinion; it implied that the Emigration Commissioners approved of the principle of employing Pacific islanders in Queensland, and that these islanders were capable of furthering their own interests by a contract, the provisions of which would be protected by law. This was the first occasion on which the imperial government had made a decision on these matters. Hitherto it had been concerned only with factors on the fringe of the problem— the abuses associated with recruiting—whereas this was a decision on the very principle of engaging these people as laborers. However, it is too much to say that the Emigration Commissioners considered any of these questions very thoroughly, especially the ability of the islanders to understand a contract. To the emigration commissioners the Pacific

28. *Ibid.*
29. *Ibid.*
30. Minute on Bowen to Buckingham and Chandos, 13 July 1867, C.O. 234/18.
31. Murdoch to Rogers, 24 Oct. 1867, *P.P.* 1867-1868, XLVIII, 391.

islanders were no different from the Indian coolies; both were emigrant colored laborers. Indian coolie labor had been regulated successfully; if Pacific island labor was regulated according to the same principles, it would prove equally beneficial to all parties.

This was also the opinion of Rogers. At a later date, in reply to Admiralty criticisms of the indenture of Pacific islanders, he wrote:

I need hardly refer to Capt. Powell's observations that the importation and contract are sure to lead to abuse—he has probably not heard of Mauritius and the West Indies. I believe importation of labourers under contract is a system capable of conferring on humanity benefits almost incalcuable....[32]

The Admiralty view was based on the opinion of Captain Richards,[33] who had been in command of the *Hecate* on the Pacific station at the time of the Peruvian atrocities, and on the enquiry carried out by Captain Blake into the murders of Europeans in the New Hebrides.[34] The Emigration Commissioners paid scarcely more heed to these warnings than did Rogers. They admitted the possibility of abuses, but they were confident these would not occur if licenses were issued for recruiting only in the more settled islands where Europeans were resident.[35] These of course were not considered the best recruiting areas, and there was little practical possibility of confining recruiters to them.

With agreement therefore between the Colonial Office and the Emigration Commissioners, the Queensland government was advised to prepare a bill on the model of the act passed for the introduction of Indian coolies.[36] Before the despatch was received by the governor of Queensland such

32. Minute on Admiralty to C.O., 28 Oct. 1868, C.O. 234/21.
33. Richards' minute on Rogers to Admiralty, 15 Nov. 1867, Admiralty 1, 6026.
34. Enclosure 1 in Admiralty to C.O., 7 Dec. 1867, P.P. 1867-1868, XLVIII, 391.
35. Murdoch to Rogers, 23 Dec. 1867, P.P. 1867-1868, XLVIII, 391.
36. Buckingham and Chandos to Bowen, 9 Nov. 1867, P.P. 1867-1868, XLVIII, 391.

a bill had been introduced into the Queensland Parliament.[37] It included all the suggestions made by Buckingham except that the laborers should not be employed inland, where supervision would be difficult.[38] The pastoral interests in Parliament opposed this as it would preclude them from employing Pacific islanders. John Douglas, who was later to lead the party representing urban and working-class interests, spoke in favor of restricting the employment of Pacific islanders to tropical agriculture.[39] But it was not until Douglas himself formed a ministry in 1877 that regulations to this effect were issued.

None of the members of the Queensland legislature opposed the introduction of Pacific islanders, although the members for East Moreton and Brisbane said the majority of their constituents were not in favor of it.[40] It was generally assumed by most members that the Pacific islander was capable of understanding and making a contract. The differences in Parliament were on the degree of protection it was the duty of the state to provide for the native. One member of the Legislative Council held so strongly to the doctrine of laissez faire as to oppose the bill as an unwarranted interference with freedom of contract;[41] but this view was exceptional. In the committee stage of the bill in the Assembly[42] concessions were made to those who wanted more protection for the native. The bill received the governor's assent in March 1868.[43]

The act was welcomed by the Colonial Office, particularly as protests against the unregulated introduction of Pacific islanders had been received from a number of quarters. The

37. *Queensland Parliamentary Debates,* 2nd Series, VI, 626-627, 21 Nov. 1867, 2nd reading in Legislative Council. (*Queensland Parliamentary Debates* hereinafter will be referred to as *Qd. P.D.*)
38. Copy of bill enclosed in O'Connor to Buckingham and Chandos, 27 Jan. 1868, *P.P.* 1867-1868, XLVIII, 391.
39. *Qd. P.D.,* 2nd Series, VI, 895.
40. *Qd. P.D.,* 2nd Series, VI, 894 (Francis), 896 (O'Doherty).
41. Hon. W. Wood, *Qd. P.D.,* 2nd Series, VI, 658.
42. *Qd. P.D.,* 2nd Series, VI, 912 ff.
43. 31 Vict., No. 47.

governors of Queensland and New South Wales had for-warded reports of public meetings held in Brisbane[44] and Sydney deploring the absence of any government supervision of the labor trade in Queensland. The Colonial Office had received a petition addressed to the governor of New South Wales from the missionaries of the Presbyterian Church in the New Hebrides asking for an investigation of the engage-ment of natives of the New Hebrides for service in Queens-land and Fiji.[45] In England similar representations were made by the Anti-Slavery Society[46] and the Aborigines Pro-tection Society.[47] It was the view of the former that the un-regulated recruiting and employment of Pacific islanders was a violation of the principles laid down for the emigration of coolies from India. It had more affinity with the "free emi-gration" from Africa conducted by France which Her Majesty's Government had regarded as analogous to the slave trade, and which had been suspended on representation to France.[48] The Emigration Commissioners and the Colonial Office were happy to be able to answer all these representa-tions by reference to the Queensland act.[49]

It is true that the act compared favorably with the ordi-nances of Mauritius and the West Indies for the introduction of coolies. The term of service under the Queensland act was shorter, but it did not provide, as the coolie ordinances did, for the medical care of the laborers, nor for a fixed proportion of females to accompany the male workers.

But the significant difference between the two systems was not in the details of the regulations but in the circum-

44. Report on Public Meeting, Brisbane, *Brisbane Courier*, 26 Nov. 1867, 3199, C.O. 234/20; also *Colonial Intelligencer*, March 1868. Report of Public Meeting, Brisbane, 16 Jan. 1868, enclosure in O'Connor to Buckingham and Chandos, 27 Jan. 1868, *P.P.* 1867-1868, XLVIII, 391.
45. Enclosure in Belmore to Buckingham and Chandos, *P.P.* 1867-1868, XLVIII, 391.
46. Bennett and Chamerovzow to Buckingham and Chandos, 13 March 1868, *P.P.* 1867-1868, XLVIII, 391.
47. No. 2963, C.O. 234/21.
48. Chamerovzow to Buckingham and Chandos, 29 April 1868, *P.P.* 1867-1868, XLVIII, 391.
49. Murdoch to Rogers, 6 May 1868, *P.P.* 1867-1868, XLVIII, 391.

stances to which they referred. The coolie had a recognized government that carefully supervised recruiting and kept a watchful eye on the conditions under which he worked while abroad. He belonged to a relatively advanced society, and it was reasonable to assume that he understood the nature of a contract and that he could expect to improve his position by emigrating from a country with a surplus of population. The position of the Pacific islander was quite different. He had no government to supervise recruiting in the islands or to protest, if necessary, against conditions in Queensland. There was little in the primitive life of the island communities to acquaint him with the meaning of a contract; and his emigration tended to depopulate rather than relieve population pressure in the islands.

It was this difference which the Colonial Office and the Emigration Commissioners did not really consider, although they vaguely recognized its existence when they assumed that recruiting would not be carried on in the more backward islands or where there was no European resident.[50]

There had been no clear statement of this difference at this time from any source. The Admiralty withheld approval because it believed slave-dealing inevitable among the islands seldom visited by Her Majesty's ships. The Anti-Slavery Society criticized the act as unique in allowing private individuals to recruit, and *ultra vires* in affecting the independence of foreign subjects.[51] Perhaps these criticisms show a vague awareness of the differences in circumstances outlined above. The Emigration Commissioners admitted that colored emigration to other parts of the Empire was not left in private hands, and stated that "if the [Pacific] emigration was to become extensive the same restrictions would become necessary."[52] Whether it occurred to them that this might not be

50. Murdoch to Rogers, 23 Dec. 1867; Murdoch to Rogers, 6 May 1868, *P.P.* 1867-1868, XLVIII, 391.

51. Chamerovzow to Buckingham and Chandos, 23 May 1868, *P.P.* 1867-1868, XLVIII, 391.

52. Murdoch to Rogers, 16 June 1868, *P.P.* 1867-1868, XLVIII, 391.

possible without wholesale annexation is not clear; and this remark suggests that no really serious thought had been given to the problem.

Therefore, when the act was received from Queensland, Rogers had no hesitation in advising that Her Majesty's pleasure should be signified.[53] But in deference to the wishes of the Foreign Office, the decision on the act was deferred until the latter had enquired into the whole question of the recruitment of labor in the Pacific,[54] a course decided upon on receiving from the secretary of the Reformed Church of Scotland a copy of a petition from the Presbyterian mission in the New Hebrides.[55] The Foreign Office sent a circular despatch to all British consuls in the Pacific asking for full information on the recruiting of islanders.[56] The Admiralty was asked to make similar enquiries of naval commanders in the Pacific.[57]

The reports of the consuls revealed no serious abuses,[58] but Commodore Powell, commanding the South Pacific station, repeated what he had heard from the French naval authorities of illegal recruiting by British vessels in the Loyalties and New Caledonia.[59] These charges were later conveyed by the French ambassador to the Foreign Office,[60] and at the instance of the Colonial Office, the governor of New South Wales appointed a Royal Commission, but this enquiry revealed no great abuse.[61] At the time, the Admiralty used the evidence supplied by Powell to press the Colonial Office to forbid such recruiting, but Rogers was certain that

53. Minute by Rogers on Murdoch to Rogers, 16 June 1868, C.O. 234/21.
54. F.O. to C.O., 8 July 1868; C.O. to F.O., 18 July 1868, C.O., 234/21.
55. Enclosure in Kinnaird to Stanley, 26 June 1868, *P.P.* 1868-1869, XLIII, 438.
56. Circular despatch to Consuls in Islands on Shore of Pacific, 8 July 1868, *P.P.* 1868-1869, XLIII, 438.
57. F.O. to Admiralty, 8 July 1868, *P.P.* 1868-1869, XLIII, 438.
58. For replies, see Nos. 5, 6, 7, 17, 18, 21, 23, of paper 438, *P.P.* 1868-1869, XLIII.
59. Enclosure in Admiralty to C.O., 28 Oct. 1868, *P.P.* 1868-1869, XLIII, 438, and C.O. 234/21.
60. French Ambassador to F.O., 10 Jan. 1869, 24 Jan. 1869, C.O. 234/23.
61. Granville to Belmore, 15 March 1869, *P.P.* 1868-1869, XLIII, 408.

recruiting could be carried on without abuse and to the advantage of all concerned.[62]

Early in 1870 the Queensland act was submitted to the Law Officers, who recommended that Her Majesty's pleasure be signified,[63] and so almost eighteen months after the act was received, Lord Granville, the Secretary of State for the Colonies, informed the governor of Queensland that it would not be disallowed. The imperial government was committed to the Colonial Office view that it was possible to conduct this emigration free of abuse.

The Colonial Office had accepted the view put to it by Sir George Bowen that colored labor was essential for the development of Queensland's resources. It regretted that Queensland had rejected Indian coolie labor after legal provision had been made for it. Pacific island labor was accepted as a substitute in the belief that it could be regulated as successfully as Indian coolie labor. In this faith the Colonial Office stood firm against doubts raised by the Admiralty and the Foreign Office, though it conceded that the measure adopted might be sufficient only if the immigration remained on a relatively small scale.

62. Rogers' minute on Admiralty to C.O., 28 Oct. 1868, C.O. 234/21.
63 L.O. to C.O., 11 Jan. 1870, C.O. 201/560.

CHAPTER IV. CRITICISM OF INDENTURE

The Queensland act of 1868 came into operation when it received the governor's assent in March. It involved the imperial government in some responsibility because of the possibility of abuses connected with recruiting beyond Queensland territory. The Emigration Commissioners and the Colonial Office were confident that the provisions of the act were sufficient to prevent these; but in view of a petition from the Presbyterian mission in the New Hebrides, and at the instance of the Foreign Office, the Colonial Office agreed that Her Majesty's assent should be withheld until the consuls and naval commanders had made further enquiries into labor recruiting.

The provisions of the act were not well-adapted to the circumstances under which recruiting was done. They required a prospective employer to take out a license to import laborers which was granted when he gave a bond of £10 to return the natives at the end of their contract.[1] Another bond of £500 against kidnaping was required from the master of the recruiting vessel.[2] On the vessel's return to port the recruiting agent had to produce the license, the bonds, an agreement to work made between the native and the recruiting agent, and a form signed by a missionary or European resident in the islands that the native had engaged voluntarily. It was the responsibility of the immigration agent in Queensland to satisfy himself that the forms were in order, and that the native understood the contract and had engaged willingly.[3]

The weaknesses of the act were, first, the assumption that the islander had sufficient understanding to make a fair con-

1. 31 Vict., No. 47 s. 6.
2. *Ibid.*, s. 15.
3. *Ibid.*, s. 8.

tract, and second, the absence of any provision for effective supervision at the place of recruitment. The first assumption implied a failure by the Queensland government and the Colonial Office to appreciate the conditions in the islands. It is true that the Emigration Commissioners assumed that recruiting would not take place in the more backward areas;[4] yet it was precisely from such islands—the Melanesian, particularly the New Hebrides and the Solomons—that recruiting had been going on for the previous five years, and there was nothing in the act to prevent its continuing.

I

The islands of Melanesia stretch from New Guinea to New Caledonia. Between these two extremities lie the Solomons, the Santa Cruz, Torres, Banks, New Hebrides, and Loyalty islands, forming an arc roughly parallel with the coast of Queensland and about 1,200 miles from it. A few of the islands are tiny low-lying reefs, but most are large volcanic outcrops like Guadalcanal in the Solomons, where Mount Popomanasiu rises to eight thousand feet. In New Guinea mountain peaks rise to almost twice this height.

The people of these islands are a racial mixture defying neat classification. The earliest arrivals in the area were probably a small-statured Negroid race similar to the pygmies who still survive in central New Guinea and Bougainville. They were followed by people of mixed Mongoloid Mediterranean stock who moved through Malaysia and into the islands, mingling with the earlier inhabitants. The characteristics of these later arrivals are most apparent among some of the natives of New Caledonia. This mixture of races in all its variety is commonly called Melanesian. However some of the smaller islands of eastern Melanesia—Rennell, Sikaiana, Tikopia, Anuda, Duff, Ontong Java—are inhabited by Polynesians, who occupied the further islands of the Pacific at a

4. Murdoch to Rogers, 6 May 1868, *P.P.* 1867-1868, XLVIII, 391.

much later date, and probably drifted back westward into this part of Melanesia.

There were no reliable population figures for the Melanesian islands in the nineteenth century, except in the smallest of them where a resident missionary could without difficulty know every individual. In 1910 the population of the New Hebrides was estimated at between 60,000 and 67,000, but it was probably four or five times this figure in 1860 before the labor trade began.[5] The Solomons, which were more populous than the New Hebrides, suffered a similar decline.

Among the Melanesians the institution of hereditary chieftainship was not highly developed; in some islands there were no chiefs,[6] and the social unit did not extend much beyond the family group ruled by an informal council of its senior members. Between these groups there was little intercourse, and they were further cut off from each other by a remarkable variety of dialect and language. In the New Hebrides alone there were twenty different languages and over a thousand dialects.[7] Language was therefore the most obvious barrier to the natives' understanding of the contract to work in Queensland. The act did not require recruiting ships to carry interpreters, if indeed there existed any person capable of understanding more than one or two of these dialects.

The main economic occupation of the islanders was fishing and the cultivation of small garden plots. Ownership was not a simple institution, but a combination of individual and communal rights. Land was held by the largest social unit, whether that was the tribe or the clan, which alone

5. F.O. *Handbook*, No. 147. For discussion of depopulation, see W. H. R. Rivers, ed., *Essays on the Depopulation of Melanesia* (Cambridge, 1922); G. Pitt-Rivers, *The Clash of Culture and the Contact of Races* (London, 1927); C. S. Belshaw, *Changing Melanesia* (Melbourne, 1954).

6. Goodenough, Report on visit of H.M.S. *Pearl* to New Hebrides, 1875, C.O. 83/7.

7. J. Copeland in answer to Anti-Slavery Society Questionnaire, printed in the Reverend J. Kay, *Slave Trade in the New Hebrides* (Edinburgh, 1872), pp. 48 ff.; C. Wilson, *The Wake of the Southern Cross* (London, 1932), p. 16.

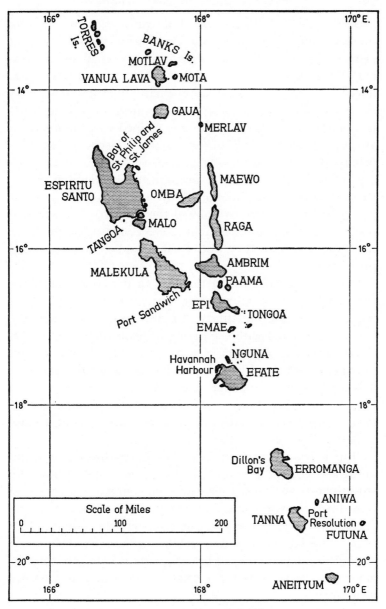

MAP 2. The New Hebrides

had the right of alienation. This unit allocated land to smaller groups or even to individuals who enjoyed the right of usufruct, but who had no authority to assign this to anyone else except perhaps by inheritance. Large objects produced by communal labor were usually held in common by those who contributed labor. Where ownership of such objects was not common, those who helped to produce them at least preserved a right of use. Smaller objects, individually produced, were individually owned, yet even here the concept of outright ownership, prohibiting use by anyone else without permission, did not apply. Living objects, such as plants and trees, were considered the property of those who planted them. Communal rights were vested in chiefs where such existed, and they could command both labor and property.[8]

The island societies—particularly in the New Hebrides—were graded into social and religious levels. Entry into these was not as a rule hereditary, but was secured through the prestige associated with the giving of feasts or the possession of certain kinds of object such as spiral-tusked pigs or shell ornaments. Those with such prestige could acquire the symbols used in the ceremonies marking progress from grade to grade. The native was therefore not without some motive for acquiring certain kinds of property, nor without a sense of barter to be used to this end.[9]

But it was a motive that he could not abstract from the social and economic pattern of his island home. When the Queensland labor recruiter came and offered a contract to work for three years on a Queensland sugar plantation at £6 per annum it meant nothing to him. He did not think in terms of his labor as a mobile, salable commodity, or in terms of continuous work. Accustomed to measuring his time in moons, three years was a period of time he could hardly imagine.

8. For summary of Melanesian property rights, see Belshaw, *Changing Melanesia*, pp. 7-9.
9. A. B. Deakin, *Malekula* (London, 1934), *passim*.

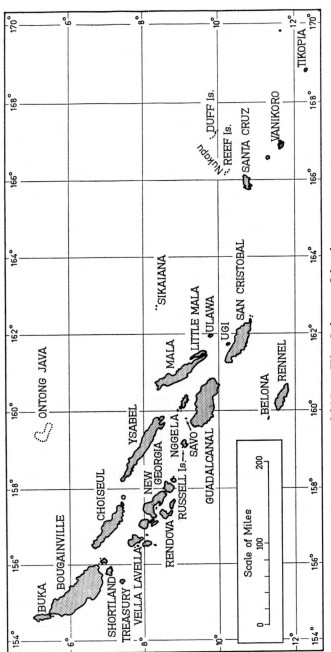

MAP 3. The Solomon Islands

In some cases the native's labor was not his own to offer; the chief or the elders could command labor for communal purposes, and their consent was necessary for its use. The recruiters recognized this, and offered gifts, known as trade, to the chief, the elders, or the relatives of the natives they wished to recruit.[10] This was in no sense a sale, as neither the chiefs nor elders had power to alienate the person of their subjects as such. It was merely a gift in return for the loan of the labor of a number of their tribe or clan. It does indicate how inapplicable was the notion of a contract clearly understood and fully entered into by each individual.

The native as a rule did not engage through any economic motive beyond the presents offered to his chief or relatives. He was not at first drawn by what there was to earn in Queensland,[11] nor was he pushed by the pressure of population to leave his own island. Yet he often went willingly enough. Missionaries in almost every island from which natives were recruited spoke of the eagerness of the islanders "to see the world."[12] This passion for travel combined with a childlike curiosity about anything new and strange made relatively easy the task of the labor recruiter who did not care whether the native understood the contract. It was kidnaping without violence.

Another factor that could be used to advantage by the labor recruiter was the opportunity recruiting offered a native to escape punishment for the breaking of a tribal taboo. This was one of the ways in which recruiting tended to break down the social structure of the island communities. Where other methods failed, force was often used, either to take natives on board or to constrain them once they had been enticed on board.[13]

10. Enclosure 1 in Kinnaird to Clarendon, 27 May 1869, *P.P.* 1868-1869, XLIII, 438.

11. Later the muskets, tools, and Manchester goods brought back by returning natives did act as an incentive to recruit.

12. Mullens to Lawes, 1 April 1867. L.M.S. Western Outgoing Letters, VIII, 89.

13. For an account of the different methods used by recruiters, and for an

Of the early years of recruiting it is safe to say that the native understood little or nothing of the engagement. He recruited because the chief commanded him to, because the recruiter took him by force, or from the motives of curiosity or the desire to escape punishment for some offense against his fellow tribesmen. As natives returned from service they passed on to others some knowledge of what was involved in the contract,[14] but this tendency toward better understanding was countered by the continual opening of new recruiting areas as the ships moved northward through the New Hebrides and into the Solomons.[15]

The provisions of the Queensland act to ensure that the native understood the contract were quite inadequate. They consisted of the bond of £500 against kidnaping, the certificate signed by the missionary or European resident that the native had engaged freely, and the examination by the immigration agent on the vessel's return to Queensland.

The missionaries, to a man, refused to be honorary civil servants of the Queensland government. There were no resident missionaries in the Solomons at the time the Queensland act was passed, and those in the New Hebrides belonged to the Presbyterian mission, which was resolutely opposed to the labor trade. As they took every opportunity to report any abuse, recruiting vessels were careful to avoid them. There being very few European residents apart from missionaries, this provision of the Queensland act was seldom observed. Without it the bond against kidnaping could not be enforced.

The only check against kidnaping that remained was the examination carried out by the immigration officer at a Queensland port. Here the act did not require an interpreter; the examination was carried out by signs, and it was an easy

---

estimate of the percentages of islanders recruited by those means, see Belshaw, *Changing Melanesia*, pp. 33-35.

14. By 1875 Goodenough thought the contract was fairly understood in the southern New Hebrides, but in any place north of Sandwich the natives remained entirely ignorant. Report on visit of H.M.S. *Pearl* to New Hebrides 1875, C.O. 83/7.

15. See Appendix, Table 1.

task for the recruiting agent on the voyage home to teach the natives the signs they were to give in response to the immigration agent's questions.

The inadequacies of the Queensland act were made worse by the number of persons who, though repeatedly accused of malpractices, continued to receive licenses to recruit. No one illustrates this better than Ross Lewin. Before the passage of the act he had been under suspicion for kidnaping and violence in connection with natives brought to Queensland by the *King Oscar*[16] in November 1867. Twelve months later he was the recruiting agent on the *Daphne*[17] when that vessel attempted to land Pacific islanders in Queensland without a license. Under the act the penalty for this was a fine of £20 for each native on board, but in this case the Crown Solicitor reported that no action could be taken, other than forbidding the natives to land, as the *Daphne* had not proceeded from a Queensland port to procure natives. However, since the natives were allowed to land, the sincerity of the Queensland government was brought into question. Early in 1869 Lewin was tried in Brisbane for a crime of violence against a native girl, but the charge was dismissed through lack of evidence other than that of natives, which was not acceptable to the court.[18] A few months later he was recruiting agent on board the *Daphne* when it was seized by Commander Palmer for slave-dealing. Only then, while he was awaiting trial, did the Queensland government suspend Lewin's license.[19]

The confidence of the Emigration Commissioners and the Colonial Office in the Queensland act was not justified. This fact was brought home to them by pressure exerted by the

16. Appendix A. Report of Select Committee on Working of 1868 Act, *Queensland Votes and Proceedings of Legislative Assembly,* 1869, II, 23. (*Queensland Votes and Proceedings of Legislative Assembly* hereinafter will be referred to as *Qd. V. & P.*)

17. Enclosure in Blackall to Granville, 9 July 1869, *P.P.* 1871, XLVIII, 468.

18. Enclosure in Granville to Blackall, No. 21, 23 April 1869, *P.P.* 1868-1869, XLIII, 408.

19. Blackall to Granville, 9 July 1869, *P.P.* 1871, XLVIII, 468.

missionary and anti-slavery societies who had perhaps the best opportunity of knowing the conditions under which recruiting was carried on. The missionary activity in this respect was typical of the way the societies organized their forces in the Australian colonies and in Britain to bring pressure to bear on both the imperial and the Queensland governments. As a result, the Colonial Office asked Queensland for a detailed report on the working of the act, while the Queensland government informed the Colonial Office that it intended to amend the act.

II

It was the missionaries who supplied most of the evidence of how recruiting was carried on in the Loyalties, New Hebrides, and Solomons. There was no British consul or government official resident in these islands before the late 1880's, and patrols by Her Majesty's ships were few and irregular before 1872. Three Protestant missionary societies—the Presbyterian, the Melanesian, and the London—had resident missionaries in these islands in 1868. The London Missionary Society was first in the field.[20] In 1836 it set up a mission in the southern New Hebrides which, in 1842, was taken over by the United Presbyterian Church of Nova Scotia, which was joined a little later by the Reformed Church of Scotland. From 1870 an increasing share of the responsibility for the Presbyterian missions in these islands was assumed by the Presbyterian churches of Victoria and New Zealand. The London Missionary Society continued to support three missionaries in the Loyalties, but it was forced by differences with the French government of the islands to withdraw gradually and to leave finally in 1884. The Melanesian Mission began its work in the northern New Hebrides, the Banks and Torres Islands, and the southern Solomons in 1849. It

20. R. Lovett, *History of the London Missionary Society* (London, 1899), I, 407 ff.

worked through trained native teachers, Europeans being resident only at the headquarters of the mission on Norfolk Island. The Bishop of Melanesia or a senior European missionary visited the island missions annually.

All these missionary societies opposed the labor trade as it was carried on, though they differed on the principle of indentured labor. The aim of the missionaries was to convert the heathen and civilize the savages. The point of difference between them was whether the labor trade could be a valuable means to this end. It had been the boast of Towns, the first to recruit for Queensland, that he would do more in one year to convert and civilize the natives than the missionaries could possibly do in ten.[21] The Melanesian Mission, particularly Bishop Patteson,[22] were at first inclined to the view that, if properly regulated, the labor trade could be of immense value by bringing the native into contact with a higher and a Christian civilization. The Presbyterian missionaries, on the other hand, believed the labor trade could never be regulated satisfactorily, and that it would always hinder their work, since it withdrew the native from their teaching, but provided none for him on the plantation. The native returned with the vices and not the virtues of Christian civilization.[23]

Experience of the labor trade brought Bishop Patteson gradually round to this view.[24] He did not think the native could understand the contract, nor did he know of any native who had benefited from his time on a plantation. Yet the missionaries did not want to segregate the natives completely from the outside world that exercised such an attraction for them. They sought, therefore, to encourage the

---

21. See p. 55, above.

22. Enclosure in Bowen to Granville, 24 July 1870, *P.P.* 1871, XLVIII, 468.

23. See answers of Presbyterian missionaries in New Hebrides to Anti-Slavery Society questionnaire printed in Kay, *Slave Trade in the New Hebrides*, pp. 48 ff.

24. Memorandum by Bishop Patteson for General Synod of New Zealand, Jan. 1871, *S.P.G. Annual Report* 1871, p. 141.

natives to grow cotton in their own islands,[25] which they could then trade for the tools and Manchester goods previously offered as inducement to recruit, or as wages for work on foreign plantations. The missionaries hoped this legitimate trade would remove the incentive for what they regarded as a slave trade.[26]

In this respect their view was similar to that of the 1842 West African Committee,[27] though in general they had some of the skepticism of the report of the 1837 Committee on Aborigines[28] as to the benefits of contact with Europeans, and welcomed the natural isolation of the islands. Though they differed slightly in their views about the nature of the labor trade, the missionaries were united in their opposition to the way it was carried on, and their representatives combined in a meeting of protest held in Sydney early in February 1869.[29] The mayor of the city presided, and representatives of the churches, including the Bishop of Sydney, spoke critically of the Queensland act and the abuses, including the crimes of Ross Lewin, which it failed to prevent.

The report of this meeting was an important factor in causing the Colonial Office to question, for the first time, the effectiveness of the Queensland legislation. Rogers drafted a despatch to the governor of Queensland, Colonel Samuel Blackall,[30] in which he asked for detailed information about Ross Lewin, how licenses were issued, and what enquiries were made about the way immigrants were engaged and the conditions of the voyage.[31] In another despatch of the same day, enclosing the *Times* report of the Sydney meeting, he

25. Powell to Mullens, 20 Jan. 1870, L.M.S. South Seas Correspondence 32/5/A.
26. Chalmers to Mullens, 9 Dec. 1874, L.M.S. South Seas Reports I.
27. *P.P.* 1842, XI, 1.
28. *P.P.* 1837, VII, 425.
29. Enclosure in Belmore to Granville, 26 Feb. 1869, *P.P.* 1868-1869, XLIII, 408.
30. Colonel Samuel Wensley Blackall, 1809-1871, 85th Light Infantry; M.P. for Longford (Ireland), 1847-1851; lieutenant-governor of Dominica, 1851-1867; Sierra Leone, 1862-1865; West African Settlements, 1865-1867; Queensland, 1868-1871.
31. No. 21, Granville to Blackall, 23 April 1869, C.O. 201/551.

stressed that the matter was not a "mere Queensland question"; it involved the honor of the British name, and the governor as an officer of Her Majesty's Government was under "the most serious responsibility" to use his

utmost influence to secure that these emigrants receive that special protection which immigrant labour [needs] in Queensland and in other colonies to which coloured immigrants, as they are called, proceed and without which they must be at the mercy of those about.[32]

Rogers here wrote to the governor as an imperial officer whose authority extended beyond the bounds of Queensland, and who in such matters could act without the advice of his ministers.[33] At the same time Rogers raised the question whether the labor trade to Queensland ought to be permitted unless the government took it wholly into its own hands.[34]

This firm stand on the moral responsibility of the imperial government was taken by Rogers alone. The Secretary of State, Lord Granville, as was so often the case, had no comment to make, and the Emigration Commissioners were not moved from their complacent satisfaction with the provisions of the Queensland act.[35]

When Rogers retired from the Colonial Office in 1871, no one remained among the permanent officials who combined his sympathetic appreciation of the aims of the missionary societies with his careful and patient sifting of the information they supplied. Herbert, Rogers' successor as Permanent Under-Secretary, Bramston, and Malcolm[36] had little sympathy with the missionary viewpoint and were only

32. No. 22, Granville to Blackall, 23 April 1869, C.O. 201/551.
33. Minute by Herbert on Bowen to Carnarvon, 16 June 1874, C.O. 309/112.
34. Minute by Rogers on Belmore to Granville, 26 Feb. 1869, C.O. 201/551.
35. Emigration Commission to C.O., 14 April 1869, 20 May 1869, P.P. 1868-1869, XLIII, 408.
36. John Bramston, Attorney-General, Queensland, 1870-1873; Assistant Under-Secretary of State for Colonies, 1876-1897. W. R. Malcolm, Assistant Under-Secretary of State for Colonies, 1875-1878. A characteristic minute by Malcolm on Cairns to Carnarvon, 10 Sept. 1875, C.O. 234/35: "Another mare's nest has been discovered by this useful and active society" (A.P.S.).

too ready to dismiss their evidence as untrustworthy. Unfortunately this was often the case.

The missionaries probably had more influence at the Colonial Office in the early years of the labor trade than at any other time, partly because Rogers was sympathetic, but also because this was a formative period before Her Majesty's assent had been given to the Queensland act, and when careful consideration was given to reports of all kinds on its working. Not again until 1892, when the Queensland government revived the labor trade after a two-year interval during which it had been forbidden, did the missionaries have an opportunity to influence an important decision. Though they could not prevent its resumption, they were able to ensure that the law was strictly enforced. This was the kind of function they performed throughout the period, and though Carnarvon and Kimberley were sorely tried by them, Kimberley admitted "they perform a useful function as a perpetual opposition."[37]

Missionary pressure was also brought to bear on the Queensland government. The resolutions of the Sydney meeting were addressed to the Queensland Parliament, both Houses of which refused to receive "a lecture delivered to the Parliament of Queensland by people residing in another colony."[38]

Early in March 1869 a public meeting had been held in Brisbane at which the Polynesian Labour Act was declared to have failed, and a resolution was passed asking for its repeal.[39] The meeting had been organized by the correspondents of the Anti-Slavery Society in Brisbane, R. Short, W. Brookes, and A. Davidson. Short was a journalist who had been writing and lecturing against the labor trade for over two years. Brookes was a small tradesman, Methodist

37. Minute by Kimberley on Anti-Slavery Society to Kimberley, 6 Sept. 1873, C.O. 234/33.
38. *Qd. P.D.*, VIII, 193 and 317.
39. Enclosure in Blackall to Granville, 16 April 1869, *P.P.* 1868-1869, XLIII, 408.

local preacher, and a member of the Legislative Assembly. The opposition of Short and Brookes to Pacific island immigration arose as much out of a narrow racialism and jealous regard for working-class standards as out of humanitarian motives. Brookes was later a committee member of the Anti-Chinese League,[40] suggesting it was to colored immigration rather than colored labor that he was opposed. Davidson's interest was more broadly humanitarian.

The Queensland Legislative Assembly at first refused to accept a petition from the Brisbane meeting on the grounds that the language of the petition showed disrespect to the House.[41] However, the Assembly[42] later followed the Council[43] in accepting an amended version.

About this time the Queensland government had received from the naval officer in command on the Australian station the charges of kidnaping made by the Presbyterian missionary, McNair, against the Queensland licensed ship *Lyttona*.[44] As a result of the enquiry into this case, and of the public opinion aroused by the Sydney and Brisbane public meetings, the Queensland government announced that it intended to amend the act. Recruiting vessels would carry a government agent and an interpreter, and females were to be introduced in the proportion of 25 per cent of the males.[45]

These amendments were suggested, and a motion agreed upon to appoint a Select Committee to enquire into the working of the 1868 act,[46] before the governor of Queensland received Rogers' despatch about the Sydney meeting and the Ross Lewin case. They were therefore the result of pressure

40. *Brisbane Courier*, 6 Jan. 1880.
41. *Qd. P.D.*, VIII, 223.
42. *Ibid.*, 277.
43. *Ibid.*, 241.
44. Lambert to Blackall, 28 Jan. 1869, enclosure in Blackall to Granville, 16 April 1869, *P.P.* 1868-1869, XLIII, 408.
45. Enclosure 4 in Blackall to Granville, 16 April 1869, *P.P.* 1868-1869, XLIII, 408.
46. *Qd. V. & P.* 1869, II, 23.

exerted in the Australian colonies rather than from the Colonial Office.

But the missionary and humanitarian forces in England were also active. The organs of the various societies—*The Chronicle* of the London Missionary Society, the *Reformed Church Magazine,* the *Anti-Slavery Reporter,* the *Colonial Intelligencer,* and the *Island Voyage* of the Melanesian Mission—published full reports about the labor trade. Some individual members of the societies such as Thomas Harvey of Leeds, who had visited the West Indies with Sturge in 1836 to enquire into the condition of the Negroes, were in direct touch with correspondents in Queensland, and had material published independently.[47] Harvey supplied information to the *Leeds Mercury,* whose proprietor, Edward Baines, was Liberal member for Leeds and one of the early Liberal Imperialists.

The most direct pressure from these interests on the imperial government came from a group of members of the Aborigines Protection Society in the House of Commons— P. A. Taylor, E. H. Eastwick, Vice-Admiral Erskine, R. N. Fowler, who was treasurer of the Aborigines Protection Society, and Sir Charles Wingfield, a vice-president. They were given support by the Hon. A. Kinnaird and by Sir John Simeon. The latter was a great nephew of the famous Cambridge divine who was one of the members of the Clapham sect.

Some of these people—Fowler,[48] Kinnaird—had connections with Quaker families who had a traditional interest in humanitarian questions. Some—Eastwick,[49] Kinnaird, Fowler, and Wingfield[50]—had special knowledge or experience of Indian affairs, and were led on from that to an interest in the

47. Harvey to Anti-Slavery Society, 29 Jan. 1872, Anti-Slavery Archives.
48. *Times* obituary, 23 May 1891. Son of a Quaker banker, he had visited the colonies and India, and wrote *Japan, China and India.*
49. *D.N.B.* His family had a long connection with the East India Co. He was an Orientalist and an Assistant Political Secretary, India Office, 1859.
50. *Times* obituary, 1 Feb. 1892. Bengal Civil Service, 1840; 1859-1866, Chief Commissioner of Oude.

Pacific island laborer. Erskine's interest derived from his experience of the Pacific while posted to the Australian station in the forties.[51]

In June 1869 Taylor initiated a debate in the House of Commons on the Queensland labor trade.[52] His main criticism of the Queensland act was that it provided no supervision of recruiting in the islands. He repeated a suggestion made at the Sydney meeting that recruiting should not be allowed unless government depots similar to those in India were set up in the islands. In reply Monsell, the Under-Secretary of State for the Colonies, announced the proposed amendments to the Queensland act. The appointment of government agents, he thought, would go some way to meet Taylor's criticisms.

In January 1870 the Law Officers[53] recommended that Her Majesty's assent should be given to the Queensland act, and that it should be amended as the Queensland government had suggested. But the Colonial Office had heard nothing more of the proposed amendments. It therefore urged upon the government of Queensland the necessity of adopting the amendments which that government had agreed upon largely as a result of pressure from the missionaries, who had produced evidence of the inadequacy of the provisions of the original act relating to recruiting.

51. *Times* obituary, 4 July 1887.
52. *Hansard*, 3rd Series, CXCVII, 633.
53 L.O. to C.O., 11 Jan. 1870, C.O. 201/560.

CHAPTER V. THE RELATION OF THE QUEENSLAND AND IMPERIAL GOVERNMENTS ON THE REGULATION OF RECRUITING

In February 1870, at the same time as he informed the governor of Queensland that the 1868 act would not be disallowed, the Secretary of State for the Colonies, Lord Granville, remarked that he was not aware that the amendments to the act promised in March 1869 had yet come before the Queensland legislature.[1]

Of these the most important affecting recruiting was the one providing for the appointment of government agents on recruiting ships. It was hoped by this means to ensure that the native engaged voluntarily; the provision of the existing act which made this the responsibility of a missionary or European resident in the islands had not been generally observed. The imperial government hoped that this measure would be an effective substitute for setting up depots in the islands—a project urged upon it by Taylor in the debate in the House of Commons in June 1869, and rejected as likely to involve a degree of responsibility it was unwilling to accept.

But the imperial government was prepared to take some additional steps to curb recruiting abuses. It grasped the opportunity offered by the proposal to appoint government agents to suggest that, as the labor trade was "not a mere Queensland question" but an imperial one and involved the other Australian colonies and France, the imperial government should appoint the government agents.[2] Presumably it was intended that these appointments should be made by the governor as an imperial officer and independently of the

1. Granville to Blackall, 18 Feb. 1870, *P.P.* 1871, XLVIII, 468.
2. Granville to Blackall, 15 March 1870, *P.P.* 1871, XLVIII, 468.

advice of his ministers.[3] Another part of Granville's proposal was that the salaries of government agents should be paid by Queensland. So often imperial action had been stifled by Treasury economy; this was a neat move by which the imperial government could assume more responsibility for recruiting under the Queensland act without making any demands on the imperial treasury.

If the Queensland government had agreed to this proposal, suitable regular appointments would have been made immediately; but it was reluctant to have government agents appointed at all.[4] The Colonial Office therefore had to press first for the appointment of government agents, and then over a number of years for a measure to ensure that a suitable type of person was appointed.

I

When Granville's reminder about the proposed amendments to the act was received in Queensland, the Lilley[5] administration was in power. This government had succeeded that of Mackenzie,[6] which had passed the 1868 act. In Mackenzie's government squatter and planter interests were well represented. Mackenzie himself was a partner in a firm of agents importing Pacific islanders, and some of his ministers were employers of this labor. It is a paradox, though an understandable one, that, until 1884, all legislation covering Pacific islanders in Queensland was passed by administrations representing the squatting and planting interests. It was their policy, by minimum regulation, to eradicate the worst abuses in order that the employment of Pacific islanders might be allowed to continue. On the other hand, Lilley's

3. See p. 78, above.
4. Blackall to Granville, 1 July 1870, *P.P.* 1871, XLVIII, 468.
5. Charles Lilley, 1834-1897, M.P. for Fortitude Valley, 1859-1874; attorney-general, 1865-67; premier, 1868-1870; judge of Supreme Court, 1874-1879; chief justice, 1879-1893; K.B., 1881.
6. Mackenzie, Robert Ramsay, 1811-1873, Colonial treasurer, 1859-1862; premier, 1867-1868; succeeded brother as 10th Baronet in baronetcy of Coul and returned to Scotland in 1871.

government represented urban interests opposed to the introduction of Pacific islanders. Lilley himself was perhaps the most uncompromising opponent of their employment in the Queensland legislature. He was a graduate of University College, London, and had twice been attorney-general. He left politics in 1874 to become a judge of the Supreme Court and later chief justice. In 1893 he resigned from this position and fought an unsuccessful election with Sir Thomas McIlwraith on the specific question of the employment of Pacific islanders. Lilley's opposition to colored labor was part of his democratic nationalism; he wanted Queensland to be an independent nation of European smallholders, not a colony governed by a small group of planters employing a large force of colored laborers. His administration therefore would do nothing to ameliorate the condition of the Pacific islanders because it feared this would prolong the practice of employing them. This is why his ministry had not adopted the amendments recommended to it by the immigration officer in March 1869.

In view of Granville's reminder, Lilley included in the governor's speech at the opening of Parliament in April 1870 a passage to the effect that in deference to the wishes of the imperial government the Polynesian Labour Act would be amended.[7] Shortly after the opening of Parliament his government resigned and was succeeded by the planter-squatter party, led on this occasion by A. H. Palmer, general manager of a large pastoral concern, described by Herbert, who knew him, as a "very able, pig-headed, upright, and drunken man,"[8] and by a clerk at the Colonial Office who had just read a typical personal letter from him, as "one who appears to have recently learned writing and not to have learned manners at all."[9] Palmer was not one to defer to the Colonial Office, and in July 1870 his government refused to consider

7. Blackall to Granville, 6 May 1870, C.O. 234/24.
8. Minute on Kennedy to Hicks-Beach, 4 March 1878, C.O. 234/38.
9. Minute by Ebden on Kennedy to Hicks-Beach, 4 March 1878, C.O. 234/38.

the amendments on the grounds that they had become unnecessary because the number of Pacific islanders introduced had recently declined.[10] The reply of Kimberley, who had succeeded Granville at the Colonial Office, was equally firm. The imperial government was considering measures[11] to control the labor trade in the Pacific, and if the Queensland government wished it to continue, it might be advisable for it to reconsider the question of appointing government agents.[12]

In December 1870, shortly after receipt of Kimberley's despatch, regulations were issued for the appointment of government agents,[13] just twenty-one months after the immigration officer had made his recommendation. Before he could obtain a license, a prospective employer had to place a deposit of 10s. with the immigration agent for each laborer required, as well as the bond of £10 to return the native. From the fund thus provided the government agent was to be paid £10 per month, while the owner of the recruiting vessel had to provide him with a free cabin and board. The government agent was responsible to the Queensland government to see that the provisions of the act with respect to recruiting were observed. He was required to inspect the accommodation and food and clothing provided for natives, to explain the contract to the native, who was to be engaged freely in his presence, and to ascertain that the native was fit in body and mind. Returning natives were the responsibility of the government agent, who was furnished with a list of names, property, and islands to which the natives were to be returned. Certificates that the islanders had been returned to their own islands had to be supplied by the government agent to the immigration officer on the vessel's return to Queensland. He was also required to keep a log.[14]

10. Blackall to Granville, 1 July 1870, *P.P.* 1871, XLVIII, 468.
11. The bill which became 35 and 36 Vict., c. 19.
12. Kimberley to Blackall, 3 Oct. 1870, *P.P.* 1871, XLVIII, 468.
13. Enclosure in Blackall to Kimberley, 27 Dec. 1870, *P.P.* 1871, XLVIII, 468.
14. Instructions to Government Agents. *Qd. Government Gazette,* 1871, p. 202.

Kimberley expressed satisfaction that his threat had achieved its purpose. The minute of the Queensland Executive Council was ambiguous, and the Colonial Office was in some doubt as to whether the government agents were to supervise the return of natives to their islands. Dealtry, the principal clerk, thought the necessity of this provision should be pointed out to Queensland; but Kimberley, having achieved his main objective, thought that now the Colonial Office's wishes were being met, undue pressure should not be applied.[15]

To appoint government agents was one thing, for them to perform the functions expected of them was another. The latter implied an independence and authority which they could hardly have in relation to the master of the recruiting vessel. As appointments were casual—made by the Colonial Secretary on the recommendation of some local person—many government agents were the nominees of some party interested in the recruiting. Even where a government agent began with some independence it was difficult for him to retain it against the wish of the master. One government agent in evidence to the 1876 Queensland Select Committee said that, on appointment, he was told by the master that other government agents had always given him a free hand, and he was expected to do the same.[16] Unless the government agent complied, the master could make his life on board almost unbearable. It was for this reason that Layard, the British consul in Fiji at the time of annexation when the Queensland Polynesian Labour Act was adopted, did not appoint government agents on Fiji labor vessels;[17] and that Des Voeux, an experienced colonial administrator, when governor of Fiji doubted whether the function of government agents was intended "to be other than make believe."[18]

The ineffectiveness of the early appointments in Queens-

15. Minute on O'Connell to Kimberley, 25 Jan. 1871, C.O. 234/28.
16. Evidence of William Matson to Select Committee on the General Question of Polynesian Labour, Qd. V. & P. 1876, III, 117-122.
17. Layard to Liardet, 3 Dec. 1874, Anti-Slavery Society Archives.
18. G. W. Des Voeux, My Colonial Service (London, 1903), II, 92.

land was illustrated by the voyage of the *Jason* between April and July 1871.[19] Meiklejohn, a retired squatter and a person of some standing in Maryborough, was appointed government agent for this voyage. When the ship returned to port he was held in irons in the hold in a seriously weakened physical condition—a state he had been in for the last month of the voyage. The registered owner of the vessel, Travis— the campaign secretary of W. H. Walsh, Minister for Works in Palmer's government—asked for a board of enquiry, the three members of whom were nominated by Walsh with the premier's approval.[20] Meiklejohn refused to attend the enquiry. Coath, the master of the *Jason*, and Irving, the mate, gave evidence that Meiklejohn came on board the *Jason* drunk; that during the voyage he had three times threatened the master's life; and that they believed him to be insane, and had therefore put him in irons. Meiklejohn had kept a very neat and careful log which does not support the master's view of him. No irregularities had been recorded in the log, but Meiklejohn had stated that his report would be different, as on board he had been coerced.[21] As the board of enquiry had been arranged and the evidence given by interested parties, it is impossible to say whether Meiklejohn was personally quite unfitted for the post, or whether he had been driven by the master and crew to the state of distraction he apparently was in. Herbert[22] and Kimberley[23] accepted the view that from the beginning Meiklejohn was unfit for the position, and should never have been appointed. Kimberley informed the governor that unless thoroughly fit and trustworthy persons were appointed as government agents, the regulations for the protection of the immigrants would be practically useless.[24]

19. For enquiry into this voyage, see *Qd. V. & P.* 1871-1872, pp. 785 ff.
20. *Qd. V. & P.* 1871-1872, pp. 783, 784.
21. Evidence of George Faircloth, Immigration Officer, Maryborough to Enquiry, *Qd. V. & P.* 1871-1872, pp. 789-790.
22. Minute on No. 12264 (Press Reports, 14 Dec. 1871), C.O. 234/28.
23. Minute on Normanby to Kimberley, 26 Dec. 1871, C.O. 234/27.
24. Kimberley to Normanby, 5 March 1872, C.O. 423/3.

That particular voyage of the *Jason* and the preceding one which took place early in 1871 also illustrate the reluctance of the Palmer administration to enforce the provisions of the 1868 act. In November 1871, on the evidence of some European member of the crew of the *Jason*, a charge of kidnaping was laid against Coath. The first accusation was made by a seaman after the first voyage, but Coath was granted a license for the second voyage because according to the premier, Palmer, the sailor refused to lay an information on oath.[25] Further allegations were made after the second voyage, in which Meiklejohn was government agent, and Coath was charged with the common law misdemeanor of kidnaping under 12 and 13 Vict., c. 96, by which offenses committed within the jurisdiction of the Admiralty could be tried in the Supreme Court of the colony.[26] He was found guilty and fined £50 and sentenced to five years' imprisonment. But no action was taken by the Palmer government to recover the bond of £500 given by the master against kidnaping. When a member of the Opposition asked a question about this, the premier confessed the bond could not be found, and that it may have been returned when the ship arrived in port.[27]

The *Jason* case provoked a move by the Opposition to end the immigration. O'Doherty, the member for Brisbane, gave notice of his intention to introduce a bill to repeal the 1868 act.[28] The government sought to forestall this by introducing a motion for the appointment of a Select Committee to enquire into the introduction of Pacific islanders.[29] The debate on the latter was adjourned, and the former did not get beyond the second reading. But it underlined the difference between the parties at this stage. In the debate on the bill[30] the Opposition remarked that the number of white im-

25. Qd. V. & P. 1871-1872, p. 165.
26. Enclosure 1 in Normanby to Kimberley, 26 Dec. 1871, *P.P.* 1873, L, 244.
27. Qd. V. & P. 1871-1872, pp. 127, 229.
28. *Ibid.,* p. 54.
29. Qd. P.D., XIII, 162.
30. *Ibid.,* XIII, 374.

migrants in 1871 was less than the number of colored. They referred to the possibility of their responsible government's being set aside by the imperial government if colored labor overwhelmed the colony. They wanted to preserve Queensland as a self-governing colony of Europeans; they feared the government wanted it to be a planter aristocracy based on cheap colored labor. This was a contingency upon which the Colonial Office never commented.

In addition to insisting on, first, the appointment of government agents and, second, the selection of persons of suitable character, the Colonial Office made another recommendation to the Queensland government. Early in 1871 the Aborigines Protection Society had drawn the attention of the Colonial Office to letters in the Queensland press by its Brisbane correspondents, Brookes and Davidson, pointing out irregularities in the observance of the act.[31] This was forwarded to Queensland,[32] where Captain Whish moved in the Legislative Council an address to the governor expressing surprise and indignation at the charges made by these individuals, and drawing the attention of the Secretary of State for the Colonies to the approval of Queensland legislation expressed by the Emigration Commissioners.[33]

Palmer, in commenting on the charges made by the Aborigines Protection Society and also by the Presbyterian missionary John G. Paton, against Queensland recruiting vessels, stated that if the imperial government was not entirely satisfied an enquiry could be made.[34] Kimberley accepted this proposal with alacrity. He knew that the Treasury would not pay the costs of an enquiry, but he thought the circumstances demanded an independent commission ap-

31. Aborigines Protection Society to Monsell, 3 Jan. 1871, *P.P.* 1871, XLVIII, 468.
32. Kimberley to Officer Administering Govt. of Queensland, 27 Jan. 1871, *P.P.* 1871, XLVIII, 468.
33. *Qd. P.D.*, XII, 196.
34. Enclosure in O'Connell to Kimberley, 15 April 1871, *P.P.* 1871, XLVIII, 468.

pointed by the imperial government.[35] Such action had been taken in British Guiana, where the colony had paid the costs of the commission appointed by the imperial government to enquire into Des Voeux's charges about the treatment of coolies.

In July 1871 Kimberley therefore suggested to the government of Queensland that it should pay the costs of a commission appointed by the imperial government.[36] Palmer, the Queensland premier, was rather taken aback that Kimberley had accepted the suggestion; he explained that he had made it not because he thought there were any abuses, but simply to set at rest the minds of the English public stirred up by the propaganda of the Aborigines Protection Society. The matter was an imperial one and he could not recommend that his government should make any provision for the expenses.[37]

This reply was received at the Colonial Office at the end of 1871 after the news of Bishop Patteson's murder, when Kimberley was in no mood to compromise. Herbert sought to temper Kimberley's sternness by suggesting that, as opposion to the introduction of colored labor was so strong in Queensland, the government for party reasons was afraid to spend any money at all on it. Between them, Herbert and Kimberley drafted a despatch that placed the burden of responsibility for the labor trade on Queensland, while at the same time alluding to Fiji, so as to deprive Queensland of the rejoinder that all irregularities were connected with the immigration to that island group.[38] The passage of time smoothed the difference between the Colonial Office and Queensland on this question; Bramston, the Queensland attorney-general, and later Assistant Under-Secretary for the Colonies, explained in a private letter to Herbert[39] that

35. Minute on O'Connell to Kimberley, 15 April 1871, C.O. 234/26.
36. Kimberley to O'Connell, 5 July 1871, *P.P.* 1871, XLVIII, 468.
37. Enclosure in Normanby to Kimberley, 25 Oct. 1871, C.O. 234/27.
38. Minute by Herbert and Kimberley on Normanby to Kimberley, 25 Oct. 1871, C.O. 234/27.
39. Minute by Herbert on Normanby to Kimberley, 17 April 1872, C.O. 234/29.

Queensland did not object to contributing a reasonable sum toward the commission, but was not prepared to assume responsibility for an indefinite amount which might be considerable if the commissioners had to travel from Great Britain. Kimberley would not consider sharing the cost as he knew the Treasury would almost certainly refuse to authorize any expenditure for such a purpose.[40] He agreed that the officers of Her Majesty's ships who were about to be employed in enforcing the Pacific Islanders Protection Act recently passed by the imperial Parliament would have the best opportunity of obtaining information on the subject.[41]

The Queensland government did not heed Kimberley's warning that the imperial government might not allow the immigration to continue unless persons of more suitable character than Meiklejohn were appointed as government agents. A minor regulation increasing the capitation fee from which government agents were paid, to 15s. instead of 10s., was the only alteration.[42] The same casual method of appointment continued, and instances of unsuitable appointments and neglect of duty occurred. Goodenough reported that on one Queensland vessel he inspected in the New Hebrides in April 1875, the government agent was a mere inexperienced lad of twenty-one, completely dependent on the master of the vessel.[43] It was his opinion that in most cases the government agent was simply another recruiting agent paid for by the government. He recommended that a much better type of man should be appointed.[44] Carnarvon, who succeeded Kimberley in 1874, had already urged this on Queensland,[45] after receiving a report from the governor of Queensland on the *Mary Stewart* case in which the government agent had allowed natives recruited for Queensland to be

40. Minute by Kimberley on Normanby to Kimberley, 25 Oct. 1871, C.O. 234/27.
41. Kimberley to Normanby (private), 12 July 1872, Kimberley Papers.
42. *Qd. Government Gazette*, 1872, p. 1510 (5 Sept. 1872).
43. Report on visit of H.M.S. *Pearl* to New Hebrides, Ad/9253, C.O. 83/7.
44. *Ibid.*
45. Carnarvon to Cairns, 18 Aug. 1875, referred to in Cairns to Carnarvon, 16 Nov. 1875, C.O. 234/35.

taken against their will to Noumea, where the government agent himself absconded.[46] In response to this despatch six positions for government agents were created in the civil service, permanent during good conduct at a salary of not less than £200 per annum, to be met from the capitation charge, which was to be raised from 15s. to £1.[47]

But even if this ensured the appointment of government agents of good character, it did not necessarily give them the desired independence and authority in relation to the master of the recruiting vessel. Not until 1884 did the Queensland regulations give any specific power to the government over the kind of men who served in recruiting vessels as master, mate, and recruiting agent. The Anti-Slavery Society had asked that some such provision should be included in the 1868 act,[48] but the Emigration Commissioners and the Queensland government were content that the grant of the license should be discretionary.[49] But following a series of irregularities in 1883 and 1884 this negative power was made positive by a clause in the 1884 act by which no person could be employed on a recruiting vessel as master, mate, or recruiting agent unless approved by the minister.[50] This naturally strengthened the position of the government agent.

The measure to secure first the appointment of government agents, and then to give those appointments the status of permanent civil service posts was the major reform in the legislation relating to recruiting. This reform did not conduce to much improvement in the methods of recruiting. Of the other reforms relating to recruiting recommended in 1869, the appointment of interpreters was not secured until the regulations of April 1884,[51] based on the act of that year,

46. Normanby to Carnarvon, 17 Oct. 1874, C.O. 234/34.
47. Minute of Executive Council, 16 Nov. 1875, enclosure in Cairns to Carnarvon, 16 Nov. 1875, C.O. 234/35.
48. Chamerovzow to Buckingham and Chandos, 23 May 1868, P.P. 1867-1868, XLVIII, 391.
49. Murdoch to Rogers, 16 June 1868, P.P. 1867-1868, XLVIII, 391.
50. 47 Vict., No. 12, s. 6.
51. Instructions to government agents, No. 23, Qd. Government Gazette, 17 April 1884.

while the recommendation that women to the number of 25 per cent of male immigrants should be introduced was never implemented. Throughout the whole period the immigration remained almost entirely male.[52] The only other reform of any significance was made by a clause of the 1884 act prohibiting payment to any member of the crew of a recruiting vessel according to the number of natives recruited.[53] This removed an incentive to unscrupulous recruiting. The imperial government had had to press the Queensland government hard before it adopted the reform relating to government agents, but the other measures were passed on its own initiative.

II

These legislative amendments were not sufficient to prevent irregularities by Queensland recruiting vessels in 1883-1884 as serious as any that had occurred previously. Most of these took place in connection with recruiting in the New Guinea area—New Britain, New Ireland, the islands to the southeast of New Guinea, and New Guinea itself—where Queensland vessels had first appeared in 1883.[54] Natives from this area had been recruited since 1880 by German planters for three-month periods of service on adjacent islands, where they had gone willingly. When the Queensland vessels arrived, the natives believed they were going for similar short periods to nearby islands. The first Queensland ships therefore had no difficulty in getting recruits, and they were followed by many others. From the beginning of 1883 to June 1884 Queensland vessels made twenty-seven voyages to this area, and took away about 2,600 natives.[55]

The natives resisted recruiters as soon as they realized that these vessels came from a distant place and those that

52. See Figure 4, p. 146.
53. 47 Vict., No. 12, s. 7.
54. Romilly to Acting High Commissioner for West Pacific, 15 Sept. 1883, *P.P.* 1884, LV, c. 4126.
55. *Qd. V. & P.* 1884, II, 769-770.

went with them did not return within the expected time. The Queensland recruiters met this resistance by force, the worst example being the murder of two natives by the crew of the *Hopeful* at Harris Island in June 1884.[56] The case was tried in the Queensland Supreme Court in December 1884, and the two members of the crew found guilty of the murder of the natives were condemned to death, while the master and government agent were sentenced to life imprisonment, and other members of the crew to shorter terms for kidnaping.

The case assumed considerable importance as illustrating how public opinion in the colony could set aside the decision of the court. Shortly after the conclusion of the case, a public meeting attended by prominent citizens, including members of the Legislative Assembly, petitioned the governor to exercise his prerogative of mercy, and expressed the hope that the Executive Council would endorse the wishes of the people.[57] Samuel Griffith,[58] the premier, aware that such a petition might arise from a feeling that a black man's life was not worth that of a white man, sought to discover the motive behind it. The minister presenting the petition urged mitigation because the crimes of the convicted were part of a series which had been countenanced for so long that it was unjust that punishment should suddenly be exacted from these men. Griffith refused to acknowledge this, and said that if such crimes were regarded as customary, he would never sign another license. At a public open-air demonstration of three thousand people, one speaker referred to Pacific islanders as "oily wretches," "a conniving cunning smooth-tongued lot," to whom the "High Power" in Queensland

56. Enclosure in Musgrave to Derby, 17 Dec. 1884, C.O. 234/45.
57. *Ibid.*
58. Samuel Walker Griffith, 1845-1920, B.A. with first class honors, Sydney University; T. S. Mort Travelling Fellowship; called to bar, 1867; M.P. for East Moreton, 1871; attorney-general in Macalister, Thorn, and Douglas ministries, 1874-1879; also Secretary for Public Instruction in latter two ministries; Premier, 1883-1888 and 1890-1893; resigned to become chief justice, 1893; High Court of Australia, 1903-1919; K.C.M.G., 1886; G.C.M.G., 1895; P.C., 1901.

wanted to sacrifice two white men.[59] As the decision of the court was not questioned on the grounds of debatable evidence, and as the appeal for mercy seemed to be based, not on any opposition to capital punishment as such, but to capital punishment for the murder of natives, the governor, Griffith, and one other member of the Executive Council opposed the commutation of the sentences. However, in view of the strong public feeling and the petition signed by most members of the Legislature, the governor gave way to the majority in the Council, but he wrote in a despatch to Derby, the Secretary of State for the Colonies,

I had not believed it possible that now in any part of the Queen's dominions it should be openly contended that the life of a black human being is not as sacred as that of a white man—that popular meetings should be regarded as a better judge of the law of evidence than the Chief Justice, and that the Government, including presumably Her Majesty's Government are responsible for abuses of a traffic carried on with its sanction.[60]

He expressed a hope that this case would persuade the imperial government to put an end to the trade.

This was not the end of the *Hopeful* case. Four years later, the public again petitioned—this time for the release of the prisoners.[61] Although Chief Justice Lilley strongly upheld the justice of the original sentence, the report of the Minister of Justice threw some doubts on it, and on the strong recommendation of his ministers, the new governor, Sir Henry Norman,[62] pardoned the prisoners.[63] Herbert expressed doubts about the wisdom of this decision, but relief that the Colonial Office did not have to decide the issue.[64] This was of a piece with Herbert's character; he had little

59. Enclosure in Musgrave to Derby, 27 Dec. 1884, C.O. 234/45.
60. Musgrave to Derby, 27 Dec. 1884, C.O. 234/45.
61. Norman to Bramston, 23 Nov. 1889, C.O. 234/50.
62. Henry Wylie Norman, 1826-1904, K.C.B., 1873; G.C.M.G., 1887; service in army in India, 1844-1883; general, 1882; field marshal, 1902; governor of Jamaica, 1883; Queensland, 1889-1895; Chairman, Royal Commission to enquire into condition of sugar growing colonies of the West Indies, 1896.
63. Norman to Knutsford, 22 Feb. 1890, C.O. 234/51.
64. Minute by Herbert on Norman to Knutsford, 17 March 1890, C.O. 234/51.

of Rogers' moral fervor and never of his own initiative raised the question of the treatment of Pacific island labor. On the contrary he often showed some annoyance when his attention was directed toward it. This perhaps explains his animus toward representations of the missionary societies,[65] and his rather terse dismissal of the opinion of Governor Cairns that the report of the 1876 Select Committee showed a bias toward the planters' point of view.[66]

Cairns,[67] the half-brother of Disraeli's Lord Chancellor, and Musgrave,[68] who as governor of Jamaica in 1879 had tried against the wishes of the planters to end the subsidy to coolie immigration, were the only governors of Queensland who sent to the Colonial Office unfavorable reports of that colony's administration of the labor trade, and both Herbert and Bramston tended to set them aside. Bramston criticized Musgrave for leaning too much toward the party which opposed the employment of Pacific islanders;[69] but no one among the permanent officials at the Colonial Office after Rogers' retirement had suggested that any of the other governors leaned too much toward the planters' and squatters' point of view.

The *Hopeful* case provided evidence for those who thought that the Queensland government was not fit to exercise control over natives from outside her territory. About this time this view had been put forward by the commissioners, appointed to enquire into the working of the Western Pacific Orders-in-Council, who had recommended that the administration of Queensland labor recruiting should

65. Minutes on Queensland Agent-General to C.O., 10 May 1871, C.O. 234/28; Normanby to C.O., 24 Dec. 1873, C.O. 234/32.
66. Minute on Cairns to Carnarvon, 6 Dec. 1876, C.O. 234/36.
67. William Wellington Cairns, 1828-1888, K.C.M.G., 1877; governor of Trinidad, 1874; Queensland, 1875-1877; administrator of South Australia, 1877.
68. Anthony Musgrave, 1828-1888, C.M.G., 1871; K.C.M.G., 1875; colonial secretary, Antigua, 1854; administrator, Nevis, 1860; St. Vincent, 1871; lieutenant governor, St. Vincent, 1862; governor, Newfoundland, 1864; British Columbia, 1869; lieutenant governor, Natal, 1872; governor, South Australia, 1873; Jamaica, 1877; Queensland, 1888.
69. Minute on Musgrave to Derby, 24 April 1884, C.O. 234/44.

be placed directly under the High Commissioner.[70] The Queensland government protested strongly against this recommendation as an infringement of its rights of responsible government.[71] The Colonial Office, particularly Herbert,[72] had always been careful not to interfere with the colony's right of self-government. But it had never conceded that the labor trade to Queensland was entirely the business of that colony. Rogers had reminded Blackall that the labor trade was an imperial matter as well, and that the governor as an imperial officer had a special responsibility to see that the Pacific islanders received the consideration that was given to colored labor in other colonies.[73] Granville, on Rogers' advice, had proposed that the imperial government should appoint government agents on Queensland ships.[74] Now the commissioners appointed to enquire into the working of Western Pacific Orders-in-Council had suggested that the administration of the labor trade should be withdrawn from the Queensland government and given to the High Commissioner. The Colonial Office was not prepared to accept this infringement of Queensland's political rights, but it did foster a move to withdraw from the Queensland courts to the Court of the High Commission cases involving offenses by Queensland recruiters.

The *Hopeful* case was the most spectacular, but only one of a number of cases which showed how susceptible the courts and the administration were to a public opinion which cared little for the rights of the colored man. In the *Hopeful* case the jury's decision had been set aside by the display of public opinion; in another case, that of the *Alfred Vittery*,[75] the jury had failed to convict in such a way that Derby re-

70. Report of Western Pacific Royal Commission, s. 153, *Qd. V. & P.* 1884, II, 958.
71. Enclosure in Queensland Agent-General to C.O., 24 April 1884, C.O. 234/25.
72. Minute on Musgrave to Derby, 10 March 1884, C.O. 234/44.
73. See p. 78, above.
74. See p. 83, above.
75. Enclosure in Musgrave to Derby, 10 April 1884, C.O. 234/44.

ferred to it as "a failure of justice which is greatly to be deplored, and will require serious consideration when the possibility of permitting any continuance of the Western Pacific labour traffic is being considered."[76] The case had occurred in October 1883 near Malaita in the Solomons. Two natives who caused a disturbance on board had been shot dead. No sufficient evidence was adduced at the trial to show that the natives' behavior was a threat to life or to the safety of the ship, yet the jury found all the accused not guilty except one, on whom the verdict was manslaughter with a recommendation to mercy. On this failure of justice Musgrave wrote to Derby[77] that in such cases it would always be difficult to obtain convictions in the local courts. He suggested provision should be made for transferring the trial of offenders to the Court of the Western Pacific High Commission, where assessors and not jurors were employed.

The question of extradition of offenders from Queensland to the High Commission Court was under discussion at the time of the trial of the *Alfred Vittery* prisoners. It had arisen in January 1884 in connection with members of the crew of the *Caera*,[78] who had been accused of kidnaping in the Louisiade Islands. In the opinion of Griffith there was no power under the Foreign Jurisdiction and Fugitive Offenders Acts and the Western Pacific Orders-in-Council of 1877 to extradite offenders from an Australian colony to the Court of the Western Pacific High Commission.[79] The Imperial Law Officers accepted Griffith's opinion, and under the direction of the Colonial Office proceeded to draw up an Order-in-Council to remedy this.[80]

In the meantime, however, Chief Justice Lilley anticipated the content of the Order-in-Council by ruling that for the purposes of extradition the High Commission could be

76. Derby to Musgrave, 9 June 1884, *Qd. V. & P.* 1884, II, 745.
77. Musgrave to Derby, 10 April 1884, C.O. 234/44.
78. Musgrave to Derby, 9 Jan. 1884, C.O. 234/44.
79. Enclosure in Musgrave to Derby, 8 May 1884, C.O. 234/44.
80. L.O. to C.O., 17 July 1884, 28 Oct. 1884, C.O. 234/45.

regarded as part of Her Majesty's dominions, and the High Commissioner as a governor of one of Her Majesty's colonies. On this decision two members of the crew of the *Stanley*, Davies and McMurdo, against whom proceedings were taken in the Queensland Supreme Court under the kidnaping act, were extradited and tried in the Court of the Western Pacific High Commission.[81] In the words of the High Commissioner, Des Voeux, this case "made it known for the first time to ill doers of the Western Pacific, that none of the Australian colonies is now a safe refuge for them."[82]

As a result of the evidence produced at this trial, the High Commissioner made some harsh criticisms of Queensland's administration of recruiting. In his opinion, the *Stanley* case might not have occurred had earlier conduct by other Queensland vessels been censured by Queensland authorities.[83] Considerable weight was given to this criticism by the conduct of the acting immigration agent, who had written a letter to one of the prisoners in the *Stanley* case in which he had said, "There is one comfort; you did nothing dishonourable or that you need in the least be ashamed of." The Queensland government called for an explanation but chose to admonish rather than dismiss the agent from the service.[84]

There were other instances in which officials failed in their duty, and for these Griffith expressed sincere regret.[85] Griffith was himself a man of great integrity, perhaps the most eminent of all Australian statesmen of that period. The maladministration had occurred in spite of his efforts to see the law properly administered. In some cases, such as the commuting of the sentences of the *Hopeful* prisoners, he had to bow to the will of his colleagues. Enquiry had been held into many of the incidents that occurred in recruiting in 1883-1884, and many of those concerned had been dismissed from

81. Enclosure in Musgrave to Derby, 20 June 1884, C.O. 234/44.
82. Quoted in minute on Norman to Knutsford, 1 April 1892, C.O. 234/53.
83. Des Voeux, *My Colonial Service*, II, 91.
84. Enclosure in Musgrave to C.O., 9 March 1885, C.O. 234/45.
85. Griffiths to Musgrave, enclosure in Musgrave to Derby, 18 Feb. 1884, C.O. 234/44.

the service. In 1884 Griffith appointed a Royal Commission to enquire into the activity of Queensland vessels in the New Guinea area in 1884.[86] Most of the evidence supplied to the commission came from the natives who had been brought to Queensland. The commissioners reported that these natives had been sent against their will, and they were returned at Queensland's expense under the supervision of H. H. Romilly, who had assumed the administration of the New Guinea Protectorate on the death of Sir P. Scratchley. The Queensland government also paid compensation to the employers.[87]

But these were belated attempts to make amends for crimes which the Queensland legislation relating to recruiting had not been able to check. The events of 1883-1884 confirmed the growing impression in Queensland that recruiting could never be adequately regulated by colonial legislation, and that if the colony was to preserve, or rather regain, its good name, then recruitment must stop. Griffith introduced a bill for this purpose in October 1885. No more licenses to recruit were to be issued after 31 December 1890.[88]

Griffith had accepted the view of the party opposed to the introduction of Pacific islanders that sugar could be grown without black labor, and his government had already introduced measures to promote the small cane farm in preference to the large plantation. In 1884 a land selection act[89] was passed to make land available for cane-growing to the small farmer, and to complement it in 1885 the government made available a sum of money to set up its first central sugar mill.[90] Such central mills had been first set up in the French colony of Martinique, and an unsuccessful attempt had been made to set them up in St. Lucia under the guidance of the

86. *Qd. V. & P.* 1885, II, 797 ff.
87. 49 Vict., No. 3.
88. 49 Vict., No. 17, s. 11.
89. 48 Vict., No. 28.
90. *Qd. V. & P.* 1885, I, 1157. For earlier private central mills, see p. 135, below.

administrator, G. W. Des Voeux.[91] In Queensland they became part of the successful plan which enabled that colony to become the only major sugar producer to use white labor exclusively.

Griffith had as little sympathy with the extreme opponents of Pacific island labor as he had for those who wanted Queensland to become another South Carolina. He was prepared to accept colored labor—Pacific islanders, but not Indian coolies —until he reorganized the sugar industry, when it would no longer be necessary. In the event, the five years he allowed for this was not long enough; he then had the courage, against strong popular opinion, to postpone the end of the system for a further ten years.[92]

The measure of 1885 to end the labor trade was not the result of any direct pressure from the imperial government; like the original proposal for amending the 1868 act the initiative was with the colonial government. In the debates in the Queensland Parliament[93] there was little difference of opinion on the clause to end the labor trade, and this clause evoked little comment at the Colonial Office.

On the whole one must conclude that the attempt by the colonial legislature to regulate recruiting was a failure. It was early brought home to the imperial and the Queensland governments by missionary representation that the provisions of the original act were inadequate. It was Queensland that suggested the amendments, which were adopted, however, only under strong pressure from the imperial government. This pressure stopped short of any interference with the colony's rights of self-government, but the imperial government tried to exercise some authority through the governors, most of whom, however, were sympathetic to the employment of colored labor. The withdrawal from the Queensland courts to the High Commission Court of cases involving crimes by

91. Des Voeux, *op. cit.*, I, 212 ff.
92. Griffiths' manifesto enclosed in Norman to Knutsford, 13 Feb. 1892, *P.P.* 1892, LVI, c. 6686.
93. *Qd. P.D.* XLVII, 1076 ff.

Queenslanders against natives in the Pacific reflected un-favorably on that colony's treatment of natives, but in Griffith it had a statesman who spared no effort to see justice done, and who answered the failure of recruiting legislation by the reorganization of the sugar industry to make the recruitment of colored labor unnecessary.

CHAPTER VI. THE QUEENSLAND LABOR TRADE AND THE ANNEXATION OF NEW GUINEA

The fear that Germany might annex New Guinea was the ostensible reason why the McIlwraith[1] government of Queensland annexed the territory in the name of the Queen in April 1883. But the close connection in time between this action and the appearance of Queensland recruiting vessels in New Guinea waters raised suspicions in some quarters that the Queensland government wanted to secure for its planters a supply of cheap colored labor free from any restrictions placed on it by the imperial government. These suspicions were strengthened as the McIlwraith government, in which planter interests were well represented, were negotiating at the same time for Indian coolie labor to come to Queensland in spite of strong popular feeling against it. A change of government in November 1883 brought Griffith to office, and he opposed the importation of Pacific islanders. But the question of annexation remained, in spite of Derby's refusal to confirm McIlwraith's action, and with it the fear that the administration of New Guinea and its native population might pass to the Queensland government.

The permanent officials at the Colonial Office seemed at first not to be disturbed by this possibility. They suggested that a solution of the agitation of the Australian colonies for the annexation of New Guinea might be to allow Queensland to assume responsibility for both its cost and administration. But strong representations by influential people, pointing out the unsatisfactory nature of Queensland's administration of the Pacific island immigration, convinced the Colonial

1. Thomas McIlwraith, 1835-1900, M.P. for Maronoa, 1868; Secretary for Public Works and Mines, 1874; premier, colonial treasurer, colonial secretary, 1879-1883; second ministry, 1888; coalition with Griffith, 1890; third ministry, 1893; K.C.M.G., 1882.

Office that the welfare of the natives of New Guinea would be secure only if the imperial government were to assume responsibility for it.

I

The proclamation by the Queensland government of New Guinea as part of Her Majesty's domains[2] aroused suspicion in some quarters where it was assumed that the territory was to be annexed to, and administered by, the Queensland government. It was seen as a move made in the interests of Queensland planters—well represented in the government of the time led by McIlwraith—to secure undisputed control of an ample supply of cheap colored labor. Those who held Queensland's motive suspect included Sir Arthur Gordon, the High Commissioner for the Western Pacific, who was in England at the time, representatives of the London Missionary Society in New Guinea, and Lord Lamington,[3] who spoke on the subject in the House of Lords. Their views were given sufficient publicity for Derby, who refused to approve the Queensland action, to advance them as one reason why New Guinea should not be annexed to Queensland.[4]

These suspicions also were strengthened by the coincidence in time of Queensland's annexation and the appearance of Queensland recruiting vessels in New Guinea waters, a fact brought to the notice of Derby by the Aborigines Protection Society.[5] The *Hopeful*, the first of these vessels, returned to Queensland in May 1883. The comparatively short voyage and quick return to port aroused much interest among planters, and in the succeeding 15 months 27 voyages were made and 2,600 natives from the islands immediately east and

2. *Victorian Parliamentary Paper* No. 25, 1884, p. 76. (*Victorian Parliamentary Paper* hereinafter will be referred to as *Vict. P.P.*)

3. *Hansard*, 3rd Series, CCLXXXI, 3 (2 July 1883).

4. Derby to Officer Administering Government of Queensland, 11 July 1883, *Vict. P.P.* No. 38, 1884, p. 19.

5. A.P.S. to Derby, 12 Sept. 1883, C.O. 234/43.

north of the mainland of New Guinea were taken to Queensland.[6]

To the missionaries in the area this, coinciding with the move for annexation, was sufficient proof that Queensland intended to gain possession of New Guinea to secure an adequate supply of labor. The missionaries had received enquiries from planter associations in Queensland about the possibility of recruiting labor from the mainland of New Guinea.[7] When the proclamation followed soon after, and Queensland recruiting vessels appeared in nearby waters, they concluded that the government was acting on behalf of the planters.[8]

There were other facts that might support this view. It was well-known that the existing sources of colored labor were inadequate to meet the needs of the expanding sugar industry, and the government between 1882 and 1883 had been conducting negotiations for the introduction of coolie labor from India. There was, however, stronger popular opposition in Queensland to the immigration of Asian labor than to Pacific island labor. In the face of this resistance might not the government regard New Guinea as politically a safer source of labor than India?

The early eighties were for the Queensland sugar industry a period of expansion comparable with that of the first years of the seventies, when the area under sugar increased from some 6,000 to 14,000 acres.[9] Between 1880 and 1884 the area under sugar increased from 20,000 to 57,000 acres[10] and the export of sugar rose from 6,000 tons in 1881 to 30,000 in 1885.[11] Although the price of sugar was never again as high as it had been in 1872, there was some recovery in

6. Qd. V. & P. 1884, II, 769-770.
7. Letter in Queenslander, 31 March 1883, by W. G. Lawes, L.M.S. Archives, London, Papua 2.3.C.
8. Macfarlane to L.M.S., 8 April 1883, L.M.S. Archives, London, Papua 2.3.C.
9. Qd. V. & P. 1889, II, 985.
10. G. H. Knibbs, Prices, Price Indexes and Cost of Living in Australia (Commonwealth Bureau of Census and Statistics, 1912), p. 63.
11. Appendix 33, Qd. Royal Commission on Sugar Industry, 1889.

the years 1879-1880. In this period Queensland outstripped Jamaica and Natal and was third to Mauritius and British Guiana among Empire sugar producers,[12] and began to compete seriously with Mauritius and Java in the sugar markets of the Australian colonies. This expansion severely strained the labor resources available. The immigration of Pacific islanders was heavier between 1881 and 1884 than at any other period,[13] yet it was not sufficient to meet the demand.

The McIlwraith government therefore promulgated regulations under the act passed in 1862[14] for the introduction of laborers from India and sought to have these approved by the Indian government.[15] Much of the initiative for this move had come from the Mackay Planters Association, and in particular from its president, J. E. Davidson. Davidson was a director of the Melbourne-Mackay Sugar Company, which had a number of large plantations in Queensland. In 1872, when returning from England, he had visited Mauritius, where he hoped to arrange for Indians who had completed their contract there to migrate to Queensland, but the Indian government had vetoed the plan. When McIlwraith's regulations to introduce coolie labor were repealed by Griffith in November 1883,[16] Davidson made representations direct to Lord Derby and the government of India to be allowed to introduce Indians into Queensland privately.[17] When this too failed,[18] he revived the movement for the separation of North Queensland.[19] Davidson represented that small group of planters who wished to establish in Queensland a planta-

12. *P.P.* 1888, XCIII, No. 353, p. 3.
13. See Appendix, Table 1.
14. 26 Vict., No. 5.
15. India Office, Government of India, Proceedings of Revenue and Agriculture Department, 1881-1884.
16. Griffith to Secretary to Government of India, 13 Dec. 1883. Government of India, Proceedings of Revenue and Agriculture Department, March, 1884.
17. Davidson and Jeffray to Derby, 9 July 1884. Government of India, Proceedings of Revenue and Agriculture Department, Oct. 1884. Cf. Jeffray to Secretary to Government of India, 31 March 1884. Government of India, Proceedings of Revenue and Agriculture Department, May 1884.
18. Secretary to Government of India to Jeffray, 5 May 1884, *ibid.*
19. Davidson and Lawes to Derby, 14 Jan. 1885, C.O. 234/46.

tion economy based on cheap colored labor. Those who wanted Queensland to develop into a democracy of small-holders distrusted the McIlwraith government for the influence that such men as Davidson had with it. If the McIlwraith government were prepared to introduce coolies to satisfy this planter minority, then it was equally capable of annexing New Guinea to secure cheap labor for the planters. McIlwraith himself denied this when Derby repeated what the missionaries and Sir Arthur Gordon had suggested. McIlwraith said his primary motive was to forestall annexation by a foreign power.[20]

II

The full explanation for Queensland's annexation of New Guinea in April 1883 is to be sought elsewhere than in the labor supply question. Queensland was not alone in pressing for New Guinea to be declared British territory; the other Australian colonies joined in with varying degrees of enthusiasm. Moreover, it was not in respect to New Guinea alone that they desired action; they pressed for the annexation of all the islands of Melanesia that were unoccupied by any European power. In all cases the principal reason advanced for such action was strategic: that the security of the Australian colonies depended on these islands' being under British control. The desire for cheap labor was a motive restricted to Queensland, and if the question of annexation is placed in its larger perspective, this particular motive seems incidental and secondary.

From 1858 Presbyterian missionaries in the New Hebrides had from time to time petitioned the imperial government to annex those islands before the French took action.[21] The first definite approach to the imperial government to annex New Guinea came from an Australian-born London barrister,

20 McIlwraith to Administrator, Government of Queensland, 28 Sept. 1883. *Vict. P.P.* No. 38, 1884, p. 46.
    21. F.O. to C.O., 17 Aug. 1860, C.O. 201/514.

Francis P. Labilliere, in 1874. Labilliere, a foundation member of the Royal Colonial Institute and later one of the chief advocates of Imperial Federation, had called a private meeting at the Royal Colonial Institute of people who were interested in and knew something about New Guinea. He then wrote to the Secretary of State for the Colonies urging annexation on both economic and political grounds.[22]

Herbert gave careful attention to Labilliere's arguments, noting that New Guinea, because of its wealth and strategic position, was a more important question for the Australian colonies and the Empire than the annexation of Fiji.[23] Carnarvon therefore sought the opinion of the governments and the governors of the Australian colonies.[24] The executive councils of the Australian colonies expressed themselves in favor of annexation, but the governors were more hesitant. Governor Cairns of Queensland, however, while questioning the economic attraction of New Guinea, advised annexation in order to keep out any foreign power.[25]

In minutes on this reply of Governor Cairns the permanent officials at the Colonial Office expressed the views which were to underlie Colonial Office policy toward New Guinea for the next ten years. Neither Malcolm nor Herbert appreciated Cairns's apprehension that if Britain did not annex New Guinea, one of her maritime rivals would, and would thus threaten the security of the Australian colonies. Malcolm assumed that Cairns's reference to half a dozen European powers as possible intruders showed that he had no definite information that any of them were really interested, while Herbert ridiculed the "prevailing idea of Australian statesmen . . . that their country must perish if any foreign power hoists her flag within a week's sailing. . . ." However,

22. Labilliere to Secretary of State for Colonies, 26 March 1874, C.O. 234/34.
23. Minute by Herbert on Labilliere to Secretary of State for Colonies, 26 March 1874, C.O. 234/34.
24. Circular despatch, Carnarvon to Governors of Australian Colonies, 17 April 1874, P.P. 1876, LIV, c. 1566.
25. Cairns to Carnarvon, 22 Feb. 1875, C.O. 234/35.

Carnarvon was more appreciative of this danger. A few days later he received a deputation from the Council of the Royal Colonial Institute. Writing privately to Carnarvon the following day, the Duke of Manchester, the president of the council, underlined what he thought had not been made clear the day before: the council thought the occupation of two strategic points commanding Torres Strait with a declaration of a protectorate over the mainland not occupied by Holland would be sufficient to keep other naval powers out.[26]

Carnarvon accepted the first part of the suggestion and it was passed on to the Foreign Office,[27] but nothing came of it. It was revived in 1876 when the Australian colonies feared French action, and was partly carried out in 1878 when, by Letters Patent, the boundary of the colony of Queensland was extended to include the islands within sixty miles of her coast.[28]

But the real obstacle to any imperial action in this matter, as in so many others in the sixties and seventies, was expense. If the colonies had been willing to pay the expenses of any form of annexation of New Guinea, the Colonial Office might have given such a plan greater consideration. Herbert did not see why the British taxpayer should defray the expenses of occupying a country from which the Australian taxpayer would reap the benefit.[29] There was, moreover, the fear—and this was present in Derby's mind in 1883—that if the imperial government accepted the expense of annexing New Guinea, it would drift into meeting the wishes of the Australian colonies in respect to the other islands of Melanesia.

All these views were brought together in Carnarvon's despatch to the governor of Queensland early in 1876.[30] Here Carnarvon anticipated an argument that the Australian

26. Manchester to Carnarvon, 30 April 1875, Carnarvon Papers, P.R.O. 30/6, 45.
27. C.O. to F.O., 7 Aug. 1875. C.O. Confidential Print No. 53, C.O. 808/15.
28. Letters Patent, 10 Oct. 1878, C.O. 234/38.
29. Minute by Herbert on Cairns to Carnarvon, 22 Feb. 1875, C.O. 234/35.
30. Carnarvon to governor of Qd., 13 Jan. 1876. Qd. V. & P. 1876, III, 15.

colonies were to use in favor of annexation, particularly after the discovery of gold in 1878: the need for good government among the Europeans in the area. Carnarvon pointed out that under the Pacific Islanders Protection Act of 1875, the imperial government had power to establish a High Commission for the good government of territory in the Pacific not governed by any recognized power. The High Commission was thus to become the imperial government's alternative answer to any petition for annexation. Kimberley had welcomed it in debates on the 1875 act as a means of preventing the conditions arising in other islands of the Pacific that had forced the imperial government to annex Fiji.[31] With regard to New Guinea, the imperial government held firmly to this policy until German action forced her to establish a protectorate in 1884.

Queensland again pressed for annexation early in 1883, when the agent-general was authorized to place Queensland's case before the Colonial Office.[32] The same argument in respect to the danger of foreign intervention was used, but now it was more definite because of the growth of German influence in the area since 1874. Since 1857 the Hamburg firm of Godeffroy & Son had been trading in Samoa and extending its trading posts westward toward New Guinea. This process was accelerated after 1880 when Godeffroy's assets were taken over by Deutsche Seehandels-gesellschaft, which by 1883 had eighteen trading posts in the islands immediately east of the mainland of New Guinea. Attempts had been made to get state support for German companies which might take the form of annexation of territory in which their trading interests were established, but these efforts had been frustrated by the rejection of Bismarck's Samoan Subsidy Bill. Queensland's fears of German intervention had been aroused by an article in *Augsburger Allgemeine Zeitung* toward the end of 1882 advocating German expansion in the area, and

31. *Hansard,* 3rd Series, CCXXIV, 3.
32. Agent-General to C.O., 28 Feb. 1883, C.O. 234/43.

by general rumors that Germany and Italy were contemplating action.[33]

The agent-general gave more weight than formerly to the argument anticipated by Carnarvon in 1876: the need for order and justice among Europeans in the areas. Upon this and the strategic argument the agent-general based Queensland's case, but he enormously improved it in the eyes of the Colonial Office by introducing a new factor—Queensland's willingness to meet the costs of annexation. This removed the principal obstacle to annexation, and Mercer, one of the clerks at the Colonial Office, thought annexation of New Guinea to Queensland would be the most satisfactory solution to a question that could not be staved off indefinitely.[34] He recalled, however, that Carnarvon had objected to the plans of Armit's New Guinea Colonising Co. because they provided no effective guarantees for the welfare of the native population, and he supposed that some such guarantees would be required from Queensland. Mercer showed more concern to be rid of a troublesome problem than to secure the interests of the natives. Much the same is true of Bramston; Herbert and Derby were both more hesitant, feeling the question required more consideration.[35]

At this stage, while these negotiations were in progress, Chester, the Queensland magistrate at Thursday Island, acting on instructions from the Queensland Executive Council, landed at Port Moresby and took possession of the portion of New Guinea and the islands lying between the 141°W. and the 155°W. meridians.[36] The reason for this precipitate action was the rumor that the German corvette *Carola*, which left Sydney on March 18, intended to take possession of the territory on behalf of Germany.[37] This action caused sur-

33. *F.O. Handbook* No. 42.
34. Minute by Mercer on Agent-General to C.O., 28 Feb. 1883, C.O. 234/43.
35. Minutes on Agent-General to C.O., 28 Feb. 1883, C.O. 234/43.
36. McIlwraith to Kennedy, 13 April 1883, *Vict. P.P.* No. 25, 1884, pp. 70-71.
37. Administrator, Government of Queensland, to Derby (telegram), 4 June 1883, *Vict. P.P.* No. 25, 1884, p. 72.

prisingly little opposition at the Colonial Office. Herbert criticized the governor for not first communicating with the Secretary of State before taking such unusual action, but he thought that ultimately the imperial government would be obliged to confirm the action.[38]

The Queensland government sought and obtained the support of the other Australian colonies for its action.[39] As a result the agents-general waited upon Derby, who asked them to submit a memorandum of their case. This they did,[40] and in the process extended the demand for annexation to include all the other islands of Melanesia unoccupied by a European power. This caused Derby to suspect the motives of the Australian colonies, who he thought were deliberately trying to assert their independence of the mother country. In no other way could he explain why the colonial politicians should set up these new demands with which they knew the imperial government could not comply, when they had all but obtained what they wanted in New Guinea.[41]

The colonies, however, did not obtain what they wanted. The Foreign Office stated there were no grounds for the rumors that other European powers were about to annex New Guinea.[42] But the Colonial Office feared that the failure of Britain to take action would be interpreted by other powers as giving them the right to proceed if they so desired.[43] Derby bowed to the will of the Foreign Office, but in announcing the decision of the imperial government not to ratify Queensland's proclamation, he stated that any action by a foreign power in the area would be regarded as an unfriendly act.[44] Derby's alternative to annexation was the same as Carnarvon's—the High Commission. This he said

38. Minute by Herbert on Kennedy to Derby, 16 April 1883, C.O. 234/43.
39. *Vict. P.P.* No. 25, 1884, p. 40.
40. Agents-General to Derby, 21 July 1883, *P.P.* 1883, XLVII, c. 3814.
41. Derby to Gladstone, 13 Sept. 1883, Gladstone Papers, 44321.
42. F.O. to C.O., 5 May 1883, 14 June 1883, 25 June 1883, C.O. 234/43.
43. Minute by Bramston on F.O. to C.O., 14 June 1883, C.O. 234/43.
44. Derby to Officer Administering Government of Queensland, 11 July 1883, *Vict. P.P.* No. 38, 1884, p. 19.

provided a jurisdiction sufficient for the immediate needs of the territory.

Mcllwraith, the Queensland premier, was not at all satisfied with Derby's statement. He could not put aside the danger of foreign intervention which only annexation by Britain could prevent. The High Commission gave no security from this threat. Moreover, to regard such an act by a foreign power as an unfriendly gesture would be no consolation to Queensland after the event. The High Commission too had no power over non-British subjects whether they were Europeans or natives. Mcllwraith therefore declared that Queensland would not contribute toward the cost of setting up a Deputy High Commissioner in New Guinea.[45]

His successor, Griffith, however, acceded[46] to Derby's suggestion of May 1884[47] that Queensland should contribute toward the cost of the Deputy High Commissioner in New Guinea. Upon this agreement, plans were drawn up for the administration of the protectorate declared late in 1884 after the German government had stated its intention to annex the territory of the Neu Guinea Kompagnie formed in May 1884.

III

Seen in this larger perspective the need for labor was a very secondary motive in Queenland's interest in New Guinea. Annexation had been pressed for by successive Queensland governments since 1874, some of which had been opposed to the introduction of Pacific island labor. Even if the Mcllwraith government's motive was suspect—in spite of Mcllwraith's own statements that the primary concern of his government was Queensland's security—the action of his successor, Griffith, removed any doubt that Queensland intended to use New Guinea as a reservoir from which to draw

45. Mcllwraith to Officer Administering Government of Queensland, 28 Sept. 1883, *Vict. P.P.* No. 38, 1884, p. 46.
46. Musgrave to C.O., 4 Sept. 1884, C.O. 234/45.
47. Circular Derby to governors of Australian colonies, 9 May 1884, *P.P.* 1884, LV, c. 3839.

supplies of cheap labor. Following irregular recruiting by Queensland vessels in the New Guinea area in 1883 and the early months of 1884, the Griffith government issued regulations in June forbidding recruiting by Queensland vessels in New Guinea,[48] New Britain, New Ireland,[49] and Louisiade archipelago.[50] When rumors spread in 1885 that Queensland planters intended to recruit from the German protectorates in this area, effective action was taken by the Queensland government to prevent it.[51]

As evidence of its good faith in the administration of the labor trade, the Griffith government appointed a Royal Commission in 1884 to enquire into the conditions under which labor was recruited in the New Guinea area. As a result of the findings of the commission, the government returned more than six hundred natives to their islands, and paid compensation to employers who had engaged such natives in good faith.

IV

If the desire to secure native labor was at most a very secondary motive in Queensland's proclamation of April 1883, her administration of the immigration of Pacific islanders had an important bearing on whether, in the event of annexation by the imperial government, New Guinea should be annexed to Queensland, or administered as a crown colony or by some authority other than the Queensland executive.

From early in 1883 when Queensland offered to meet the costs involved in the annexation of New Guinea,[52] the permanent officials at the Colonial Office were inclined to favor the annexing of New Guinea to that colony, with just a passing regret that this might not be in the best interests of

48. 27 June 1884, *Qd. Government Gazette* 1884, p. 1924.
49. 19 June 1884, *Qd. Government Gazette* 1884, p. 1855.
50. 24 Dec. 1884, *Qd. Government Gazette* 1884, p. 2040.
51. Musgrave to C.O., 14 July 1885, C.O. 234/46.
52. Queensland Agent-General to C.O., 28 Feb. 1883, C.O. 234/43.

the native inhabitants.[53] This preference for an expedient settlement at possible risk to native interests was not new. In 1872 Kimberley had wanted to annex Fiji to New South Wales, fully aware that he was handing over a large native community to a colony with responsible government.[54] New South Wales, however, was unwilling to accept the responsibility. Herbert, too, had been prepared to accept that course or to leave Fiji to be governed by the *de facto* government.[55]

Only once between February and May 1883, when the question of annexing New Guinea to Queensland was being discussed at the Colonial Office, did a permanent official mention Queensland's record in dealing with her own aborigines as a possible reason why that colony should not be entrusted with the affairs of the natives of New Guinea; and even then that official, Mercer, concluded that Queensland would probably be more careful to study moderation and listen to directions from the imperial government in the case of New Guinea natives than she had been in connection with her own aborigines.[56] The more immediate and relevant question of Queensland's administration of the immigration of Pacific islanders was not raised by the permanent officials. But there were people outside the Colonial Office who used this argument very cogently and successfully as a reason why Queensland should not be allowed to administer the affairs of the natives of New Guinea.

One of the most influential of these people was Sir Arthur Gordon, a friend of Gladstone, with whom he regularly corresponded. As governor of Fiji, he had complained to Gladstone that none of the permanent officials at the Colonial Office had the breadth of vision of Sir James Stephen, Sir

53. Minutes by Mercer, Bramston, Herbert on Queensland Agent-General to C.O., 28 Feb. 1883, C.O. 234/43.
54. Kimberley to Gladstone, 26 July 1871, Gladstone Papers, 44224.
55. Minute by Herbert on Belmore to Kimberley, 28 April 1871, C.O. 201/563.
56. Minute by Mercer on Aborigines Protection Society to C.O., 14 May 1883, C.O. 234/43.

Henry Taylor, or Lord Blatchford;[57] and on another occasion that none of the permanent officials, with the exception of Herbert, when supported by Carnarvon, had any sympathy with native interests.[58] Soon after Queensland annexed New Guinea, Gordon wrote privately to Gladstone to say how unfit Queensland was to be entrusted with the welfare of a native community. The affairs of a large community of natives should not as a general rule be entrusted to a small "ignorant and selfish oligarchy of another race, having interests directly opposed to those of the natives themselves."[59] Particular circumstances making annexation inadvisable in the case of Queensland were her treatment of her own aborigines and her incentive to use native labor on sugar plantations. In this letter to Gladstone, and in a column, contributed anonymously to the *Times*[60] in a similar vein, Gordon made one false accusation against Queensland—that its courts did not accept native testimony. The chief justice of Queensland, in London at the time, was quick to correct this error.[61] The Aborigines Protection Society also protested against Queensland's being allowed to administer New Guinea,[62] as did the missionaries of the London Missionary Society in New Guinea.[63] They were both, however, in favor of annexation by the imperial government, under whom they felt the interests of the natives would be safeguarded.

Derby took account of these views when he refused to ratify the action of the Queensland government in annexing New Guinea.[64] This marks a change from the attitude at the Colonial Office under Carnarvon when it was prepared to allow Queensland to administer the territory if it was an-

57. Gordon to Gladstone, 22 March 1876, Gladstone Papers, 44320.
58. Gordon to Gladstone, 17 May 1878, Gladstone Papers, 44320.
59. Gordon to Gladstone, 20 April 1883, Gladstone Papers, 44321.
60. London *Times*, 15 May 1883.
61. London *Times*, 23 May 1883. Lilley also wrote to C.O., 19 May 1883, C.O. 234/43.
62. Aborigines Protection Society to C.O., 14 May 1883, C.O. 234/43.
63. Chalmers wrote to Derby, 1 June 1883; see Chalmers to L.M.S., 25 June 1883, L.M.S. Archives, Papua 3.3.A.
64. Derby to Officer Administering Government of Queensland, 11 July 1883, *Vict. P.P.* No. 38, 1884, p. 19.

nexed.[65] It is quite possible that the views of Sir Arthur Gordon, the Aborigines Protection Society, and the missionaries weighed with Derby, but more probable that he was glad to be able to offer them as an excuse for delay.

For a time the question of the part Queensland was to have in the affairs of New Guinea lapsed, but it revived again in the period from 1885 to 1888 when plans were discussed between the Colonial Office and the colonies for the administration of the protectorate and later the annexed territory. In this period it was Sir Anthony Musgrave, the governor of Queensland, who firmly opposed any surrender of native affairs in New Guinea to Queensland control.

The first plan for the administration of the protectorate was drawn up by the agents-general in consultation with Colonel Stanley, the Secretary of State for Colonies, in December 1885.[66] As Queensland had agreed to be responsible for the expense of administration to the extent of £15,000 per annum for ten years, this plan provided for dual control.[67] Lawes, the London Missionary Society missionary in New Guinea, had protested against Queensland's contributing anything toward expenses, as this would lead to a demand for a share in the administration.[68] Musgrave also opposed dual control, and suspected that the Queensland agent-general had been used by "the sugar planters of Queensland and their capitalist supporters in Victoria."[69] He recited Queensland's bad record in the labor trade and the low moral tone of the community as illustrated by the public demonstrations in favor of those members of the *Hopeful* crew accused of murdering natives. He concluded, the "only way in which the acquisition of New Guinea can be prevented

65. McIlwraith to Officer Administering Government of Queensland, 28 Sept. 1883, *Vict. P.P.* No. 38, 1884, p. 46.

66. Queensland Agent-General to Griffith, 31 Dec. 1885, *Qd. V. & P.* 1886, II, 996-998.

67. Colonial Office memorandum on financial proposals referred to in Musgrave to C.O., 13 Jan. 1886, C.O. 234/47.

68. Lawes to Anti-Slavery Society, Nov. 1885, Anti-Slavery Society Archives.

69. Musgrave to C.O., 11 March 1886, C.O. 234/47.

from becoming a disgrace to the British people will be to retain control of administration in the hands of Her Majesty's Government."[70]

The plan of the agents-general was adopted by Griffith in his draft plan drawn up in March 1886 and submitted to Victoria and New South Wales, who were to contribute toward the sum guaranteed by Queensland.[71] This was in essence the plan adopted at the Colonial Conference of 1887[72] and passed by the colonial legislatures later that year.[73] It provided for an administrator and executive council in New Guinea who were to receive instructions from, and were to report to, the governor of Queensland, who was to accept the advice of his ministers on all matters where it was consistent with the welfare of the natives. In certain questions of native affairs the administrator was directly responsible to the imperial government.

Some misunderstanding occurred when the bill embodying this arrangement was before the Queensland Parliament. A strong section of the Queensland Parliament desired Queensland to have full direction of the affairs of New Guinea.[74] In order to get this bill through, Griffith had said, "The control of New Guinea would be under the direction of Queensland ministers," which was only a half-truth. The governor, Musgrave, who had always suspected that the imperial government would surrender to Queensland, protested very strongly to the Colonial Office.[75] About the same time Sir George Campbell in the House of Commons had accused the imperial government of handing over New Guinea to Queensland, but in reply Sir Henry Holland, the Secretary of State for the Colonies, explained the limitations on Queens-

70. *Ibid.*
71. Griffith to Queensland Agent-General, 30 March 1886, *Qd. V. & P.* 1886, II, 999.
72. *P.P.* 1887, LVI, c. 5091.
73. The Queensland act was 51 Vict., No. 9.
74. Enclosure in Musgrave to C.O., 10 Sept. 1887, C.O. 234/48.
75. Musgrave to C.O., 20 Oct. 1887, C.O. 234/48. Cf. Musgrave to Herbert (private), 2 April 1888, C.O. 234/49.

land's authority.[76] The Colonial Office allayed the governor's misgivings by making it clear that Sir Henry Holland and not Sir Samuel Griffith had given the true account.[77]

With the passage of the Queensland New Guinea Act of 1887[78] the territory was formally annexed, and Dr. William MacGregor was appointed as the first administrator. One of his early ordinances forbade the deportation of natives of New Guinea.[79] In 1892 Musgrave's successor as governor of Queensland, Sir Henry Norman, suggested that New Guinea natives might be brought to Queensland for short periods of labor,[80] but the suggestion was very cautiously put aside by the Colonial Office. The Queensland planter was not to be allowed access to this labor supply.

80. Norman to C.O., 24 Feb. 1892, C.O. 234/53.
77. Minutes on Musgrave to C.O., 20 Oct. 1887, C.O. 234/48.
78. 51 Vict., No. 9.
79. Ordinance III, 1888.   Enclosure in Musgrave to C.O., 27 Aug. 1888, C.O. 234/49.
80. Norman to C.O., 24 Feb. 1892, C.O. 234/53.

CHAPTER VII. THE PACIFIC ISLANDER IN QUEENSLAND

I

The main burden of responsibility for the welfare of Pacific islanders in Queensland rested with the colonial government. When dissatisfied with Queensland's conduct of the immigration of islanders, the imperial government had from time to time threatened to end it, presumably by taking action to prevent Queensland ships recruiting in the islands. But once the islanders were within the colony, the imperial government acknowledged it had no power to interfere.[1] The colony itself was very sensitive to any infringement of its right of self-government, while at the Colonial Office, Herbert, in particular, was careful never to give offense in this respect. Herbert espoused the principle of self-government partly from genuine admiration and partly from expediency; when humanitarians protested against the treatment of Pacific islanders in Queensland, he could tell them that the colonial government and not the Colonial Office was responsible.

However, officials at the Colonial Office were not indifferent to the treatment of Pacific islanders in Queensland. Though they could not compel the government of Queensland to any particular course of action, and sometimes despaired of offering advice because it was so often disregarded,[2] they made clear the points on which they differed from the colonial government on the treatment of islanders.

The Colonial Office expected, in general, the same standard of treatment for the Pacific islander in Queensland as was required by the government of India for its emigrant

---

1. "... the responsibility of looking after the labourers so long as they are in Queensland is entirely rested in the colonial authority under the power of self government...." Minute by Mercer on Question on Notice Paper, March 1893, C.O. 234/58.
2. Bramston's minute on Norman to C.O., 13 May 1894, C.O. 234/59.

laborers in the West Indies and Mauritius.[3] Indian coolie
emigration had begun in the thirties when the principle of
the free contract was most in favor. The original engagement
was to be freely made; the coolie was to be free to choose his
employment; he was to enjoy the same rights and privileges
as the indigenous laborer; and on expiration of his contract
he was to be free to remain in the colony or to return to
India.[4] From time to time as these privileges were denied,
the Indian government protested or the colonial government
appointed a commission of enquiry. The government of
India protested against the Mauritius ordinance of 1847 because it infringed the principle of the free choice of employment by making the free return passage dependent on the
coolie's serving his five-year contract in the sugar industry.[5]
On the recommendation of the governor, Sir Arthur Gordon,
the Colonial Office appointed a commission of enquiry in
Mauritius after the 1867 ordinance compelled coolies to re-
engage themselves upon the expiration of their indenture.[6]
Following charges of ill treatment made by a British Guiana
stipendiary magistrate, G. W. Des Voeux, who like Gordon
was later High Commissioner for the Western Pacific, Granville appointed a commission to enquire into the conditions
of coolies in British Guiana.[7] These commissions mark a
revival of interest in the condition of the coolie after a slack-
ening, in the fifties and early sixties, of the concern shown
when the indentured system began after emancipation.

Throughout the history of coolie indenture the tendency
to discriminate against the immigrant was met by an in-
sistence on his rights both as a free laborer and citizen. In
1875 Lord Salisbury, at the India Office, insisted that Indian
immigrants were "in all respect free members with privileges

3. Granville to Blackall, No. 22, 23 April 1869, *P.P.* 1868-1869, XLIII, 408.
4. G. R. Mellor, *British Imperial Trusteeship* (London 1951) chap. iv,
passim.
5. *Ibid.,* p. 200.
6. *P.P.* 1875, XXXIV, c. 1115.
7. *P.P.* 1871, XX, c. 393.

no whit inferior to those of any other class of Her Majesty's subjects resident in the colonies."[8]

In Queensland, however, the status of the Pacific island immigrant was quite different, and the reason for this is to be sought in the difference between that colony and the West Indies or Mauritius. Queensland was a colony of settlement with a diversified economy. It was only partly tropical, and it had more in common with the other Australian colonies than with the West Indies or Mauritius. There was a division of opinion in Queensland between those who wished the colony to develop along the lines of the other Australian colonies, and those who wished to introduce colored labor to develop the colony's tropical resources. The outcome was a compromise in which colored labor was accepted as a temporary expedient, and the laborer's freedom hedged about by more and more restrictions until finally he was excluded from the colony altogether.[9] The permanent officials at the Colonial Office deplored this discrimination[10] which compared so unfavorably with the treatment of coolie laborers in other colonies, but like prominent English visitors to Queensland, such as Trollope,[11] they showed little appreciation of the dilemma which the government and people of Queensland faced.

This may be accounted for by the fact that there was not the same concern at the Colonial Office about Queensland as there was, for example, about the West Indies or Mauritius, partly for the reason already mentioned—that the imperial government's responsibility for what happened in Queensland was limited by that colony's self-government—and partly because the sugar produced in Queensland was sold entirely in the markets of the Australian colonies, and the condition of the colony's sugar industry did not depend

8. Quoted in N. Gangulee, *Indians in the Empire Overseas* (London, 1947), p. 45.
9. Commonwealth of Australia Act, No. 16, 1901.
10. See pp. 128, below.
11. B. A. Booth, ed., *The Tireless Traveller* (Berkeley, 1941), Letter XV.

as much on the economic policy of the imperial government as did the sugar industries of the West Indies and Mauritius, whose principal market was in Britain. In the case of the West Indies and Mauritius this dependence was accentuated, as sugar cultivation was so basic to the colonies' economies. On the other hand, as British capital was invested in Queensland sugar, the Colonial Office might be pressed by those interests to take notice of developments in Queensland's sugar industry.

The planters and squatters of Queensland, who most desired colored labor, were less interested in restricting the numbers and freedom of colored laborers than were the urban and working-class interests. But not even a government dominated by planting interests could ignore the colony's obligations to its European immigrants, and every government of Queensland agreed that all public monies set aside for immigration should be reserved to bring Europeans and not colored immigrants to the colony. This was the main factor in the failure to implement the regulations passed in 1862 for the introduction of Indian coolies into Queensland.[12]

These regulations gave the same freedom to the coolie as he enjoyed in other colonies, and for this reason they aroused considerable opposition among the working-class elements in Queensland. Whereas the attempt to bring Indian coolies to Queensland failed, employers were successful in introducing Pacific islanders, partly because it was first done privately and did not require government action, and partly because the white worker did not see in the Pacific islander quite the same threat to his living standards as he did in the vast and industrious population of Asia.

The first legislation regulating the employment of Pacific islanders placed no restrictions on their choice of employment.[13] Their original contracts were almost exclusively for work of all kinds on sugar plantations or as shepherds on

12. Bowen to Newcastle, 4 Oct. 1863, C.O. 234/8.
13. 31 Vict., No. 47.

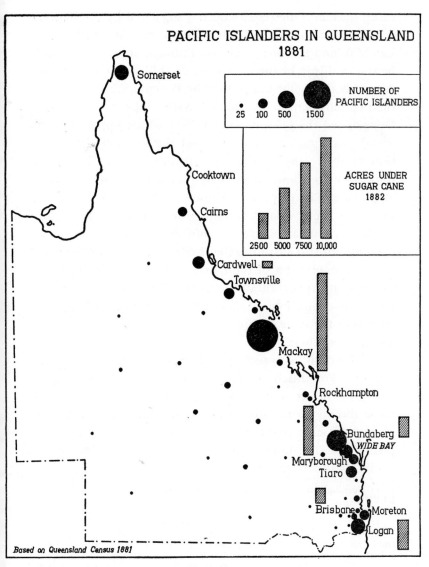

FIGURE 1.

sheep stations. One restriction was suggested by the imperial government: that the islanders should not be employed on lonely inland stations where government supervision would be impossible.[14] In the debate on the bill in the Queensland Assembly this point was pressed by Douglas, who also wanted their employment to be confined to sugar plantations.[15] When Douglas led the government of 1877 which opposed Pacific island immigration, he introduced the first definite restriction of their employment by refusing to grant licenses to import, or to allow transfers of Pacific islanders, except for employment in tropical or subtropical agriculture.[16] Until this time Pacific islanders were employed in roughly equal numbers on sugar plantations and sheep stations with an increasing but still small number finding employment in towns after the expiration of their first contract.[17] It is impossible to say what proportion of the natives remained in the colony after the expiration of their first agreement, either to re-engage in the same occupation or to seek work on their own account elsewhere.

McIlwraith, who succeeded Douglas, set aside these regulations.[18] For this he could advance the reason that he was acting on the recommendation of the 1876 committee that there should be no restriction on the kind of employment given to Pacific islanders.[19] This was the committee whose members, with one exception, were either employers of Pacific islanders or connected in some way with their em-

14. Buckingham and Chandos to Bowen, 9 Nov. 1867, *P.P.* 1867-1868, XLVIII, 391.
15. *Qd. P.D.*, VI, 912.
16. Executive Council minute, 12 April 1877, *Qd. V. & P.* 1880, II, 413.
17. On 4 March 1868 of the 1,539 Pacific islanders in Queensland, 771 were employed in agriculture, 697 in pastoral undertaking, and 71 in urban occupation. Enclosure in Blackall to Granville, 16 April 1869, *P.P.* 1868-1869, XLIII, 408. Another analysis of the occupations of Pacific islanders is not available until the 1881 census—three years after Douglas' regulation was passed—when 5,075 were in agriculture and 370 in pastoral industry of a total of 6,348. *Qd. V. & P.* 1882, I, 1078-1079; see also Figure 1.
18. Griffith, Legislative Assembly, 6 July 1880, *Qd. P.D.*, XXXII, 5-11.
19. *Qd. V. & P.* 1876, III, 51.

ployment, and whose report Cairns, the governor, called "rose coloured."[20]

Nevertheless, it was in the McIlwraith government's bill of 1880 that the former regulation was given legislative form.[21] Palmer, who introduced the bill, and some of the members of the government were opposed to this clause,[22] which discriminated principally against squatters, the largest employers of Pacific islanders other than the sugar planters. This government, representing planters and squatters, promoted such a measure in the hope that by granting a little to the opposition, they would be left with something for themselves. Squatters would still be able to employ islanders who had served their first contract and who were then free to seek employment where they chose, as the clause applied only to islanders serving under contracts made when they first engaged for service in Queensland. But the opposition wanted more. Griffith introduced an amendment[23] that the clause should apply to all Pacific islanders in the colony, so that on the expiration of their original contract the Pacific islander would have to re-engage for service in tropical or subtropical agriculture, or return to his native island. Though Griffith's amendment was lost on this occasion, it became law with the passing of the bill which he introduced in 1884. Here he confined the occupations open to Pacific islanders still further by enumerating kinds of works in tropical or subtropical agriculture which were closed to them.[24]

The governor, Musgrave, and the permanent officials at the Colonial Office took strong exception to Griffith's legislation. To Musgrave this act arbitrarily withdrew certain privileges from a limited class of people whom he thought

20. Cairns to Carnarvon, 6 Dec. 1876, C.O. 234/36.
21. 44 Vict., No. 17, s. 7.
22. Legislative Assembly, 11 Aug. 1880, *Qd. P.D.*, XXXII, 326-330.
23. Committee stage of bill, 28 Sept. 1880, reported in *Brisbane Courier*, 29 Sept. 1880.
24. 47 Vict., No. 12, s. 2.   Under s. 11 Pacific islanders who, on 1 Sept. 1884, had resided continuously in the colony for five years, were exempted from the act.

should receive the special protection of Her Majesty's Government. They were denied the right enjoyed by the coolie to choose freely to remain or not to remain in the colony when their engagement was completed;[25] and if they chose to remain, then to choose their employment.[26] A Colonial Office official, Fuller,[27] pointed out that the act might place under a particular penalty a native who had left his island to escape punishment and now was faced with the alternative of returning home to be murdered or continuing to work on a sugar plantation. Bramston[28] thought the act was a curious illustration of the workings of free institutions, but acknowledged that the imperial government could not interfere. Herbert[29] thought more of how the act discriminated against squatters than against natives as laborers.

Musgrave, Fuller, and Bramston thought in the same terms as those who, in the Queensland Parliament, spoke against these discriminatory clauses in the 1880 and 1884 bills—in terms of free competition in labor. Labor legislation in England could be justified on the grounds that it corrected unequal bargaining power, and thus created the best conditions for the operation of free competition. But the Queensland legislation was simply discriminatory; its object was to prevent free competition. The people in Queensland who used this argument did so from interested motives, but to Musgrave and the Colonial Office officials these views were accepted principles. Yet the principles of political economy current in England were not relevant to the Queensland environment. This Musgrave and the Colonial Office officials did not appreciate any more than did the Anti-Slavery Society. The latter was petitioned by the Queensland Labour

25. In 1894 the Natal government desired to introduce a clause into labor contracts that coolies must return to India at the end of their indenture. The Indian government finally agreed to this provided failure to comply with it was not made a criminal offense—see R. L. Buell, *The Native Problem in Africa* (New York, 1928) I, 23.

26. Musgrave to C.O., 10 March 1884, C.O. 234/44.

27. Minute by Fuller on Musgrave to C.O. 10 March 1884, C.O. 234/44.

28. Minute by Bramston on Musgrave to C.O., 10 March 1884, C.O. 234/44.

29. Minute by Herbert on Musgrave to C.O., 10 March 1884, C.O. 234/44.

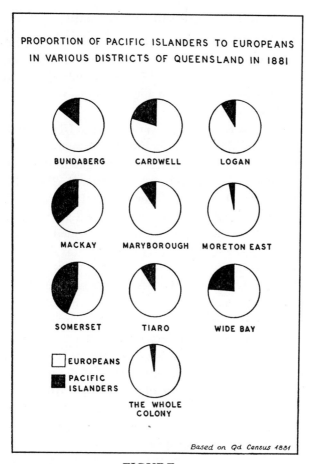

PROPORTION OF PACIFIC ISLANDERS TO EUROPEANS
IN VARIOUS DISTRICTS OF QUEENSLAND IN 1881

BUNDABERG   CARDWELL   LOGAN

MACKAY   MARYBOROUGH   MORETON EAST

SOMERSET   TIARO   WIDE BAY

☐ EUROPEANS
■ PACIFIC
  ISLANDERS

THE WHOLE
COLONY

Based on Qd Census 1881

FIGURE 2.

League, an organization of European immigrants, for support
in its effort to exclude colored labor from Queensland. The
Anti-Slavery Society refused to co-operate, as it claimed under
British law "men of every colour should have equal freedom,
equal rights, and equal protection."[30]

The object of the Queensland law was to segregate colored labor, to prevent its coming into competition with white
labor by providing that some work was to be done only by

30. *Anti-Slavery Reporter,* 15 May 1876.

colored labor, while all other work was to be reserved exclusively for white labor. This was based on the assumption that two systems of free labor of different standards could not exist side by side without the higher being reduced to the standard of the lower.

The total cost to the employer of Pacific Island labor was about 2/4d. per day. This included the islander's passage money to and from the islands, all charges under the acts, and the laborer's wage and maintenance.[31] The cheapest white labor cost about 5/2d. per day.[32] The Pacific island laborer worked slightly longer each day, and a few days more each year, and for the type of work performed was held to be as efficient as the white laborer. It is natural therefore that the employer should prefer him.

While the Pacific islander remained free to choose his employment, he was a potential threat to the white worker. How real a danger he actually was is difficult to gauge.[33] In 1881 the male Pacific islanders were 4.78 per cent[34] of the total male population, but the male and female Pacific islanders together were only 2.99 per cent of the total Queensland population. Those who opposed restricting their employment tried to demonstrate that their introduction was no threat to white labor, but in fact created further employment opportunities for Europeans.[35]

From the introduction of Douglas' regulation in 1877 the Pacific islanders became concentrated in tropical and subtropical agriculture. Whereas in 1868 as many were employed on sheep stations as on plantations, in 1881 79 per cent of the Pacific islanders in Queensland were employed in tropi-

31. Report by Walter Maxwell, Commonwealth of Australia, *P.P.* 1901-1902, II, 967.   There was no significant variation in wages or costs throughout the period.
32. *Ibid.*
33. The commissioners appointed to enquire into the Queensland Sugar Industry in 1889 disagreed on this question, *Qd. V. & P.* 1889, IV, 37 ff.
34. Table CXLIII, 1881 Qd. Census, *Qd. V. & P.* 1882, I, 1181; Table I, 1901 Census, Commonwealth of Australia, *P.P.* 1901-1902, I, 835.
35. Hume Black to Colonial Secretary, 28 Sept. 1881, *Qd. V. & P.* 1881, I, 1122.

cal or subtropical agriculture, and by 1891 the proportion had risen to 88 per cent.[36] In the Mackay district in 1881 90 per cent of the agricultural laborers were Pacific islanders.[37] Thus the purpose of the Queensland legislation to segregate the Pacific islander was being achieved. But it was not intended that some kinds of work should be left exclusively and permanently to the Pacific islanders. Such labor was still regarded as a temporary expedient. By section eleven of the 1885 act[38] no more licenses to introduce Pacific islanders were to be issued after 31 December 1890. Griffith hoped, by that time, for the success of the second part of his policy: the reorganization of tropical and subtropical agriculture by replacing the plantation with the small cane farm which could be worked without colored labor.

II

Griffith's plan for sugar cultivation in Queensland was in sharp contrast to that of his predecessor as premier, McIlwraith. Under the McIlwraith government of 1879-1883, negotiations had been reopened with the government of India to frame regulations under the Queensland act of 1862 for the introduction of laborers from India.[39] These negotiations began in April 1881,[40] and in October Queensland sent a representative to discuss the proposed regulations with the government of India.[41] As the 1884 act confined the employment of Pacific islanders to tropical or subtropical agriculture, so these regulations proposed to restrict the coolie's choice of employment by imposing a penalty on any coolie

36. See n. 17 above; Qd. Census 1891, *Qd. V. & P.* 1892, II, 825.
37. Table LXXXVI, Qd. Census 1881, *Qd. V. & P.* 1882, I, 1063. Table XCI, Qd. Census 1881, *Qd. V. & P.* 1882, I, 1078-1079.
38. 49 Vict., No. 17.
39. 26 Vict., No. 5.
40. Palmer to Secretary of Government of India, 25 April 1881, Government of India, *Proceedings of Revenue and Agriculture Dept.*, Sept. 1881, India Office, London.
41. Palmer to Secretary of Government of India, 24 Oct. 1881, *Proceedings of Revenue and Agriculture Department*, Feb. 1882, India Office, London.

who engaged for any other work. The Indian government protested against this[42] but accepted a nominal retraction of this clause,[43] the purpose of which was preserved by shifting the penalty to the employer who engaged an Indian laborer for any other kind of work. The regulations were then approved by the Indian government in September 1883,[44] but they could not become law without the express approval of the Queensland Parliament. This was necessary under an act of 1882[45] which incorporated a resolution moved by McIlwraith earlier in that session on the defeat of a bill brought in by Griffith for the repeal of the 1862 act.

Parliament, however, was dissolved before the regulations could be submitted to it. Although the proposal to introduce Indian laborers was not the question that caused the dissolution, it was perhaps the most important question on which the ensuing election was fought. The success of the opposition was interpreted as a definite expression of opinion by the electorate against the use of Asian labor in sugar cultivation. Griffith announced that his government did not intend to submit the regulations to Parliament.[46] Instead he introduced a bill for the repeal of the 1862 act.[47] Although this passed the Assembly it was rejected by the Council, and Griffith had to wait until the session of 1886 before he could remove this act from the statute book.[48]

The Council's rejection of this bill revived the hopes of those planters who had been the prime movers behind the

42. Secretary of Government of India to Colonial Secretary, Qd., 16 Oct. 1882, *Proceedings of Revenue and Agriculture Department,* Oct. 1882, India Office, London.
43. Secretary of Government of India to Colonial Secretary, Qd., 15 Sept. 1883, *Proceedings of Revenue and Agriculture Department,* Sept. 1883, India Office, London.
44. Secretary of Government of India to Colonial Secretary, Qd., 15 Sept. 1883, *Proceedings of Revenue and Agriculture Department,* Sept. 1883, India Office, London.
45. 46 Vict., No. 14.
46. Colonial Secretary, Qd. to Secretary of Government of India, 13 Dec. 1883, *Qd. V. & P.* 1883-1884, 1423.
47. *Qd. P.D.,* XLI, 55.
48. 50 Vict., No. 4: An Act to Repeal the Acts relating to the introduction of labourers from British India.

McIlwraith government's negotiations—Jeffray of Sloane & Co., Melbourne, and J. E. Davidson of the Melbourne-Mackay Sugar Co. Sloane & Co. wrote directly to the government of India proposing that it be allowed to introduce laborers from India privately.[49] The government of India rejected the proposals.[50] Some months later when in England Davidson and Jeffray wrote jointly to Derby, outlining the conditions of the sugar industry and its need for labor if the investment of British capitalists was to be safeguarded.[51] By stating what the McIlwraith government had done and that there were no legislative obstacles to the introduction of Indian laborers, they implied that the Griffith government was prepared to accept such labor. The government of India again refused to act without the approval of the Queensland government,[52] and Griffith again made it clear that, although he had been unable to repeal the act, his government had no intention of promulgating the regulations.[53]

Davidson was undeterred. Early the next year, this time in association with J. B. Lawes, he petitioned Derby for the separation of North Queensland, in order that the new colony so formed might develop its resources by the introduction of labor from India.[54] Since the early seventies frequent petitions for the separation of North Queensland had been made. If the motive presented had been a desire for a plantation economy, then it had been carefully concealed among a variety of other complaints about administrative and financial neglect. Other supporters of the movement criticized

49. Sloane & Co. to Secretary of Government of India, 12 May 1884, Government of India, *Proceedings of Revenue and Agriculture Department,* July 1884, India Office, London.

50. Secretary of Government of India to Sloane & Co., 30 June 1884, Government of India, *Proceedings of Revenue and Agriculture Department,* Oct. 1884, India Office, London.

51. Davidson and Jeffray to Derby, 9 July 1884, Government of India, *Proceedings of Revenue and Agriculture Department,* Oct. 1884, India Office, London.

52. *Qd. V. & P.* 1885, II, 989.

53. Colonial Secretary to Government of Qd., 30 Sept. 1884, *Qd. V. & P.* 1884, II, 929.

54. Davidson and Lawes to Derby, 14 Jan. 1885, C.O. 234/46.

Davidson and Lawes for a tactless admission of their true motives, which would make the separation movement unpopular among working classes, without whose support it was not likely to be successful.[55]

In commenting on this letter from Davidson and Lawes, Herbert expressed the hope that separation would not be necessary.[56] He criticized the policy of the Griffith government toward colored labor as one "bringing a great deal of trouble upon itself and us." He thought that Griffith, for the sake of the white workingman's vote, was ruining the sugar industry, in which some millions had been invested in the confidence that colored labor would not be prohibited.

Herbert had no more sympathy with votes for the working class than did his cousin Carnarvon, who had opposed both extensions of the franchise in Britain—by his own party in 1867, and by the Liberals in 1884. Twenty years earlier Herbert had lead a planter-squatter government in Queensland, and his sympathies remained with this class as possessing more than any other in the colony the qualities he associated with the ability to govern. He had little patience with the white workingman's fear of competition from the colored laborer, and he did not appreciate Griffith's attempt to show that sugar could be produced economically by white labor alone, and that Queensland need not run the risk of losing her free institutions by introducing large number of colored laborers to develop her tropical resources.

Griffith's first two measures had been negative: to exclude Indian labor and to confine Pacific island labor to a narrower

55. Reference by Griffith in debate on Macrossan's motion for separation, Aug. 1886. Qd. P.D., XLIX, 451.
56. Minute by Herbert on Davidson and Lawes to Derby, 14 Jan. 1885, C.O. 234/46. As further approaches were made to the Colonial Office on this subject, advice was sought from the Law Officers, whose final opinion was that though the imperial government could create a new colony out of Queensland, it would not be advisable to do so without some action first being taken by the Queensland Parliament. The colony's part in the administration of New Guinea and the Federation movement made the question of separation more difficult, although Griffith made a statesmanlike attempt in 1892 to meet the genuine grievances of the separationists by his bill to create two provinces on the Canadian model. See p. 194, below.

range of occupations within tropical and subtropical agriculture. Negativeness was characteristic of some of the opponents of colored labor; but when Griffith opposed a certain course he usually put forward a constructive alternative. He did not intend to leave the sugar industry without labor. He did not accept the theory held by many desiring black labor—that white men could not do field work in the tropics. He therefore proposed to encourage the immigration of European agricultural laborers, and for this purpose he introduced in mid-1884 an Immigration Amendment Bill.[57] These immigrants would first work as laborers and later become small cane growers, for already there was a tendency among planters to solve their labor problem by concentrating on milling and leasing their plantations in small lots to cane growers who would supply the mill.

The second part of Griffith's constructive policy was to encourage the development of central mills. The system of central milling had been first introduced into the French colony of Martinique in the 1860's to provide machinery too expensive for any individual smallholder to acquire. It had been so successful that Des Voeux, the lieutenant-governor of St. Lucia, had in 1870 recommended its introduction there. By this means he hoped to promote the more efficient production of sugar to meet the threat of falling prices likely to follow the bounty adopted by certain countries to foster domestic sugar production. The colony made a loan, and Des Voeux and his friends contributed capital, but the venture failed partly through mismanagement, but also because of uncertain cane supplies and the falling price of sugar.[58]

From 1880 the system had been tried in Queensland by a number of planters, not from any direct experience of the West Indian experiment, but as a means of meeting a shortage of labor. Unlike the West Indian planters in those islands where there was no labor shortage, the Queensland planters

57. Second Reading Debate, 6 Aug. 1884, *Qd. P.D.* XLIII, 273 ff.
58. Des Voeux, *My Colonial Service*, I, 212 ff.

preferred to concentrate on the milling of cane grown by small farmers to whom their plantations were let. However, with two or three exceptions these early experiments failed because the planters could not get the farmers to grow sufficient cane for milling to give an adequate return on the amount invested in machinery.[59]

There was one successful example of a central mill worked on a co-operative basis by a group of small farmers. But generally the cultivation of cane itself required all the capital a small farmer could raise, so that the setting up of a central mill was impossible for any unaided group of small farmers. To meet this difficulty, the Griffith government in 1885 allowed two groups of cane farmers to take shares in two central mills by mortgaging their land to the government, who advanced £25,000 for the erection of each mill. The price to be paid by the milling companies for the shareholders' cane was fixed by the articles of association, and it was intended that the cane should be grown entirely by white labor. In both cases, however, the shareholders were unable to provide sufficient cane, and the mills purchased Kanaka-grown cane at a higher price. Neither company was able to show a profit, nor was it able to pay to the government the interest on the loan, which in effect became a subsidy.[60] Griffith had failed to demonstrate that sugar could be grown economically by white labor.

It was unfortunate that his experiment should coincide with the depression in the sugar industry. This depression was felt by all the cane sugar-producing countries; the fall in prices was generally ascribed to the system of bounties granted by European countries to home-produced beet sugar.[61] Queensland sugar on the Australian market was indirectly affected as it faced keener competition from Mauri-

59. Report of Queensland Royal Commission on Sugar Industry, p. xxxii, *Qd. V. & P.* 1889, IV, 37.

60. *Ibid.*

61. Memorial from Jamaica Society of Agriculture and Commerce enclosed in Norman to C.O., 21 Jan. 1887, *P.P.* 1888, XCIV, c. 5059 (Correspondence relating to Conference on Sugar Bounties).

tius and Javan sugar excluded from the European market. Although Australian colonies had power to make reciprocal trade treaties since the Australian Custom Duties Act of 1873, Queensland sugar received no preference in the Melbourne market,[62] where most of Queensland's sugar exports were sold. Greater proximity to the market was the only advantage it enjoyed over the coolie-grown sugar of Mauritius and Java. The price of sugar on the Melbourne market fell sharply in 1884-1885, and in the following years showed no sign of recovery.[63] In 1886-1887 Queensland sugar production was adversely affected by drought and disease.

In these circumstances the McIlwraith government, which was returned in the election of 1888, appointed a Royal Commission to enquire into the condition of the sugar industry.[64] The principal question it addressed itself to was whether the sugar industry could dispense with colored labor at the end of 1890, as provided by Section 11 of the 1885 act. Two of the commissioners—one of them a large planter—ascribed the depression to the loss of confidence in the industry by capitalists because of the uncertainty about the supply of colored labor, without which, in their opinion, sugar could not be economically produced. The other commissioner, the chairman, dissented, ascribing the depression to bounties granted by European powers. With the ratification of the Sugar Convention against bounties in August 1890, he expected prices to recover. He recommended that the government set up more central mills, and that legislation excluding Pacific islanders should not be repealed.

The majority report was not acted upon until early in 1892, when Griffith, the premier, announced his intention to lift the ban on the introduction of Pacific islanders that had come into operation at the end of 1890.[65] Griffith had not

62. Appendix 32, Qd. Royal Commission on Sugar Industry.
63. G. H. Knibbs, *Prices, Price Indexes and Cost of Living in Australia* (Commonwealth Bureau of Census and Statistics, 1912), p. 63.
64. *Qd. V. & P.* 1889, IV, 37.
65. Enclosure in Norman to Knutsford, 13 Feb. 1892, *P.P.* 1892, LVI, c. 6686.

abandoned his earlier policy; but he admitted that a temporary resumption of Pacific island immigration was necessary to save the sugar industry. He reiterated the grounds of his opposition to colored labor, particularly Asian, and remarked on the tendency of the large plantations to give way to small farms worked by white labor. He criticized some planters who had opposed this trend and those workers who, through jealous fear of competition, had opposed the immigration of European agriculture workers.[66] As these people were partly responsible for the failure of his plan to make the sugar industry independent of colored labor, he had no alternative but to allow the re-introduction of Pacific islanders for a limited period in order to save the sugar industry.

The Griffith government extended the provisions for setting up central mills by the Sugar Works Guarantee Act of 1893,[67] under which the government guaranteed debentures—secured on the land of cane farmers—to provide the capital for mills. This measure, together with the amending act of 1895,[68] radically altered the organization of the sugar industry. In 1892 there were 480 cane farmers in Queensland; in 1897 there were 1,450.[69] There was a similar rise in the number of employers of Pacific islanders—from 195 in 1892[70] to 1,264 in 1899.[71] During this period the number of Pacific islanders in the colony remained constant at about 8,700,[72] the average number employed by each employer falling from about forty-four in 1892 to seven in 1899. This meant almost certainly that many of the small cane farmers who sent their cane to central mills employed at least one or two Pacific islanders. In 1897 Lord Lamington, the governor, remarked

66. See Kinnaird on Rose to C.O., 18 May 1892, *P.P.* 1892, LVI, c. 6808, for the point of view of organized labor.
67. 57 Vict., No. 18.
68. 59 Vict., No. 14.
69. Appendix C, 137, Royal Commission on West Indies, *P.P.* 1898, L.
70. Budget Summary, *Brisbane Courier*, 29 July 1893.
71. Qd. *V. & P.* 1901, IV, 1097.
72. See Appendix, Table 2.

that many who formerly opposed the introduction of Pacific islanders were happy to use two or three on their small holdings.[73] They were also contravening the intention of the framers of the Sugar Works Guarantee Act that only cane grown by the white labor should be accepted. As in the first experiment, not all the central mills were able to make a profit and some of them did not pay interest on government loans.[74] But at the cost of this subsidy the Queensland government had converted sugar cultivation from plantations to small farms which could if necessary dispense with colored labor, and had provided the cane farmers with modern machinery for the milling processes. The system was sufficiently successful to be judged worthy of emulation by the Royal Commissioners appointed to enquire into the affairs of the West Indies, whose chairman, Sir Henry Norman, was a former governor of Queensland.[75]

The Colonial Office scarcely noticed this change in the organization of the Queensland sugar industry. It accepted the assumption of all the Queensland governors—including the two who criticized Queensland's administration of the Pacific island immigration, Cairns and Musgrave—that tropical agriculture could not be carried on without colored labor. It had no patience with the white workingman's desire to exclude cheap labor whether it was colored or European, and it did not seem to appreciate the political and social complications that would follow if colored labor was freely introduced.[76] The initiative for the reorganization of the sugar industry, which in time would make it possible to dispense with colored labor, came from Griffith. For twenty years a party in the Queensland Parliament had opposed the introduction of Pacific islanders, but Griffith was the first member of this party to offer a constructive alternative to the

73. Lamington to C.O., 15 May 1897, C.O. 234/65.
74. Appendix C, 61, Royal Commission on West Indies, *P.P.* 1898, L.
75. Report of Royal Commission on West Indies, s. 93, *P.P.* 1898, L.
76. Mercer's minute on W. Moloney to Ripon, 12 Jan. 1893, C.O. 234/58. "The writer represents the class which sees competition in the introduction of Polynesians. It is a short-sighted and mistaken view."

negative criticism of his predecessors. He followed this through in spite of some criticism from the Colonial Office.

III

As the imperial government could not intervene in the interests of the Pacific islander in Queensland, it lacked the motive either to protest very definitely against restrictions placed on the islander's choice of employment, or to understand the reason why the Queensland government insisted on these measures. It was in much the same position as regards the general treatment of the Pacific islander in Queensland; the imperial government criticized and advised, but it never had to make clear its attitude by decisive action.

Those provisions of the 1868 act affecting the conditions of the laborers in Queensland were modeled on the regulations for the immigration of Indian coolies sent to Bowen in 1861.[77] They were not as comprehensive as the latter, but the Emigration Commissioners and the Colonial Office were satisfied, as they considered them adequate for the small scale on which they expected the immigration of Pacific islanders to remain. After less than twelve months' experience with the act, the Queensland immigration officer reported that it had not been found to answer all expectations; he therefore recommended, among other amendments, some affecting the condition and welfare of the laborers in Queensland: security for the payment of wages, provision for the return of natives introduced before the act, the introduction of women at the rate of one-fifth of the number of men introduced, and provision for hearing cases between Pacific islanders and their employer under the Polynesian Labourers Act rather than the Masters & Servants Act, and for the admission of evidence by Pacific islanders in such cases.[78] As the colonial government appeared to have no intention of

77. Newcastle to Bowen, 26 April 1861, *P.P.* 1861, XL, 2890.
78. Enclosure in Blackall to Granville, 16 April 1869, *P.P.* 1868-1869, XLIII, 408. For other recommendations concerning recruiting, see chap. v.

implementing these recommendations, the imperial government pressed for their adoption. They indicated that some improvements were needed in the condition of the laborers in Queensland.

With respect to wages, the 1868 act provided for payment at the rate of £6 per annum in coin of the realm,[79] but the act contained nothing about when the wages should be paid. Consequently the employers did not pay until the end of the three-year engagement, when the laborer spent the entire wage on a variety of goods ranging from shirts and tools to useless trinkets or dangerous firearms.[80] The demand for the latter increased, and their sale and consequent use against white traders in the Pacific was a constant source of friction between the Queensland and imperial governments between 1876 and 1884, when the former prohibited their sale. Usually employers sold goods for fair prices, but occasionally they gave the natives no choice except to buy at exorbitant prices or not at all.

While there was no provision for the regular payment, the laborer had little security for his wages. One of the few rights the laborer had under the Masters & Servants Act—the provisions of which governed his engagement—was a claim for wages unpaid.[81] But the act provided that no claim could be made for any offense more than six months after it was committed,[82] so that the laborer could not recover wages owing for more than that period, though they might be unpaid for three years. If a mortgage on an estate was resumed, the mortgagee was not liable for the unpaid wages of the laborers, and in one instance at least the laborers on such an estate received no wages whatever for three years' work.[83] Before they were returned to their islands the immi-

79. 31 Vict., No. 47, s. 9. and Form D.
80. See description of pay day enclosure 2 in Blackall to Granville, 1 July 1870, *P.P.* 1871, XLVIII, 468.
81. 25 Vict., No. 11, ss. ix-xii.
82. 25 Vict., No. 11, s. xxii.
83. *Qd. V. & P.* 1876, III, 23. Laborers were similarly deprived of wages by the many bankruptcies in Fiji in 1874—see Steel to S.M.H., 25 Sept. 1874.

gration officer found them work for one year at £9, whereas
their four years' work should have returned them £24. Again,
if a laborer died during his three-year contract, his employer
paid no wages at all.[84]

Though in 1869 the immigration officer had pointed out
the lack of security for the payment of wages, and the imperial government had pressed for some amendment in the
following year,[85] nothing was done. The matter was raised
again in 1876 in a report submitted by Richard Brinsley
Sheridan as assistant immigration officer at Maryborough.[86]
The mortality rate among laborers had been exceptionally
high in 1875, and Sheridan had hinted that the prospect of
saving three years' wages and the return passage was an
obstacle in the way of any effort by the planters to lower the
death rate. Statements made in this report were ridiculed by
the Select Committee of 1876[87] appointed to enquire into
the treatment of Pacific island laborers in Queensland, but
in the opinion of the governor, Cairns, Sheridan was fully
justified in everything he wrote and said.[88] Sheridan resigned
early in the following year in protest against the difficulties
placed in the way of carrying out his duties,[89] but he was
vindicated by the adoption of most of his recommendations
in the legislation after 1880.

In view of the committee's treatment of Sheridan and the
tendentious questions asked of other witnesses,[90] it is difficult
to understand Herbert's curt dismissal[91] of Cairns's remark
that the report was "rose coloured." It is probably to be explained by Herbert's desire to avoid controversy. Herbert

84. Assistant Immigration Officer, Maryborough to Colonial Secretary, 28
Jan. 1876, *Qd. V. & P.* 1876, III, 28.
85. Granville to Blackall, 18 Feb. 1870, *P.P.* 1871, XLVIII, 468.
86. Assistant Immigration Officer, Maryborough to Colonial Secretary, 28
Jan. 1876, *Qd. V. & P.* 1876, III, 28.
87. *Qd. V. & P.* 1876, III, 51 ff.
88. Cairns to C.O., 6 Dec. 1876, C.O. 234/36.
89. *Qd. V. & P.* 1877, II, 1209.
90. A question asked by a member of the committee of a witness, R. Cran,
"Do you consider that statement of Mr. Sheridan a palpable affront to all
employers of Polynesians?"
91. Minute by Herbert on Cairns to C.O., 6 Dec. 1876, C.O. 234/36.

never himself raised the question of the treatment of Pacific islanders, and showed some reluctance to becoming involved when it was raised by others.

The committee, however, recommended that wages be paid every six months. The Emigration Commissioners in their minute on this report which was the basis of the Secretary of State's despatch, considered three months a more desirable period for payment.[92] Even this was considerably longer than the monthly payments general among Indian coolie labor. The Emigration Commissioners also recommended that wages be paid in the presence of an inspector, and that unpaid wages be given a preferential lien on the estate to protect the laborers' claims in the event of the transfer of the estate. They suggested, as a further safeguard, that the bond for the payment of the laborer's return passage might be amended to include wages.

The legislation of 1880 incorporated the recommendation of the 1876 committee that wages be paid every six months[93] in spite of the Secretary of State's expressed preference for three-month payments. Wages were to be paid to the natives—an amendment in the Council that they be paid into savings bank accounts was lost—in the presence of the inspector, who was given power to sue on behalf of the natives for wages that were overdue for more than fourteen days. Wages owing to a deceased islander were to be paid to an inspector or immigration officer.[94]

These provisions were accepted at the Colonial Office, but Edward Wingfield, an Assistant Under-Secretary of State, thought the latter provision unjust to the laborer's relatives.[95] This implied a standard of property rights for the native which the Queensland authorities had not, at this time, recog-

---

92. Walcott's minute on Cairns to C.O., 6 Dec. 1876, incorporated in Carnarvon to Officer Administering Government of Qd. 29 March 1877, C.O. 234/36.
93. 44 Vict., No. 17, s. 21.
94. 44 Vict., No. 17, s. 33.
95. Minute by Wingfield on Kennedy to C.O., 7 Dec. 1880, C.O. 234/40.

nized. They accepted this view five years later when the immigration officer was given discretion to pay a deceased native's wages to his next of kin.[96]

This was the sum of legislation by the Queensland Parliament covering the wages of Pacific island laborers. Their wages tended to rise slightly above the £6 minimum, and those who took work on their own account after serving their first contract were able to earn considerably more. This opportunity was closed to them with the passing of the 1884 act. The laborers were encouraged to open savings bank accounts. Throughout the nineties about one-third of those under engagement had such accounts, in which the average balance was about £8.[97]

In commenting on the 1880 act Wingfield regretted the absence of any clauses limiting the hours of work by Pacific islanders.[98] The usual length of a working day throughout the period was from 7 A.M. to 6 P.M. with a one-hour break at midday. Although the Indian coolie's hours were usually prescribed by ordinance, they were no shorter than these. A clause limiting the hours of the Pacific islander to eight had been introduced into the 1880 bill in the Council,[99] but the planters petitioned so strenuously against it that it was dropped. The planters objected to it for its own sake, and also because white agricultural workers who did not enjoy an eight-hour day would also want it.[100] There was never in any Queensland law relating to Pacific island laborers any clause limiting hours.

This one attempt in 1880 to limit hours sprang from the report of Drs. Hill-Wray and Thompson on the very high mortality among Pacific islanders employed on the planta-

96. 49 Vict., No. 17, s. 8.
97. See Annual Reports of Pacific Island Immigration Department published in *Qd. V. & P.* from 1889.
98. Minute on Kennedy to C.O., 7 Dec. 1880, C.O. 234/40.
99. Qd. Legislative Council, Committee stage, 30 Oct. 1880, *Qd. P.D.*
100. Qd. Legislative Council, 3rd Reading, 3 Nov. 1880, *Qd. P.D.*, XXXI, 198.

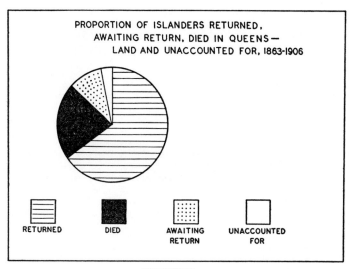

FIGURE 3.

tions of R. Cran & Co. at Maryborough.[101] These two doctors had been appointed to enquire after the Secretary of State had brought to the notice of the governor of Queensland[102] an extract from a letter received from the Aborigines Protection Society pointing out the high mortality rate among Pacific islanders, particularly in the Maryborough district.[103] Among the causes advanced in the report were the long hours worked by natives unaccustomed to strenuous and continuous physical work.

The mortality rate among islanders on plantations twice rose above 85 per thousand in the seventies, and in 1884 reached 147 per thousand.[104] This high rate existed among an almost entirely male population, over 70 per cent of whom were classified as being between the ages of fifteen and thirty-five,[105] and it is reasonable to assume that a good proportion of the 20 per cent not classified into any age groups were

101. *Qd. V. & P.* 1880, II, 414 ff.
102. Hicks-Beach to Kennedy, 2 June 1879, *P.P.* 1883, XLVII, c. 3641.
103. A.P.S. to Hicks-Beach, 4 April 1879, C.O. 201/589.
104. See Appendix, Table 3.
105. For age groups see Figure 4.

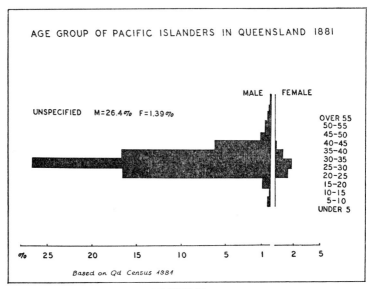

FIGURE 4.

also in the prime of life.[106] The death rate for the whole of the white population never at any time rose above 25 per thousand. Again the Pacific islander death rate represented only the deaths reported. Until the 1880 act no death certificate or enquiry into death under the Inquests of Death Act was compulsory in the case of Pacific islanders in Queensland,[107] and over the whole period some 2,200 of 60,000 islanders who came to Queensland were not accounted for in any way,[108] and it must be presumed that the greater part of this number represented unreported deaths.

A variety of reasons was advanced for this high mortality. The Colonial Office was sensitive to any reports of ill treatment, and noted the evidence of Sheridan to the 1876 committee concerning occasions when natives were whipped. One of the Colonial Office clerks, F. W. Fuller, pointed out that the Queensland legislation was silent on the question of

106. Table CXXI, 1881 Qd. Census, *Qd. V. & P.* 1882, I, 1148.
107. 44 Vict., No. 17, s. 35.
108. See Figure 3, p. 145.

ill treatment of Pacific islanders.[109] Though subsequent Queensland legislation did not provide penalties for ill treatment, there is no evidence that the few isolated cases of ill treatment had anything to do with the high mortality. The deaths were rather to be ascribed to the islanders' inability to adapt themselves to a different environment and to strenuous and continuous work to which they were unaccustomed.

Once the natives fell ill they succumbed very quickly. The provisions for medical care in the 1868 act were inadequate. The act did nothing more than state that the employer was responsible for the medical treatment of his colored employees. There was no provision, as in New Caledonia, for the medical examination of Pacific island laborers on their arrival in the colony, and no one was charged with seeing that the native received adequate medical attention on the plantation. If the employer chose to give hospital treatment to his colored employees, they were admitted to public hospitals at a charge of 1/6d. per day, which the employer paid.[110]

Attention was drawn to these deficiencies in the debate on the bill in the Queensland Assembly in 1868,[111] but the Colonial Office did not comment on them until it reviewed the evidence given to the 1876 Select Committee. As a result of that committee's report, the Queensland government, through its immigration officer, asked inspectors to insist on medical treatment being given if they thought it necessary.[112] The 1880 act gave the inspectors power to order hospital treatment—at the employer's expense—for natives requiring it.[113] It became obligatory also for the master of the recruiting vessel to produce a health certificate from the port medi-

109. Minute by Fuller on Cairns to C.O., 6 Dec. 1876, C.O. 234/36.
110. Evidence of Joseph Bancroft, M.D., to Qd. Select Committee, 1869, 34-36, Qd. V. & P. 1869, II.
111. Qd. P.D. VI, 916.
112. Circular from Immigration Agent to Police Magistrates, Qd. V. & P. 1877, II, 1219.
113. 44 Vict., No. 17, ss. 24-32.

cal officer for every native landed.[114] The framers of the act adopted another suggestion made by Sheridan in his report as assistant immigration officer at Maryborough in 1876: that a capitation fee should be levied on all employers for the support of a hospital for Pacific islanders in any district where the governor declared it necessary.[115] Hospitals were established in a number of districts, but their administration in some cases was extremely bad.[116]

This act created the pattern of medical treatment for the Pacific islanders. The effect was reflected in a steady decline in the mortality rate among Pacific islanders in Queensland after 1886.[117] However the 1880 act did not require returning natives to undergo a medical examination. They thus took back to the islands, often with disastrous results, diseases which they had contracted in Queensland. Such a compulsory medical examination was introduced[118] following a recommendation by Commodore Wilson in his Report on the Labour Trade in the Western Pacific in 1882.[119]

In 1869 the immigration agent, in the report already referred to, had drawn attention to the unsatisfactory provision in the 1868 act for the return of native laborers to their islands. There was no provision for the return of islanders introduced before the passage of the act. This was corrected by the issue, soon after the immigration agent's report, of new regulations[120] for which the imperial government claimed, without justification, some credit.[121] Early in 1870 the imperial government drew the attention of the

114. *Ibid.*, ss. 15-16.
115. *Ibid.*, s. 28.
116. *Qd. V. & P.* 1884, II, 697.
117. See Appendix, Table 3.
118. Regulation No. 42 enclosed in Norman to Knutsford, 20 May 1892, *P.P.* 1892, LVI, c. 6808.
119. *Qd. V. & P.* 1882, II, 580.
120. Enclosed in Blackall to Granville, 16 April 1869, *P.P.* 1868-1869, XLIII, 408.
121. In a minute on Kinnaird to Granville, 18 March 1870, C.O. 234/25, Pennell lists these regulations as being passed as a result of pressure by the imperial government, whereas they were drawn up and passed on the initiative of the Queensland government.

governor of Queensland to the immigration agent's recommendation[122] relating to the return of the natives, apparently
without realizing that in the meantime the Queensland
government had issued new regulations. As it happened
there was still much to amend, but nothing was done. This
question was one of the number on which Sheridan urged
amendments in his report of 1876. The 1868 act had offered
a choice between paying 15s. per quarter or giving a bond
of £10 to meet the cost of the return passage.[123] The planters,
almost without exception, had chosen the latter, for if the
native's contract was canceled under the Masters and Servants
Act, or his services transferred, the planter was freed from
responsibility for the cost of the return passage, though no
one else assumed it.

The provision of the return passage was more necessary
in the case of the Pacific islander in Queensland than it was
for the Indian coolie in Mauritius or the West Indies. In
1851 the Indian government had accepted the abolition of
the free return passage for Indian immigrants in Mauritius
on condition that it was given to those who from sickness
or destitution were unable to pay their own.[124] Though the
coolie's return passage cost more than the Pacific islander's,
in terms of their respective wages it cost the latter twice as
much. The return passage meant more to the Pacific islander,
for he was seldom accepted, like the coolie, as a permanent
settler.

To prevent some natives' being left without any provision
for their return passage, Sheridan had suggested that the
return passage money should be deposited with the immigration officer. The 1880 act achieved Sheridan's purpose by
retaining the bond, but refusing a transfer of the natives'
services unless a new bond was taken out by the transferee,
and requiring the return fare to be deposited with the im-

122. Granville to Blackall, 18 Feb. 1870, *P.P.* 1871, XLVIII, 468.
123. 31 Vict., No. 47, Form K.
124. Sanderson report, pp. 3-4, *P.P.* 1910, XXVII, Cd. 5192.

migration officer if the native did not return to the islands when his service under the act ended.[125]

Apart from raising it as one of the series of amendments which Queensland had suggested but had not adopted, the imperial government showed no further interest in whether the natives received a free return passage. Of the remaining amendments referred to in Granville's despatch of February 1870 the introduction of women at the rate of one-fifth of the male immigrants, which was the rule in Indian immigration, was never adopted. Such an amendment would increase the danger of permanent settlement, which the Queensland government wished to avoid. The final proposed amendment—the admission of evidence given by Pacific islanders in Queensland courts—raised the question of the natives' legal rights.

As their contracts came under the Masters and Servants Act they had the same rights as the European servant. Under this act a breach of the contract by the servant was a criminal offense. In this respect both European and Pacific islander suffered alike, but the former had a clearer conception of his rights, however limited they were, and was able to protect them in the courts. Not until 1876 was the evidence of Pacific islanders admitted in Queensland courts,[126] and even then there were instances where a native's evidence could not be received because no interpreter could be provided for the particular dialect spoken by the native.

Ignorance of language and local custom prevented the native from taking advantage of what rights he possessed. In the 1881 census more than 85 per cent of the Pacific islanders in Queensland were listed as heathen,[127] which meant that before recruitment they had had little or no contact with Europeans and almost certainly spoke no English. As it was often the policy of missionaries to teach natives some island

125. 44 Vict., No. 17, ss. 19, 23.
126. 40 Vict., No. 10.
127. Table XCL, Qd. Census 1881, *Qd. V. & P.* 1882, I, 1176.

language other than their own, rather than English,[128] many classified as Christians had little knowledge of English.

Even where natives realized they had recourse to a higher authority than their employer, the plantation was often too far away from the office of the inspector for them to be able to make the journey without absenting themselves from work, thus enabling the employer to charge them with breach of contract. Because of the locality of the plantation, the laborer was often in fact confined to it outside his working hours. Such a restriction on freedom of movement was imposed on Indian laborers in Mauritius and the West Indies, but it was never accepted by the government of India.

A justice of the peace before whom any case involving a native laborer was brought was almost certain to be an employer of native labor himself. In an attempt to remove the possibility of a biased judgment in such cases, Griffith introduced a clause into the 1885 bill by which all cases involving Pacific islanders were to be tried before police magistrates rather than justices of the peace. The Assembly at first refused to accept the Council's rejection of this clause, but were forced to give way when the Council's intransigence threatened the complete rejection of the bill.[129]

As there were so many reasons why the native's rights might be disregarded, it was particularly desirable that the inspectors appointed under the 1868 act should do their work carefully. The reports of the 1869[130] and 1876[131] committees showed that this was not the case; visits by inspectors were infrequent and returns often incomplete, and the imperial government in commenting on the 1876 report drew special attention to the need for careful inspection.[132] The

128. Reverend E. Griffith to Mullens, 10 June 1869, Australian Correspondence, Box 7, L.M.S. Archives.

129. Qd. P.D., XLV, 171, 207, 221-222; XLVII, 1076.

130. Evidence of O'Donnell, pp. 8-12. Qd. Select Committee, 1869, Qd. V. & P. 1869, II, 23.

131. Report of Qd. Select Committee 1876, Qd. V. & P. 1876, III, 51 ff.

132. Carnarvon to Officer Administering Government of Qd., 29 March 1877, C.O. 234/36.

general standard can be gauged from the reaction to the efficient work of Sheridan, which was an embarrassment to the immigration agent. There is no doubt that the standard of administration improved greatly after 1885 and particularly after 1892.

It had been claimed, in favor of the introduction of Pacific islanders into Queensland, that they would benefit from contact with a higher civilization. However, very little was done to teach the natives anything that would be useful to them on their return to their islands. Bishop Patteson had not entirely opposed the labor traffic because he saw in the sojourn in Queensland an opportunity to train natives for service as teachers on their return. But nothing was done in Queensland for the natives, although some Christian natives working in Brisbane regularly attended the Congregational Church, where the Reverend Edward Griffith, father of Sir Samuel, was the minister.[133] The Headquarters of the London Missionary Society in London asked that native teachers be sent to Queensland[134] to work among the laborers, but the missionaries in the islands at first opposed this move as implying that they sanctioned the labor traffic.[135] Neither did the planters welcome the proposal, for they feared a teacher might become a labor leader or trouble maker. In fact, native teachers did not adopt this role, though they sometimes brought injustices to the notice of the inspectors.

Any schools or chapels for natives were provided on a voluntary basis either by the planters themselves or by churches, some of which had in the nineties special missions to the Pacific islanders in Queensland.[136] The most notable example was the work of Florence Young, a planter's wife,

<hr/>

133. E. Griffith to Mullens, 10 June 1869, Australian Correspondence, Box 7, L.M.S. Archives, London.
134. Mullens to Sutherland, 27 Nov. 1868. Outgoing letters, Western, Vol. 8, L.M.S. Archives, London.
135. Creagh to Mullens, 13 Oct. 1869, South Seas Correspondence, 23/3/B, L.M.S. Archives, London.
136. See A. C. Smith, *The Kanaka Labour Question*, enclosed in Norman to C.O., 19 Jan. 1893, C.O. 234/56.

who began a mission which continued its work in the Solomons when Pacific islanders were finally repatriated between 1901 and 1906. In one instance the natives themselves subscribed the money necessary to build their own hall.

These efforts on behalf of the islanders were exceptional; they were never accepted as citizens, although a small proportion married Europeans and lived permanently in the colony as leaseholders, small traders, or laborers.[137]

The assumptions of the imperial and Queensland governments about the treatment of Pacific islanders in Queensland were often at variance. The imperial government held that, like the Indian indentured laborer, the Pacific island laborer should have equal rights with the local laborer. For this reason it had no sympathy with the policy of restricting the choice of employment open to the Pacific islander in order to shield the white laborer from competition. Similarly it insisted that the property rights of the laborer should be safeguarded to the extent that the wages of the deceased laborer should be paid to his next of kin. Other points raised by the imperial government—a statutory limitation of working hours and legislative protection against ill treatment— were not held to be of sufficient importance by Queensland to require legislation. To the Queensland government, on the other hand, Pacific islanders were a temporary and inferior labor supply to whom the statutory rights and privileges of European labor did not extend. They were not allowed free choice of employment, nor given either adequate legal protection against ill treatment, or any limitation on their hours of work. Only under pressure did the government provide security for the payment of their wages, reasonable medical care, and a guaranteed return passage, or accept the evidence of Pacific islanders in courts of law. They owed what social and educational amenities they enjoyed to the good will of voluntary bodies. The imperial government

137. *P.P.* 1903, XLIV, Cd. 1554.

could do little other than express regret at such differential treatment, while the missionary societies were not so much concerned about the treatment of the Pacific islanders in Queensland as they were about recruiting abuses in the islands. They knew that if their efforts to end recruiting were successful, this would solve the problem of the Pacific islanders in Queensland.

CHAPTER VIII. IMPERIAL
REGULATION IN THE PACIFIC, 1872-1893

I

The imperial government had passed the 1872 act to prevent kidnaping. Proposals for legislative action to this end had first been made twelve years earlier. During the intervening period, reports reaching the imperial government proved that the remedies under the slave trade acts could not be applied to cases of kidnaping in the Pacific, and that there were obstacles in the way of the evidence of both Europeans and natives being set before the courts authorized to try such offenses. That legislation was required to meet these needs was evident long before the bill was submitted to Parliament; the principal cause of the delay was the reluctance of the Treasury to authorize the expenses involved. It was the shock of Bishop Patteson's murder that finally brought the bill before Parliament. Subsequent legislative action by the imperial government on this question followed much the same pattern. Although it aspired, in its object, beyond the mere prevention of kidnaping, Treasury parsimony still inhibited imperial action on the scale required for the proper administration of the labor trade.

Kimberley hoped that the 1872 act in conjunction with the Queensland act of 1868 and additional patrolling by the Navy would solve the problem of the labor trade in the Pacific;[1] indeed, one naval officer, returned from the Pacific, informed Carnarvon at a personal interview late in 1873 that kidnaping had been eradicated since the passing of the 1872 act and the strengthening of the naval forces.[2] But this was a prematurely optimistic view that later reports contradicted.[3]

1. Kimberley to Normanby (private), 12 July 1872, Kimberley Papers.
2. Memorandum of conversation with Capt. Challis, Nov. 1873, Carnarvon Papers, P.R.O. 30/6, 51.
3. Letter from Reverend R. Steel, *Sydney Morning Herald*, 25 Sept. 1874, enclosed in Bowen to Carnarvon, 8 Oct. 1874, C.O. 309/112.

The inherent weaknesses of the act were soon evident. As it applied only to British subjects, those engaged in recruiting were able to continue unhindered by flying a foreign flag. Such a defect could not be remedied except by international agreement.[4] Again, the act made no provision for the supervision of the employment of the recruited labor. It assumed that this would be undertaken by the governments of the places where the natives were employed.[5] Only in Queensland was this provided for in any satisfactory way. In Fiji the treatment of immigrant Pacific island laborers was part of the general problem of the administration of those islands, which at this time had not yet been satisfactorily solved. Laborers were also employed in other island groups, such as the New Hebrides, where there had been no attempt of any kind to supervise the conditions of their employment.

While imperial legislation alone could not reach those recruiters who flew a foreign flag, the Foreign Office had approved of a suggestion of the Law Officers that the question of jurisdiction in islands where laborers were employed might be considered when drafting the 1872 bill.[6] However, nothing to that effect was included in the act; but when it was amended in 1875 such a clause, which crept in almost as an afterthought, came to be the most significant part of the new act.[7] The original purpose of the amending act, however, was to remedy less important defects in the 1872 act.

The first vessels seized under the 1872 act had been engaged in the *bêche de mer* and pearl fisheries off the north coast of Queensland. Two of these vessels were condemned in the Vice-Admiralty Court in Sydney, but the decision had been set aside by the Privy Council on the grounds that the native members of the crew had been engaged before the passage of the act, and the intention to procure licenses had

4. See pp. 176 ff., below.
5. Minute by Malcolm on Cairns to Carnarvon, 16 June 1877, C.O. 234/37.
6. F.O. to C.O., 18 Feb. 1870, F.O. 58/127.
7. 38 and 39 Vict., c. 51, s. 6.

been established.[8] There was, however, no provision under the 1872 act for the issuance of licenses to recruit labor for service on ships engaged in *bêche de mer* or pearl fishing. Although the condition of natives engaged in these occupations had been the subject of a report by a naval officer in 1868,[9] the act was passed before any complaints about kidnaping for such service had been received.

The legal position of these natives was ambiguous: they were neither members of the crew nor passengers. The purpose of the clause of the bill was to authorize their engagement by requiring the vessel on which they served to be licensed, and to provide for the method of engagement, either in accordance with the Merchant Shipping Act of 1854, or by an Order-in-Council to be issued under the act. In either case the names of the natives engaged, with particulars of their identity, were to be entered in the official log of the vessel. The latter clause was originally intended to provide an alternative arrangement to that of the other two clauses, but was made compulsory in all cases by an amendment desired by the Aborigines Protection Society[10] and proposed in the House by McArthur.

This amendment was only partly successful in achieving its limiting object: the satisfactory regulation of the engagement of natives for service in *bêche de mer* and pearl fisheries. In the first place the forms prescribed for the licensing of vessels under the act were often inapplicable because the

8. The *Melanie, Challenge, Woodbine,* and *Christina* were seized by Capt. Moresby, *H.M.S. Basilisk,* between 5 and 14 Jan. 1873; see Stirling to Admiralty, 22 March 1873 enclosed in Admiralty to C.O., 12 May 1873, C.O. 234/33. The *Melanie* and the *Challenge* were condemned in the Vice-Admiralty Court at Sydney. The *Christina,* although a *bêche de mer* fisher, was taking to Queensland natives recruited by the wrecked vessel *Active,* and was condemned in the Vice-Admiralty Court, Brisbane; it was the first conviction under the 1872 act. See Normanby to Kimberley, 11 June 1873, C.O. 234/32. No action was taken against the *Woodbine.* See also J. Moresby: *Two Admirals* (London, 1909), p. 289.

9. See enclosures in Admiralty to F.O., 16 June 1868, *P.P.* 1868-1869, XLIII, 438.

10. *The Colonial Intelligencer,* Nov. 1875. There are no accounts in *Hansard* of the 1875 bill in the Commons.

number and description of the crew were constantly changing.[11] In the second place, although most of the natives who
served in these vessels were engaged in Sydney under the
Merchant Shipping Act, many of the agreements were considered unfair by Douglas, the Queensland premier who
toured the North in 1878.[12] His report was forwarded by the
Colonial Office to New South Wales, where in the following
year an act[13] was passed requiring such engagements to be
made in the presence of a shipping master.

It was as true of this clause referring to the fisheries as of
the act in general, that it provided in no way for the conditions under which the natives worked.[14] Local acts[15] provided
for this in those fisheries within the jurisdiction of Queensland, the boundaries of which had been extended in 1878
to include islands within sixty miles of the coast; but the
employment of natives in fisheries outside these limits remained under inadequate supervision.

Other clauses in the amending bill as first presented to
Parliament referred to the jurisdiction of the Admiralty
courts[16] and to the status of Fiji.[17] The High Court of Admiralty was given the same powers as Vice-Admiralty courts
in Her Majesty's dominions in respect to vessels seized under
the 1872 act. The powers given under the 1872 act to the
supreme courts of the Australian colonies to issue commissions for the examination of witnesses, and to hear the evidence of natives, were extended to the Admiralty courts.
Power was also given to seize cargo as well as vessels[18]—an
omission in the 1872 act.

11. Hoskins to Admiralty, 4 Sept. 1878, enclosure 1 in Admiralty to C.O.,
29 Oct. 1878, C.O. 234/38.
12. Enclosure in Kennedy to Carnarvon, 14 Jan. 1878, C.O. 234/38.
13. N.S.W., 43 Vict., No. 6.
14. See report of Chester of May 1877, enclosed in Cairns to Carnarvon,
16 June 1877, C.O. 234/37.
15. Queensland, 45 Vict., No. 2; 50 Vict., No. 2; 55 Vict., No. 29; 57 Vict.,
No. 7; 60 Vict., No. 32; 63 Vict., No. 3.
16. 38 and 39 Vict., c. 51, ss. 4-5.
17. Ibid., s. 8.
18. Ibid., s. 3.

The act was also amended to take account of the fact that since its passage, Fiji had become a British colony. Fiji was included in the definition "Australian Colonies," but the act still applied to the natives of Fiji as it did to natives of islands not within the jurisdiction of any civilized power.

II

The most significant amendment was introduced by Carnarvon in the committee stage of the bill in the Lords.[19] This amendment became clause six of the amending act; it was to provide for the exercise of jurisdiction over British subjects in any islands not under the jurisdiction of any civilized power. This would be done by the issue of an Order-in-Council to create the office of High Commissioner with authority to make regulations for the government of British subjects in the islands, and to set up a court with civil, criminal, and Admiralty jurisdiction corresponding to the authority of the High Commissioner. It would be possible under the Order-in-Council for the High Commissioner to regulate the conditions of employment as well as recruiting of labor, thus meeting an obvious deficiency of the 1872 act.

The authority proposed for the High Commissioner was of the kind the Foreign Office had considered giving the consul in Fiji before annexation and as an alternative to it. The Foreign Office abandoned this plan partly because of legal difficulties—not, however, insurmountable—but principally because of Treasury opposition. As an alternative the Foreign Office hoped that some clause giving authority over the recruiting and employment of labor in Fiji might be included in the bill to prevent kidnaping which the Colonial Office were considering at that time.[20] The 1872 act contained no such clause; but the annexation of Fiji in 1874 met the problem of the administration of immigrant labor there.

19. *Hansard*, 3rd Series, CCXXII, 2-3.
20. See chap. ii, above.

In the meantime immigrant labor was being used by British subjects in other islands—at Havannah Harbor in the New Hebrides and in Samoa for example—and some form of supervision was necessary, particularly in those places where, as at Havannah Harbor, the majority of the settlers were British. It was to meet this kind of situation that Goodenough had suggested in his report[21] that the governor of Fiji should be given authority over British subjects in the islands of the South Pacific not under the jurisdiction of any civilized power.

Carnarvon was receptive to this proposal as he was aware that even an amended kidnaping act was not likely to be sufficient in itself to prevent further kidnaping, nor did it provide any means of supervising the terms of employment of natives outside British territories. The annexation of Fiji would meet this problem for those islands, but would do little or nothing for the other areas. To suggest that it would, said Herbert, was like supposing that "everyone would become sober if one out of fifty public houses in a parish were closed."[22] Further annexation was most unlikely in view of the difficulty already encountered in getting the government to accept the annexation of Fiji. This had at first been rejected because of the expense involved. When the reasons for annexation became overwhelming, Carnarvon still had to justify his proposal to annex by stating that if his plans turned out as he had reason to expect they would, no colony would have been established at so little cost to the mother country.[23] As a result the imperial government advanced £100,000 to Fiji at the time of cession which was less than the amount annually spent by France on Martinique, with a land area one thirtieth that of Fiji.[24] The cramping effect

21. *P.P.* 1874, XLV, c. 1011.
22. Quoted by W. D. McIntyre, "Disraeli's Colonial Policy: The Creation of the Western Pacific High Commission, 1874-1877," *Historical Studies*, IX, No. 35 (Nov. 1960), 281.
23. Carnarvon to Disraeli, 7 Aug. 1874, Disraeli Papers.
24. Des Voeux, *My Colonial Service*, I, 346.

this had on the work of those charged with the administration of the new colony can be gauged from the fact that Gordon recommended that his private secretary should be appointed a deputy commissioner under the proposed Order-in-Council, because he was prepared to equip and maintain at his own expense a vessel for official use in the islands.[25]

To set up the kind of authority suggested by Goodenough might prevent the conditions in other island groups reaching the point which made annexation unavoidable in Fiji. The proposal was therefore welcomed as a modest alternative to annexation, and it was used as such in dealing with deputations seeking the annexation of New Guinea in 1875.[26] It was also on these grounds that Kimberley later supported the amendment in the House of Lords,[27] while Herbert curtly dismissed a suggestion by Vogel, the former New Zealand premier, that any regulations made under the Order-in-Council should continue in force if the territory concerned became part of Her Majesty's dominions.[28] Herbert regarded this as a subtle attempt by Vogel to commit the imperial government by words in the bill to a policy of future annexation—the very policy it desired to avoid.

When the proposal was referred to the Foreign Office it was received with little enthusiasm. The Colonial Office had discussed the position with Sir Arthur Gordon at the time he was considering the governorship of Fiji. They agreed that the governor of Fiji should also be consul for the island groups, in particular Samoa, Tonga, and the New Hebrides. Gordon accepted the governorship of Fiji before the plans for the High Commissionership were complete, but he made it quite clear to Carnarvon that he desired to assume these "interesting and important duties connected with the regulation of the labour trade and our relations with the islands

25. Gordon to Carnarvon, 10 May 1875, P.R.O. 30/6, 39.
26. W. D. McIntyre, *op. cit.*, p. 284.
27. *Hansard*, 3rd Series, LCXXIV, 3.
28. Minute on Vogel's memorandum, April 1875, P.R.O. 30/6, 47.

of Melanesia and the independent groups of the Pacific."[29] Nor did he wish to share authority in these matters with any other existing officials, and he asked that no appointment affecting them should be made by either the Colonial Office or the Foreign Office without first consulting him.[30] Although there was a precedent for something like this arrangement—the governor of Labuan was also consul for North Borneo—the Foreign Office was not happy about consular functions being exercised by a Colonial Office appointee. At a conference between representatives from the Colonial Office and Foreign Office less than three weeks before Gordon left for Fiji, it was agreed that Gordon should be given the title of High Commissioner and that he would have authority over British subjects in the area in their relations with each other and with Pacific islanders, but that relations between British subjects and other foreigners would be dealt with by the consul at New Caledonia.[31] The Foreign Office agreed, however, not to appoint any other consuls in the High Commission area without consulting the High Commissioner, though they did not in fact observe this.

The new act, with Carnarvon's amendment providing for the High Commission, became law on 4 August 1875, but for another two years contention between the Colonial Office and the Foreign Office prevented issuance of the Order-in-Council. The delay might have been longer had it not been for Gordon's impatience. He wrote, "I was promised in writing that if I would start without the Commission which I had declared to be essential, and without the promise of which I declined to go to Fiji, it should be sent after me immediately, and would probably overtake me in Sydney. . . . But the Foreign Office was very unwilling to allow a Colonial Office Officer to be Consul . . . and while the bickerings between the offices went on, my appointment was month after

29. Gordon to Carnarvon, 17 Feb. 1875, P.R.O. 30/6, 39.
30. Sir Arthur Gordon, *Records of Private and Public Life 1875-1880* (Edinburgh 1897-1910), II, 407-408.
31. McIntyre, *op. cit.*, p. 283.

month postponed."[32] But for this delay, he said, he could have prevented the chaos in Samoa which continued to prevail down to 1899. After writing many letters to Carnarvon about the delay, he finally sent Maudslay, his private secretary, back to England in May 1877 to see if he could hasten the issue of the Order-in-Council.[33]

When the Order-in-Council[34] was issued Gordon was bitterly disappointed. He had been assured by Carnarvon that "within the limits of the High Commissionership . . . the authority of the officer holding such a commission from the Crown should be sole and supreme."[35] Yet he found he was without full authority on the two essentials for the effective control of the labor trade. First he was unable to make regulations for the employment of Pacific islanders anywhere outside the colony of Fiji. His powers were limited to the issue of regulations dealing with offenses against treaties with native authorities.[36] This meant that the Order-in-Council had done nothing toward solving the problem of administering the employment of immigrant native labor by British subjects in islands with no recognized government. The Colonial Office absolved itself from any responsibility for thus curtailing the power of the High Commission; the blame was attached to the Foreign Office, which was accused of both overt and covert hostility to the idea of the High Commission.[37] There seemed to be no legal reason for such restriction. At the time the Foreign Office was considering the extension of the consul's jurisdiction over British subjects in Fiji, the Foreign Jurisdiction Act in force required a valid treaty with the native ruler before such jurisdiction could be granted; but the 1875 act expressly gave to Her

32. Gordon, *Records*, loc. cit.
33. A.P. Maudslay, *Life in the Pacific Fifty Years Ago* (London, 1930), pp. 176-177.
34. Western Pacific Order-in-Council, 13 Aug. 1877, *Qd. V. & P.* 1880, I, 65 ff.
35. Gordon, *Records*, IV, 56.
36. Western Pacific Order-in-Council, loc. cit., s. 24.
37. Minutes by Bramston and Herbert on Gordon to Kimberley, 28 Jan. 1881, C.O. 225/7.

Majesty jurisdiction over British subjects in any islands not part of Her Majesty's dominions nor within the jurisdiction of any civilized power. For no apparent reason, then, the High Commissioner was without power adequately to supervise the employment of colored labor in islands with no recognized government, a state of affairs which continued until this restriction was removed by the 1879 Order-in-Council.[38]

Gordon was also disappointed with the Order-in-Council on a second point: it failed to fulfil all that he had expected of it in respect of the recruiting of labor.[39] Here the problem was what was known as "the inter-island traffic," where laborers were often recruited and employed in islands without any recognized government such as the New Hebrides and Solomons. Vessels engaged in this traffic were out of reach of any authority except the Navy. Because it was impossible to supervise, Commodore Goodenough, when he was officer commanding on the Australian station in 1874-1875, banned this traffic altogether.[40] Under the Order-in-Council responsibility for granting licenses to recruit was to be shared between the High Commissioner and the consul at New Caledonia.[41] This was too indirect a method to ensure that the licenses were issued only to people of good character. Gordon was adamant that he alone should have authority for the issue of licenses, and that enquiries into the suitability of

38. Western Pacific Order-in-Council, 14 Aug. 1879, *Qd. V. & P.* 1880, I, 702 ff.
39. In his despatch to Kimberley, 16 July 1881 (*P.P.* 1883, XLVII, c. 3641), Gordon refers to powers for the superintendence of the labor trade given at first to the High Commissioner and taken away immediately afterward and given to the governors of the Australian colonies. Ward, p. 273, n. 3, accepts Gordon's statement, and attempts to set down what these powers were. It is more probable that Gordon's statement is inaccurate. He gives a more accurate account of the powers conferred on the High Commissioner in Gordon to Secretary of State for Colonies, n.d., Gordon, *Records,* III, 245, and Gordon to Hicks-Beach 2 March 1878, C.O. 83/16. The powers Gordon refers to as at first given were probably those *proposed* but never given, while those he refers to as given to the governors of the Australian Colonies were probably the temporary right to issue licenses for the inter-island recruiting.
40. Gordon to Hicks-Beach, 19 April 1879, C.O. 201/589.
41. Gordon to Carnarvon, 28 Dec. 1877, Gordon, *Records,* II, 675.

applicants in these areas should be made by deputy commissioners who should be appointed to the New Hebrides and Solomons.

While the 1875 bill was still before Parliament both Gordon and Vogel were thinking in terms of five or six assistants to the High Commissioner in different parts of the Western Pacific. Under the 1877 Order-in-Council deputy commissioners were appointed in Tonga and Samoa; but instructions were given that no other appointments were to be made,[42] in spite of the fact that deputy commissioners were most urgently needed in the New Hebrides and Solomons in order to control the inter-island labor trade. Treasury economy was the reason for this refusal. In 1879 Hicks-Beach agreed that the temporary system of issuing licenses on the recommendation of the consul at Noumea should end if a deputy commissioner could be appointed at Havannah Harbor in the New Hebrides without cost to the Treasury.[43] This could not be done, of course, and it was left to Gordon to continue to press for such appointments, but without success.[44]

It was one of the recommendations[45] of the Royal Commission on the Western Pacific in 1884 that five resident deputy commissioners should be appointed in five administrative areas to be set up in the Western Pacific. These deputy commissioners were to have full control of labor-recruiting in their areas; they alone were to issue licenses for recruiting and recruiting vessels were to employ government agents appointed by them. Recruiting under the Queensland legislation was not to be exempt from this as it had been from the 1872-1875 acts. The colony protested vigorously

42. Report of Royal Commission on the Working of the Western Pacific Orders-in-Council, 1884, s. 38, *Qd. V. & P.* 1884, II, 948.
43. Minute by Hicks-Beach on Gordon to Hicks-Beach, 19 April 1879, C.O. 201/589.
44. Gordon to Kimberley, 11 Jan. 1881, C.O. 225/7; 16 July 1881, 16 June 1882, *P.P.* 1883, XLVII, c. 3641.
45. Report of Royal Commission on Working of Western Pacific Orders-in-Council, 1884, s. 196, *Qd. V. & P.* 1884, II, 962.

against this as an interference with its rights of self-govern-ment.[46] The proposal, however, was not implemented, and it was not until after 1893 that sufficient deputy high commissioners were appointed. The High Commission did not, therefore, provide the means for the satisfactory regulation of either the recruiting or the employment of labor in the islands. This did not come until European administrations were set up.

III

The High Commission failed in its positive task of supervising recruiting and the conditions of employment of island laborers; it also failed to maintain law and order in the Western Pacific. From the beginning the relations of black and white in the Pacific had been marred by crimes of violence, but these had become more frequent since Europeans began recruiting labor. Many natives were murdered by recruiters and others were recruited by force, and for this the natives took indiscriminate revenge. Ironically, the Europeans, by selling firearms to natives, provided them with more effective instruments of revenge. Attacks on Europeans became so frequent that toward the end of 1880 angry public opinion in the Australian colonies demanded that the High Commission be reformed or replaced by some other system more capable of preventing such outrages.

Until the High Commission was set up, the Navy had policed the Pacific, bringing British subjects to justice and punishing natives by "acts of war." Most recruiting took place within the boundaries[47] of the Australian naval station which was separated from the East Indies and China station in 1859 and placed under the command of a commodore. Until 1872 there were never more than six ships on the station, and these were of inferior rating and of obsolete

46. Copy of telegram, Griffith to Agent-General, enclosed in telegram Griffith to Victorian Premier, 24 April 1884, *Vict. P.P.* No. 38, 1884, p. 95.
47. In 1859, 10° S., 170° W., 75° E., the Antarctic, Ad. 13/4. Minor alterations occurred in succeeding years.

design.[48] Only one of these was used from time to time to visit the islands, and only when pressed by the Anti-Slavery party in the Commons did the Admiralty agree to place an additional ship on the station for the purpose of maintaining a continuous patrol.[49]

Quite apart from the inadequacy of the forces at its disposal, the officers on the Australian station were accused of indifference to kidnaping.[50] They regarded posting to the Australian station as an opportunity of visiting Australian ports and spending long leaves ashore. This perhaps was most true of the two years when Lambert was commodore between 1868 and 1870; yet indifference might easily be explained by the hopelessness of the task of putting down kidnaping with the ships available and—before the 1872 act—no legal power to seize ships engaged in kidnaping.

In spite of these difficulties and criticisms the ships sent on patrol exercised a restraining influence on kidnapers. Palmer, the commander of one such vessel, felt so strongly about recruiting—he later joined forces with the Anti-Slavery Society—that he took the risk of seizing the *Daphne* with no certainty of what the reaction of his commanding officer, Lambert, or the Admiralty would be. It transpired that Lambert, who doubted the legal validity of the seizure, was proved correct by the decision of the court; but nevertheless the Admiralty showed its sympathy with Palmer's motive by approving his action.[51]

Under the 1872 act the Navy was formally charged with seizing vessels contravening the act.[52] The Admiralty agreed to build five schooners to be manned by supernumeraries and to be employed solely to enforce the act.[53] The first of

48. Navy List for the years concerned.
49. *Hansard*, 3rd Series, CXCIX, 877-878; CC, 1427.
50. Selwyn to Gladstone, 27 Nov. 1871, Gladstone Papers, 44299.
51. See p. 19 above.
52. 35 and 36 Vict., c. 19, s. 16.
53. Admiralty memorandum, 14 Feb. 1872, Kimberley Papers; Navy List, 1874. The names of these vessels were *Alacrity, Beagle, Conflict, Reynard,* and *Sandfly.*

these ships left Sydney in June 1873 and made its first seizure two months later.[54] There was still, however, immunity from seizure for those kidnapers who desired it; before 1872 it was provided by the knowledge that the Navy had no legal power to seize; after 1872 the absence of any international agreement allowed kidnapers to avoid seizure by flying a foreign flag.

Within these limits the Navy continued its particular work of enforcing the 1872 act and its general work of maintaining peace between native and European. Humanitarians continued to criticize, on the one hand, the failure of the Navy to take action against kidnapers and, on the other, "acts of war" by which native communities were punished for violence against Europeans.[55] The Quaker influence which had opposed the use of force in the suppression of the slave trade in the forties was still strong among the humanitarians, and to it was added the voice of the missionary societies interested in the welfare of the islanders. This question of how native violence was to be restrained was to become part of the problem of the relative jurisdiction of the Navy and the High Commission.

When the High Commission was set up there were thus two imperial authorities charged with maintaining order in the Western Pacific, the functions of neither of which were clearly defined in this respect. As the High Commission's jurisdiction was limited to British subjects, the Admiralty assumed that the Navy would continue to punish natives for offenses against British subjects, while the High Commission would punish British subjects for offenses against natives.[56] This meant that legal means were used to check outrages by British subjects, but armed reprisals were used against similar acts by natives. In one case where native teachers were

54. Laird Clowes, *The Royal Navy: A History from Earliest Times to the Present* (London, 1897-1903), VII, 264.
55. *Colonial Intelligencer*, Feb. 1874; A.P.S. to Hicks-Beach, 4 April 1879, C.O. 201/589.
56. Gordon to Hicks-Beach, 19 April 1879, C.O. 201/589.

murdered by other natives the reprisal was taken by a British missionary, resulting in the anomaly of the latter's being brought before the High Commission court for punishing crimes committed by natives.[57]

Not all these crimes of course were associated with the labor trade—the problem was wider than that; but the unscrupulous labor recruiter was often the first European contact with the natives and this determined the pattern of revenge and punishment which in many cases characterized the subsequent relations of the two races.

In England there was a general distaste for the use of force against defenseless islanders. This was felt not only by humanitarians, but by upholders of the rule of law who thought crimes of natives should, like those of Europeans, be settled by law.[58] There was also a feeling that punitive measures led to fresh outrages. The Aborigines Protection Society pointed out that Commodore Goodenough was murdered on the same island where less than one year earlier H.M.S. *Sandfly* had burnt villages and killed natives as a reprisal for an attempted attack on that vessel.[59]

There was of course a simple solution to this problem of bringing natives under the law: the establishment of protectorates or the annexation of the islands. But the Colonial Office had no wish to add to its responsibilities. Much hesitation was shown before the cession of even the tiny island of Rotumah was accepted.[60] When the proposal for the High Commission was first brought before Parliament, Vogel had suggested to Carnarvon that it should have jurisdiction over natives as well as British subjects. Herbert had acknowledged the necessity for this, but rejected it because he saw no means by which it could be done except by the establishment of protectorates, the expense of which the imperial government

57. Gorrie to Hicks-Beach, 11 Nov. 1878, C.O. 225/1.
58. *Hansard*, 3rd Series, CCXXII, 1605-1606; CCLXIV, 1027.
59. *Colonial Intelligencer*, Nov. 1875.
60. Minutes of Herbert and Hicks-Beach on Gorrie to Hicks-Beach, 18 Aug. 1879, C.O. 225/3.

was not prepared to bear.[61] Most of the problems of administration in the Pacific arose when the imperial government sought a less expensive substitute for the assumption of protectorates or the annexation of new territory.

The controversy between the High Commissioner and the commodore on their respective jurisdictions probably had its origin in the view of the former that, representing as he did the rule of law, he should have authority over natives as well as British subjects. Gordon always maintained that Carnarvon intended the High Commission to be the sole authority.[62] When in 1878 a native of the Solomon Islands was executed by the Navy for being involved in the murder of a British subject, Gordon protested to the Colonial Office that no such action ought to be taken without prior consultation with the High Commissioner.[63] Though the Admiralty agreed that consultation was desirable, it pointed out that in practice it would be impossible.[64] Gordon then pressed the Colonial Office to give the High Commissioner jurisdiction over natives,[65] but the Law Officers could not suggest any means by which this could be done without assuming territorial responsibilities.[66]

The dual authority had proved most unsatisfactory: it had led to personal recriminations between Sir John Gorrie, the Acting High Commissioner, and the commodore, and it had not been successful in checking outrages, which, on the contrary, had increased. About the latter, the Australian colonies protested vigorously.[67] Whereas in England there was much misgiving about the Navy's use of force, the Australian Intercolonial Conference of 1881 passed a resolution calling for more stringent measures to check native

61. Vogel memorandum and Herbert's minute, April 1875, P.R.O. 30/6, 47.
62. Gordon to Under-Secretary of State for Colonies, 14 Feb. 1879, Gordon, *Records*, III, 249.
63. Gordon to Secretary of State for Colonies, 28 Oct. 1878, *ibid.*, III, 197.
64. Admiralty to C.O., 15 June 1878, C.O. 83/17; Admiralty to C.O., 3 Feb. 1879, C.O. 225/3.
65. Gordon to Hicks-Beach, 19 April 1879, C.O. 201/589.
66. Admiralty to C.O., 2 Sept. 1879, C.O. 225/3.
67. Loftus to Kimberley, 2 Dec. 1880, 28 Dec. 1880, C.O. 201/592.

outrages.[68] The colonial press referred to the feeling in England "that the misconduct of the black races must be corrected, not by cannon balls, but by Christian philanthropy."[69] The press opposed what it called Sir Arthur Gordon's "Exeter Hall" policy, and referred to Gorrie, the Chief Judicial Commissioner, as the nominee of the Aborigines Protection Society.[70] The difference of opinion between Gordon and the colonists on the use of force really turned on the larger question whether the interests of Europeans were always to be preferred to those of the natives. This was the assumption behind the resolution of the Intercolonial Conference, and Gordon could not accept it.[71] The Colonial Office tried to hold the balance; Kimberley thought that Gordon was as biased in favor of the natives as the Australian colonists were toward the Europeans.[72]

It was clear by 1880 that the dual authority could not continue; either the Navy or the High Commission must be made the sole authority. In 1879 Herbert had suggested that the commodore be made the High Commissioner,[73] and Kimberley entertained this view early in 1881.[74] But Gordon would have none of it;[75] this impasse was ended only when the Admiralty rejected the plan.[76] The alternative was to give the High Commissioner jurisdiction over natives. On the occasion of the reprisals inflicted by H.M.S. *Emerald* on the natives of the Solomons for the murder of Lieutenant Bower of H.M.S. *Sandfly*, the Aborigines Protection Society had made representations to the Admiralty,[77] which, acknowl-

68. Report of Australian Intercolonial Conference, Jan. 1881, *Qd. V. & P.* 1881, II, 1042.

69. Enclosure in Loftus to Kimberley, 28 Dec. 1880, C.O. 201/592.

70. Appendix to Report of Australian Intercolonial Conference, Jan. 1881, *Qd. V. & P.* 1881, II, 1089.

71. Gordon to Kimberley, 28 Jan. 1881, C.O. 225/7.

72. Minute by Kimberley on Gordon to Kimberley, 20 May 1881, C.O. 225/7.

73. Minute by Herbert on Admiralty to C.O., 2 Sept. 1879, C.O. 225/3.

74. Minute by Kimberley on Gordon to Kimberley, 28 Jan. 1881, C.O. 225/7.

75. Gordon to Kimberley, 20 April 1881, C.O. 225/7.

76. *Ibid.*, Kimberley's minute.

77. *Aborigine's Friend*, Aug. 1881, p. 408.

edging how undesirable those methods were, pressed the Colonial Office to find some means of checking native outrages in courts of law.[78] Kimberley did draw up such a bill, but it was stifled by Gladstone's alarm at the administrative and pecuniary liabilities involved.[79]

There was in this, as in other problems of administration in the Pacific and elsewhere, no satisfactory solution short of accepting full responsibility by annexation or the declaration of protectorates. In the meantime, Gordon recommended a compromise by which the authority of the naval commanders in these matters was to be brought under the direction of the High Commission by the expedient of appointing the former deputy commissioners with powers to dispense summary justice in all judicial matters and to act as committing magistrates in other matters.[80] Naval officers had previously acted for the period of one voyage as deputy commissioners. In addition Gordon asked once again for legislation to confer on the High Commission court a jurisdiction over natives similar to that exercised by courts on the West Coast of Africa.[81] However, nothing was done until the Order-in-Council of 1893 which applied the British Settlements Act of 1887 and the Foreign Jurisdiction Act of 1890 to the High Commission area. This, together with the joint naval commission, set up with France in the New Hebrides in 1887, and the declaration of a protectorate over the Solomons in 1893, helped to provide more effective means of maintaining law and order in the area.

IV

One of the reasons for the seriousness of the outrages by natives against Europeans was the natives' use of firearms

78. *Hansard*, 3rd Series, CCLXIV, 1027.
79. Gladstone to Kimberley, 26 Jan. 1882, Kimberley Papers.
80. Gordon to Kimberley, 16 June 1882, *P.P.* 1883, XLVII, c. 3641; Report of Royal Commission on Working of Western Pacific Orders-in-Council, 1884, s. 201, *Qd. V. & P.* 1884, II, 962.
81. Report of Royal Commission on Working of Western Pacific Orders-in-Council, 1884, s. 184, *Qd. V. & P.* 1884, II, 961.

supplied to them as wages for plantation work or given as an inducement to enlist for labor service. The imperial government was unequivocally opposed to these practices, but the colonial governments—Queensland in particular— were reluctant to prohibit them. This subject illustrates more clearly than any other connected with the labor trade the nature of the relations of the imperial government with a self-governing colony on a matter in which their respective policies were in opposition. To suppress the arms traffic effectively international agreement was necessary, but an approach to other powers could not be made until the imperial and colonial governments were in agreement on the subject.

The desire for firearms was so strong among the natives that the most successful recruiter was the one who could offer them as gifts to the chief or relatives of those he desired to recruit; also the natives preferred to enlist for service in places where their wages would buy the largest number of arms and ammunition.[82] Neither Fiji nor Queensland, competing keenly for the limited supply of Pacific island labor, responded willingly when the Colonial Office suggested a ban on the sale of arms to Pacific islanders.

The Colonial Office first made a direct approach to Queensland in 1877 when it expressed the hope that the colonial government would adopt the suggestion of its immigration agent that Pacific islanders employed in the colony should not be supplied with firearms.[83] The colonial government, drawn from the party opposed to the employment of Pacific islanders in Queensland, took no more notice of Carnarvon's despatch than it did of the immigration officer's report. The premier, Douglas, favored prohibiting the unlicensed sale of firearms,[84] but his colleagues did not wish to do anything to mitigate the consequences of recruiting

82. Gordon to C.O., 22 March 1878, enclosure, C.O. 384/117.
83. Carnarvon to Kennedy, 1 Nov. 1877, P.P. 1883, XLVII, c. 3641.
84. Kennedy to Hicks-Beach, 8 Sept. 1879, C.O. 234/39.

Pacific islanders and thus detract from the propaganda for its complete prohibition.

Two years later the Colonial Office made another direct approach to Queensland[85] after Sir John Gorrie, the Acting High Commissioner for the Western Pacific, had protested against giving firearms as wages in Fiji and Queensland.[86] To this Queensland replied that her native laborers were paid in coin, and it would be an infringement of the natives' freedom to forbid them to spend the produce of their labor as they chose.[87]

At this second rebuff Fuller, one of the clerks at the Colonial Office, felt nothing further could be done unless the arms trade in Fiji were prohibited, whereupon the Colonial Office might urge Queensland to conform for the sake of uniformity.[88] Fiji was not as serious an offender in this respect as Queensland, where the natives' wages were higher, and where there were no restrictions on the purchase of arms and ammunition. In Fiji there was a gun license and a gun tax; but in order to compete with Queensland for labor, the Fiji government had to allow returning natives to be paid with firearms.[89] The secretary of state might have acted on Fuller's suggestion by using the more direct influence he had in the affairs of the crown colony of Fiji to insist that arms be not supplied to native laborers. By doing so he would have further penalized Fiji in her quest for labor, and there is no evidence that he was prepared to do this.

The next approach to Queensland was made as a result of the native outrages about which the Australian Intercolonial Conference of 1881 protested to Britain.[90] Kimberley deplored the fact that the Australian colonies generally criticized the Navy for not punishing these crimes, and yet

85. Hicks-Beach to Kennedy, 2 Dec. 1879, *P.P.* 1883, XLVII, c. 3641.
86. Gorrie to Hicks-Beach, 18 Aug. 1879, *P.P.* 1883, XLVII, c. 3641.
87. Kennedy to C.O., 11 March 1880, C.O. 234/40.
88. Minute by Fuller on Kennedy to C.O., 11 March 1880, C.O. 234/40.
89. Robinson to Carnarvon, 13 Jan. 1875, C.O. 83/6; A. J. L. Gordon to Sir A. Gordon, 29 Nov. 1875, Gordon, *Records*, I, 338.
90. Kimberley to Kennedy, 16 Jan. 1881, *P.P.* 1883, XLVII, c. 3641.

refused to contribute anything toward naval expenditure,[91] while Queensland on the one hand joined in the resolution of protest, and on the other aided and abetted the outrages by refusing to ban the sale of firearms to natives.[92]

In reply to Kimberley the Queensland government again equivocated; it stated that it would be useless for Queensland to forbid the sale of firearms to natives so long as French and German nationals sold them freely.[93] In this reply the Colonial Office saw a ray of hope; if there were an international convention on the sale of arms, Queensland could hardly then refuse to prohibit the traffic.[94]

Until this time the Colonial Office view was that an approach to other powers would be premature. It felt that the colonial government might repudiate any agreement made by the imperial government.[95] Nevertheless it preferred to have agreement with Queensland before such a convention was held.

It was not until Griffith came to power in Queensland in November 1883 that Queensland prohibited the export of firearms.[96] With the change of governments Queensland ceased to be recalcitrant, and greatly to the surprise and gratification of the Colonial Office,[97] invited the other Australian colonies and Fiji to adopt a similar ban on the export of arms and ammunition, which they did early in 1884.[98]

About the same time the High Commissioner issued a regulation for the Western Pacific forbidding British vessels to carry arms or ammunition, or British subjects to sell or

91. Kimberley's minute on Loftus to Kimberley, 29 Jan. 1881, C.O. 201/595. The Australian colonies agreed to contribute at the 1887 Colonial Conference.

92. Kimberley's minute on Kennedy to Kimberley, 4 April 1881, C.O. 234/41.

93. Kennedy to Kimberley, 4 April 1881, C.O. 234/41.

94. *Ibid.*, minute by Fuller.

95. Minutes by Fuller, Herbert, Kimberley on Kennedy to Kimberley, 12 July 1881, C.O. 234/41.

96. *Qd. Government Gazette*, 22 Nov. 1883. This regulation was incorporated as s. 9 in the Qd. Act, 47 Vict., No. 12.

97. Minute by Mercer on Loftus to Derby, 3 Jan. 1884, C.O. 201/600.

98. Musgrave to Derby, 8 May 1884, C.O. 234/44.

supply them to natives.[99] Early in 1881 the High Commissioner had been asked by the Colonial Office[100] to extend a similar regulation which applied only to Samoa,[101] but he had refused on the grounds that it would prove impossible to enforce it.[102] Since that date the appointment of further deputy commissioners and the improved relations between the High Commission and the Navy made the task of enforcement less difficult.

Having achieved agreement between the Australian colonies, Fiji, and the High Commission, the Colonial Office turned to the Foreign Office to urge an early agreement with the powers on the question.[103]

V

Pacific island laborers were recruited and employed by French, German, and United States nationals. The French governments in New Caledonia and the Society Islands had their own system of labor regulation, as did the German government in the territory annexed by it in 1884. Before Fiji was annexed the American government had attempted to give its consul there power to regulate the affairs of its subjects in the islands.

From its earliest concern with the labor trade the British government realized it could not be effectively controlled without co-operative action by the powers whose subjects were concerned with it. The necessity for such action became more urgent when recruiters avoided the first British legislation by sailing under a foreign flag. The need for an approach to other powers was acknowledged in all quarters in Britain, and by colonial governors, administrators, and missionaries in the Pacific area.

In this, as in the movement for the suppression of the

99. No. 1, 1884, C.O. 808/85.
100. Kimberley to Gordon, 17 Jan. 1881, *P.P.* 1883, XLVII, c. 3641.
101. No. 5, 1879, C.O. 808/85.
102. Gordon to Kimberley, 21 April 1881, *P.P.* 1883, XLVII, c. 3641.
103. C.O. to F.O., 6 June 1884, *P.P.* 1887, LVIII, c. 5240.

slave trade, Britain took the initiative. The slave trade treaties[104] applied only to the African slave trade, and the right of search granted to the signatories of the treaties held only within a defined area. Moreover, France, the principal power other than Britain concerned in the labor trade in the Pacific, had never granted the full right of search to other powers; the most she had permitted was a limited verification of papers between 1845 and 1855. The United States had also withheld from other powers the right of search until her treaty with Britain in 1862.

It was natural, at first, that Britain should think of international action against the labor trade in terms of an extension of the slave trade treaties to the Pacific. Shortly after the passage of the 1872 act, Britain approached the United States with a view to having the 1862 treaty extended to the Pacific. The United States made co-operation conditional upon Britain's prohibiting the engagement of Chinese coolies for employment in British colonies or their transport in British ships.[105] Britain was not prepared to give up this important source of labor[106] even though, since her failure to ratify the 1866 convention with China, only one British ship, by special arrangement, had taken Chinese coolies to British possessions. Though Thornton, the British ambassador, pointed out to the American Secretary of State that strict regulations covered the engagement, transport, and employment of Chinese coolies by British subjects, the American apparently continued to confuse the British system with that of the Portuguese at Macao.[107] From his negotiations Thornton gained the impression that the United States, having just abolished slavery, was inclined to think that no other country had ever done anything in that respect.[108] Because, in official

104. For treaties, see *Instructions for the Guidance of Commanders of H.M. vessels engaged in suppression of Slave Trade*, H.M.S.O., 1892.
105. Thornton to Granville, 10 Nov. 1873, C.O. 83/4.
106. *Ibid.*, minute by Carnarvon.
107. Thornton to Granville, 10 Nov. 1873, C.O. 83/4.
108. Memorandum from Thornton enclosed in F.O. to C.O., 3 Sept. 1874, C.O. 83/5.

circles in Britain, there was sympathy for the Southern states during the Civil War, many Americans may have doubted the sincerity of Britain's traditional opposition to slavery and the slave trade, and the settlement following the Treaty of Washington may not have restored confidence. In any case the United States refused to co-operate in controlling the labor trade in the Pacific. An earlier approach had been made to the United States in 1869 following the *Young Australian* and *Daphne* cases.[109] But on this occasion nothing more was considered than the possible extension to the Pacific of an act prohibiting American citizens from engaging in the coolie trade.[110] As the act had already proved inadequate, nothing much was to be expected from its extension.

In 1870 the British ambassador to France was instructed to enquire whether the French government would co-operate for the control of the labor trade in the Pacific.[111] The two countries agreed to send similar instructions to their respective consuls and naval commanders in the region,[112] but the Admiralty was doubtful whether anything would come of this, for as the law then stood, it was practically impossible to convict offenders.[113] The 1872 act was ineffective because of the absence of similar foreign legislation. The lack of support from France in this respect led Herbert to state that the French "connive at, if they do not positively encourage kidnapping."[114]

Scarcely a year passed without someone's drawing attention to the need for an international convention on the matter. The Colonial Office thought that two conditions needed to be fulfilled before other powers were approached: there should be uniformity in the legislation of the Australian colonies, Fiji, and the High Commission on the arms traffic,[115]

109. Clarendon to Thornton, 2 Sept. 1869, *P.P.* 1871, XLVIII, c. 399.
110. Thornton to Clarendon, 23 Sept. 1869, *P.P.* 1871, XLVIII, c. 399.
111. F.O. to Lyons, 19 Feb. 1870, F.O. 58/127.
112. F.O. to Admiralty, 18 April 1870, F.O. 58/127.
113. Admiralty to F.O., 30 April 1870, F.O. 58/127.
114. Minute on Admiralty to C.O., 18 Feb. 1874, C.O. 83/5.
115. See p. 173, above.

and a thorough enquiry should be held into the "different measures which might prove most efficacious for the suppression of existing evils."[116] The first of these conditions was fulfilled early in 1884, and the second about the same time with the publication of the report of the royal commission appointed to enquire into the working of the Western Pacific Orders-in-Council.

As the arms question was most urgent, Britain communicated with the powers concerned,[117] all of whom, except the United States, were willing to enter into an agreement. The United States was not convinced of the need for such an agreement, and asked for further information,[118] which the Colonial Office supplied. When experienced British administrators from the Pacific, like Des Voeux[119] and Thurston,[120] visited the United States they made representations through the British Embassy to the United States Secretary of State, as did also missionary organizations. But these were of no avail.

Like the native, the foreigner was outside the system the imperial government had set up for the control of the labor trade. The attempts to remedy this were unsuccessful, and the problem was not solved until administrations were set up throughout the islands.

116. C.O. to Admiralty, 22 Jan. 1883, *P.P.* 1883, XLVII, c. 3641.
117. *P.P.* 1887, LVIII, c. 5240.
118. Enclosure in F.O. to C.O., 27 Sept. 1884, *P.P.* 1887, LVIII, c. 5240. No definite reason is given for the later refusal to join an international convention; Bayard to West, 11 April 1885, enclosure in F.O. to C.O., 7 May 1885, *P.P.* 1887, LVIII, c. 5240.
119. Des Voeux, *My Colonial Service*, II, 93-94.
120. C.O. to F.O., 26 March 1887, *P.P.* 1887, LVIII, c. 5240.

CHAPTER IX. FIJI AND QUEENSLAND— THE LAST PHASE

The imperial government took no decisive part in the processes that led to the end of the recruiting of Pacific islanders for employment in Fiji and Queensland. In the late sixties and early seventies representations were made to the Colonial Office to prohibit recruiting on the grounds that its regulation was impossible. At the time there was much to support that contention; there was no good government in Fiji and the Queensland act left many loopholes for abuse. But the imperial government allowed recruiting to continue, and the case for disallowance weakened as administration of the immigration improved.

It was not for any reason connected with its regulation that the labor trade came to an end. In Fiji the Pacific islander was gradually replaced by the Indian coolie. Queensland chose to exclude the Pacific islander by joining a federation pledged to a "White Australia."

I

In Fiji, after annexation, the Queensland act of 1868 was adopted for the regulation of the labor trade. But with the arrival of the first governor, Sir Arthur Gordon, the trend in the administration of the Pacific island labor immigration was away from the Queensland system, in which the government simply supervised an immigration carried on by private individuals, toward the Indian coolie emigration system, in which the government participated more directly and bore some of the cost. Gordon went to Fiji from colonies to which Indians were indented, with the definite intention of introducing Indian coolie labor to that colony as well. Although Indian labor was more costly, its ample and certain supply and general adaptability made it preferable to Pacific island labor, which it gradually displaced. In general the imperial government favored this substitution of a proved system of immigration for one which had caused it continual embarrassment. However, it was on the initiative of Sir Arthur Gordon, and not the Colonial Office, that the change from Pacific island to Indian indentured labor took place.[1]

Immediately before annexation the attempts of the consul and the *de facto* government of Fiji to administer the labor trade had completely broken down under the strain of the financial crisis of 1873-1874. In 1874 there were 3,000 laborers due to be returned to their islands for whom the planters could provide neither wages nor the cost of the return passage.[2] Nor were there ships available to return the laborers; of the ten ships engaged in the labor trade at the beginning of 1874, only two were still in commission at the end of the year.[3]

The adoption of the Queensland act of 1868 did not effectively meet this situation. Under the Queensland law labor was recruited and returned by private agencies under government supervision. In Fiji the system carried on by the planters had broken down and the circumstances demanded government intervention if the natives were to be paid and returned. From 1875 the Fiji government set aside an annual amount for Pacific island labor immigration. For the first two years about half this amount was spent on return passages.[4] Much of it was in the form of an advance to planters, which together with the interest, was to be secured by a first claim on the planter's land.[5]

---

1. Gordon at first intended that Indian labor should supplement Pacific island labor. See his speech at his swearing-in ceremony, Gordon, *Records,* I, 178. See also I. M. Cumpston, "Sir Arthur Gordon and the Introduction of Indians into the Pacific," *Pacific Historical Review,* XXV (1956), 369-388.

2. Gordon to Carnarvon, 28 April 1876, *P.P.* 1876, LIV, c. 1624.

3. Layard to Robinson, 12 Feb. 1875, C.O. Confidential Print No. 49, C.O. 808/12.

4. Gordon to Carnarvon, 28 April 1876, and Carnarvon to Gordon, 29 June 1876, *P.P.* 1876, LIV, c. 1624.

5. Gordon to Carnarvon, 27 March 1876, C.O. 83/9.

This trend away from the practice of the Queensland government, which refused to subsidize colored labor immigration, was continued after the arrival of the first governor, Sir Arthur Gordon. In an address to the planters at his inauguration ceremony[6] Gordon expressed the hope that the planters would agree to supplement Pacific island labor with Indian coolie labor. In the meantime Gordon repealed the regulations modeled on the Queensland act and replaced them by two ordinances for the introduction and employment of Pacific island immigrants. The first[7] dealt with the introduction and return of islanders and was considered by the Colonial Office to be more satisfactory than the Queensland act in respect to the regulations for the return of the natives, but less satisfactory in respect to the clauses prescribing the number of immigrants to be carried on recruiting vessels. Gordon was criticized for leaving rather too much to be provided for by the powers given to him under the ordinance to issue regulations. The Colonial Office preferred that as much as possible should be included in the ordinance, so that it came before the Council and was brought to the notice of the Colonial Office.[8] The second ordinance[9] provided for the relations between the immigrant and the employer, and was the basic ordinance in this respect until the consolidating ordinance of 1888[10]—the last important Fiji ordinance dealing with the immigration of Pacific islanders.

These two ordinances involved the government of Fiji more directly with recruiting than was the case in Queensland. In Queensland the government merely issued licenses to recruit and exercised a general supervision over the immigration; in Fiji the government acted as an agent between the employer and the recruiter. All applications for labor had to be made to the government, which arranged for the recruit-

6. Gordon, *Records*, I, 178 ff.
7. Ordinance XXIV, 1876.
8. Carnarvon to Gordon, 22 Dec. 1876, *P.P.* 1878, LV, 241.
9. Ordinance XI, 1877.
10. Ordinance XXI, 1888.

ing to be done by masters of ships under the supervision of a government agent.[11] This was very similar to the Indian coolie system without the depot at the place of recruiting. Such depots in the islands had been suggested for Queensland and Fiji recruiting as early as 1869,[12] but the suggestion was never adopted because the Colonial Office was unwilling to take any step which might increase the pressure to annex islands in the Pacific.

While the Colonial Office welcomed the trend toward bringing the regulation of Pacific island labor into line with that of Indian coolie labor, it was cautious about the practicability of the ordinance, which Walcott, the Emigration Commissioner, regarded as a "tentative and experimental measure."[13] In Bramston's opinion it was a piece of "over legislation," and he referred in particular to the provisions for the medical care of the natives, which it was beyond the resources of the colony to carry out.[14] Gordon was again criticized for reserving to himself powers to issue regulations on any matter affecting the laborer. This contrasts curiously with Queensland, where in the opinion of the Colonial Office there was "under regulation," and where the Colonial Office would have welcomed the exercise of greater power by the governor had that been possible.

The Colonial Office did, however, commend the ordinance for being in advance of Queensland legislation in restricting the hours of labor[15]—the Queensland government never legislated on this matter. The provision for payment of the wages of a deceased islander to the Treasury[16] preceded by four years a similar measure in Queensland, as did the provisions for the medical care of the immigrants. But

11. Ordinance IX, 1877, Part IV.
12. Reverend J. Graham at public meeting, Sydney, 8 Feb. 1869, report enclosed in Belmore to Granville, 26 Feb. 1869, *P.P.* 1868-1869, XLIII, 408.
13. Minute on Ordinance XI, 1877, enclosed in Gordon to C.O. 14 March 1877, C.O. 83/13.
14. Minute by Bramston, Gordon to C.O., 14 March 1877, C.O. 83/13.
15. Ordinance XI, 1877, s. LXVIII. Such a clause had been included in previous Fijian legislation, Cakobau Rex. 34, 1872.
16. Ordinance XI, 1877, s. LXXVI.

in one important respect the ordinance was criticized as being less acceptable than the Queensland legislation. The rate of wages provided for under the Fiji ordinance was £3 per annum,[17] while under the Queensland Act it was £6 per annum. Moreover the term of service for Fiji was much longer—five years; in Queensland it was three years.

These provisions were not only against the interests of the native, but they added to the difficulties of Fiji recruiters. Fiji had not been able to attract the number of Pacific islanders it needed. To help increase the supply, the government in 1877 had extended the financial help given earlier in returning natives, by voting a sum of £5,000 to be used toward the introduction of 1,000 Pacific islanders.[18] By August of that year only 110 had been recruited and the government admitted failure.[19] The low wages and long period of service provided for in Ordinance XI were partly responsible for this, for of the limited number of natives ready to recruit, most preferred the better pay, shorter service, and greater attractions of Queensland. Fiji had also lost favor because of the large number whose return was delayed by the financial failure of planters in 1873-1874. Bramston and Herbert had this in mind when they criticized the provision in Ordinance XI for the re-engagement of islanders after the first five-year period. This, they thought, would incline the islanders to believe that those who did not return at the end of their first engagement had been kidnaped.[20]

Bramston, in criticizing the method of recruiting for Fiji under this ordinance, had foreseen that the small number recruited for Fiji would not make it profitable for the masters of vessels to recruit for the government, and the latter would either have to assume full responsibility for it, or it would cease altogether.[21] The difficulty of recruiting in-

17. Ordinance XI, 1877, s. LXXIII.
18. Ordinance XIX, 1877.
19. Gordon to Carnarvon, 9 Aug. 1877, *P.P.* 1878, LV, 241.
20. Minutes on Gordon to Carnarvon, 14 March 1877, C.O. 83/13.
21. Minute by Bramston on Gordon to Carnarvon, 14 March 1877, C.O. 83/13.

creased the cost charged to the planters for the introduction of Pacific islanders. This narrowed the difference in cost between the Indian coolie and the Pacific islander, and inclined the planter toward the former.

In 1876 Gordon had drawn up a draft ordinance for the introduction of Indian coolies.[22] Carnarvon had warned him that there was strong opposition from certain sections of the public in England to the extension of the coolie system to other colonies[23] and that his plan might not be approved; but in 1878 the ordinance was approved and came into operation.[24] A few months later the first shipload of coolies arrived in Fiji.

For a time the two systems of immigrant labor continued side by side. The wages and rations of the coolie were more costly than those of the Pacific islander; but as the government contributed one-third of the cost of the introduction and return passage of coolies, and nothing toward these costs in respect of Pacific islanders[25] the latter were only slightly less expensive than the former. More Pacific islanders than Indians were introduced from 1878 to 1882,[26] but after that date the employers showed a definite preference for Indians. The Colonial Sugar Refining Co. led the way in this respect, and in 1883 threatened to withdraw its plant and equipment to Queensland if it was not assured of a steady and sufficient

22. Enclosure in Thurston to Mitchell, 13 July 1877, *P.P.* 1878, LV, 241.

23. Carnarvon to Gordon, 29 June 1876, *P.P.* 1876, LIV, c. 1624. The Anti-Slavery Society had protested against Gordon's proposals; see *Anti-Slavery Reporter*, 1 Jan. 1876.

24. Ordinance VI, 1878.

25. The amounts annually voted for Pacific island immigration were used for general administrative purposes, for special purposes, such as £500 for an enquiry to be made in the New Hebrides and Solomons as to why so few Pacific islanders recruited for Fiji (Gordon to Carnarvon, 9 Aug. 1877, *P.P.* 1878, LV, 241), and for wages and return passages unpaid by bankrupt planters. Under Ordinance XI, 1877, the planters were obliged to pay the costs of introduction and return of Pacific islanders.

26. Between 1878 and 1882 9,223 Pacific islanders were introduced (enclosure in C.O. to F.O., 27 Nov. 1884, *P.P.* 1887, LVIII, c. 5240). By the 1881 census there were only 588 Indians in Fiji; by the 1891 census there were 7,468 Indians and 2,267 Pacific island laborers. See *Fiji Legislative Council Paper* No. 35, 1947.

supply of Indian labor.[27] It was, however, two-faced about this, for, when the Queensland government temporarily discontinued the introduction of Pacific island labor, the company threatened to confine its activity to Fiji unless the Queensland government allowed the re-introduction of Pacific islanders.

By 1908 Pacific island immigration in Fiji had virtually ended. This was brought about not by any action on the part of the imperial government, but by the gradual substitution of a system of indenture found to be more satisfactory to all parties. Here there was a significant difference between Fiji and Queensland. In the former colony there was no opposition to the adoption of the alternative of Indian labor, while in the latter no government could remain in power which disregarded the strong opposition among the European working class to Asian immigration. The end of Pacific island immigration in Queensland came about in a different way.

II

In Queensland a decision to end the immigration of Pacific islanders had been taken in 1885;[28] it was to become effective at the end of 1890. The decision had been made following the Royal Commission enquiry into the recruiting of natives in the New Guinea area, where some of the worst atrocities in the history of Queensland's labor trade had been committed. Though the report of the enquiry conduced to the decision, the desire to preserve a purely European community, and the fear of the white working-class of competition from colored labor were more important factors. At the same time a move was made to replace the large plantation by the small farm, so that it would be possible to dispense with colored labor.

It was suggested at the Colonial Office that Griffith had

27. Fairgrieve to the Des Voeux, 15 Feb. 1883, C.O. 384/143.
28. 49 Vict., No. 17, s. 11.

no real intention in 1885 of stopping the immigration. He passed an act that involved no immediate responsibility, in order to keep the support of the working-class interests at a time when he needed it. As a result of the financial crisis of 1890-1891 and the Great Strike, there was a wave of reaction against the working-class program, and Griffith took advantage of this to repeal his 1885 measure.[29]

This view obscures the fact that the 1885 act was complementary to the plan put into operation at the same time by Griffith to replace the large plantations by small farms. His decision in 1892 to repeal the clause of the 1885 act prohibiting the introduction of Pacific islanders was a courageous admission that this plan was not sufficiently advanced to enable the colony to dispense with colored labor. In announcing his decision[30] Griffith reiterated his opposition to permanent reliance on colored labor in the sugar industry. He outlined what the government had done to reorganize sugar cultivation, and he stated his conviction that sugar could be grown in Queensland exclusively by white labor. But he pointed out that the laboring classes had resented the introduction of European labor to take the place of Pacific islanders, whose exclusion they had welcomed. The sugar industry therefore was threatened by a failure of its labor supply. This added to the difficulties caused by falling prices and the very serious financial crisis of 1890-1891. In view of these facts and the majority report of the Royal Commission of 1889 on the sugar industry which recommended the continuation of Pacific island labor, Griffith introduced a bill in April 1892 to enable the reissue of licenses for that purpose.[31]

The controversy that this decision aroused brought into review the whole history of the immigration to Queensland.

29. Minute by W. H. Mercer on notice of question by Kimberley in the House of Lords, 3 May 1892, C.O. 234/55.

30. Griffith's manifesto enclosed in Norman to Knutsford, 13 Feb. 1892, P.P. 1892, LVI, c. 6686.

31. 55 Vict., No. 38.

The missionary groups in Australia joined with the labor movement in petitioning the Queensland government against it. In England the Aborigines Protection Society and the Anti-Slavery Society made representation to the Colonial Office, and questions were asked in the House of Commons. This controversy in 1892 resembled very much that of 1868-1870 when the first legislation was introduced, but there were some significant differences. In the nineties the churches and missionaries were not as united in their opposition to the labor trade because the circumstances had changed. In the sixties and seventies it was true that the native had neither the command of language nor the experience of plantation life to enable him to understand the contract. The provisions for the supervision of recruiting gave him little real protection. On these grounds the missionaries could contend with some justice that the imperial government should disallow the Queensland act. But by the nineties the situation had changed. In all the islands where recruiting took place there were natives who had experience of Queensland plantations and knowledge of English. The Queensland act had been amended, and since 1886 there had been very few instances of any abuse, and no serious case at all. The regulations issued under the 1892 act further reduced the likelihood of abuse by placing Queensland recruiting ships under the jurisdiction of the High Commissioner.[32] The argument that the act should be disallowed could not be advanced with the same degree of support from the facts as in 1868.

Some of the missionaries recognized this. The churches in Queensland generally were not opposed to the resumption of recruiting.[33] The main source of the missionary opposition in Australia was J. G. Paton, who had been the principal Presbyterian missionary in the New Hebrides when the

32. No. 4, Regulations enclosed in Norman to Knutsford, 20 May 1892, *P.P.* 1892, LVI, c. 6808.
33. See pamphlet by A. C. Smith, convenor of Presbyterian Missions in Queensland, enclosure in Norman to C.O., 19 Jan. 1893, C.O. 234/56.

Queensland labor trade began. To secure the disallowance of the Queensland act he wrote personally to the premier of Queensland,[34] addressed meetings, wrote pamphlets, formed organizations, and secured a personal interview at the Colonial Office.[35] He criticized the Presbyterian Church in Queensland for not protesting against the act, and recommended the exclusion of that church from the proposed federation of Presbyterian Churches of Australia.[36] Paton sought to replace the missionary and church allies he had lost by joining forces with the labor movement in Queensland who also opposed the act. The labor paper, the *Worker*, printed a protest written by Paton that was distributed outside all churches in Queensland,[37] and Paton supplied material used by labor members in the debate on the bill in the Queensland Parliament.[38]

Paton also had an ally in the Victorian Legislative Assembly, which passed resolutions condemning the re-introduction of Pacific islanders to Queensland. These were treated by the Colonial Office[39] in the same way as the Canadian resolutions in favor of Home Rule for Ireland. On that occasion Kimberley replied that Home Rule for Ireland was no business of the Canadian Parliament.

The center of opposition in England was in the House of Commons, though the Anti-Slavery Society and the Aborigines Protection Society petitioned the Colonial Secretary,[40] and the Presbyterian Missionary Society formed the J. G. Paton Memorial Fund to raise money to campaign against the act. Those most active in the Commons were S. Smith, the member for Flintshire, and J. E. Ellis, the member for

34. Enclosure 1 in John G. Paton Mission Fund to C.O., 29 April 1892, C.O. 234/55.
35. Referred to in Paton to C.O., 16 Dec. 1893, *P.P.* 1895, LXX, c. 7912.
36. A. C. Smith, enclosure in Norman to C.O., 19 Jan. 1893, C.O. 234/56.
37. *Qd. P.D.* LXVII, 4, statement by Annear.
38. *Qd. P.D.* LXVII, 103-104.
39. Minute by Mercer on notice of question by S. Smith in Commons, 23 May 1892, C.O. 234/55.
40. A.P.S. to Knutsford, 23 May 1892, C.O. 234/55; Anti-Slavery Society to Knutsford, 3 June 1892, *P.P.* 1892, LVI, c. 6808.

Rushcliffe, Nottinghamshire. Smith was a well-known Liberal philanthropist. He was born in Scotland and trained for the Presbyterian ministry, but had become a Liverpool cotton broker. In the sixties he went to India to make a survey of its cotton resources for the Manchester Cotton Supply Association. From that time he developed and retained a keen interest in Indian affairs, like so many of those in the Commons who took an interest in the Pacific island labor trade.

At the beginning of May Smith asked the Under-Secretary of State for the Colonies whether the imperial government would stop the re-introduction of Pacific islanders into Queensland because it was indistinguishable from the slave trade.[41] The Colonial Office made quite clear, in preparing the draft reply to Smith, that it thought the labor trade to Queensland could be properly regulated and that it had no intention of disallowing the Queensland act on this or any other grounds.[42] Earlier secretaries of state had threatened to stop recruiting by Queensland ships if that colony's regulations were not satisfactory,[43] but that time had now passed.

Ellis was a member of a Midland Quaker family. He, too, had an interest in Indian affairs, and in 1905 was Under-Secretary of State for India. He was a person of independent thought and balanced judgment, and sought, not the disallowance of the act, but assurances that adequate safeguards would be provided.[44]

Earlier, in the House of Lords, Kimberley had sought a similar assurance,[45] and Lord Knutsford, the Colonial Secretary, had telegraphed to the governor of Queensland asking him to delay the issuing of licenses under the act until the Colonial Office had an opportunity of examining the act and regulations.[46] The Colonial Office was satisfied with the act

41. *Hansard*, 4th Series, IV, 1892.
42. Minutes on notice of Smith's question, 29 April 1892, C.O. 234/55.
43. See pp. 83, 98, above.
44. *Hansard*, 4th Series, IV, 972, 1515.
45. *Ibid.*, IV, 141.
46. Knutsford to Norman, 9 May 1892, C.O. 234/55.

and regulations, and made only one reservation: it remained to be seen "whether Queensland officials would report and Queensland juries convict."[47]

When the report of the first recruiting voyage was received at the Colonial Office, Mercer noted the absence of the medical report on the health of returning natives which the new regulations required.[48] The Colonial Office regarded this report as the best evidence of the way in which the labor had been treated in Queensland. The Marquess of Ripon, who had succeeded Lord Knutsford as Colonial Secretary in August, asked the governor to forward full and complete details.[49] And so from the end of 1892 until the cessation of the trade, copies of the license, the return, the government agent's report, and the medical officer's report were forwarded to the Colonial Office for every voyage made.

These documents were very carefully scrutinized. In 1900 Edward Marsh noted that one recruiting vessel returned to the islands more natives than it was licensed to recruit. This led him to calculate whether the ship was returning more natives than the law allowed a ship of that size to carry.[50] If any irregularity was noticed, this fact was carefully recorded, and when the next return referring to that ship came in, it received special attention.[51]

As a result of this very careful supervision there was not a single case of serious abuse in this final phase of the labor trade. There were minor irregularities such as the occasional failure to return a native to the exact place where he was recruited, or of recruiting wives without their husbands. There was one charge of kidnaping, and the Colonial Office watched this carefully to see whether the Queensland jury would convict. The charge was dismissed through insufficient

47. Minute on Norman to Knutsford (enclosing regulations), 20 May 1892, C.O. 234/53.
48. Minute by Mercer on Norman to Ripon, 16 July 1892, C.O. 234/53.
49. Ripon to Norman, 27 Oct. 1892, *P.P.* 1893-1894, LXI, c. 7000.
50. Minute by E. H. Marsh on Griffith to C.O., 5 March 1900, C.O. 234/70.
51. Minute by Mercer on Norman to Ripon, 22 Nov. 1894, C.O. 234/60.

evidence,[52] but as the behavior of the government agent had been brought into question, he was dismissed from the service.[53]

At the end of 1893 Paton had an interview with Buxton, the Parliamentary Under-Secretary of State for the Colonies, in an attempt to persuade the Colonial Office to forbid the immigration. He was asked to prepare a memorandum.[54] On receipt of this the Colonial Office pointed out that Paton's evidence for irregularities was, with one small exception, drawn from the period before 1885.[55] This was characteristic of the representations made against the Queensland labor trade after 1892. Evidence was advanced that may have been true of the first decade and a half of the labor trade, but no longer held true for the nineties.

There were still some unsatisfactory features of the employment of these islanders in Queensland. The mortality rate, though much lower than in the eighties, was still high; the depopulation of Melanesia was an admitted fact, and the extent to which recruiting contributed to this was under discussion. From time to time the Queensland government forbade recruiting where depopulation was serious.[56] But neither depopulation nor high mortality could bring into question the efficient regulation of the immigration. The high mortality rate arose mainly from the fact that the Pacific islander was not well-adapted to hard and continuous plantation work.

The administration of this labor system, therefore, was not sufficient ground for attacking it or advocating its abolition. Whereas in the seventies a case could have been made for bringing the immigration to an end on the ground that

52. *William Manson* case; enclosure in Norman to Ripon, 24 April 1895, C.O. 234/61.
53. Enclosure in Acting High Commission to Ripon, 22 May 1895, *P.P.* 1895, LXX, c. 7912.
54. Paton to C.O., 16 Dec. 1893, *P.P.* 1895, LXX, c. 7912.
55. C.O. to Paton, 13 Jan. 1894, *P.P.* 1895, LXX, c. 7912.
56. *Qd. Government Gazette*, 16 July 1892, announced that recruiting was prohibited in Tongoa and Santa Cruz; 10 March 1896, at Torres Island; 2 March 1898, at Efati.

its proper regulation was impossible, in the nineties there was no such case. One might have argued that the service of the islanders overseas was not in their own, nor the islands', best interests, but such considerations played little part in terminating the immigration. From at least as early as 1884 colored labor had been regarded as an interim measure to allow the sugar industry to adapt itself to the exclusive use of white labor. Recruiting was resumed in 1892 only to give the industry more time for this adjustment. In the debate on the 1892 bill it was estimated that indenture would end within ten years or with the federation of the Australian colonies.[57] It was in fact the latter that ended the system, but federation was merely the occasion of a decision which had already been accepted by Queensland governments, if not by its planters, that Queensland should be, like the other Australian colonies, a self-governing Anglo-Saxon state, and that sugar should be produced by small independent European cane farmers, rather than by planters employing large numbers of servile colored laborers.

It has been shown that on two occasions Queensland governments opened the door to Indian indentured laborers, though none actually entered. On the first occasion, in 1862, their sponsors withdrew when the Queensland government refused financial assistance.[58] On the second occasion in 1882 and 1883, McIlwraith opened the door, but when the planters came to introduce their Indian laborers they found a new host, Griffith, who politely but firmly turned them away.[59] Others wanted to bring in Chinese labor: in the early sixties an offer came from T. Gardiner Austin, the British Guiana representative in China,[60] and in 1883 another came from Messrs. Butterfield and Swire, merchants of Hong Kong.[61]

57. *Qd. P.D.* LXVII, 103, 104, 186.
58. See p. 54, above.
59. See p. 132, above.
60. Emigration Commissioners to C.O., 23 Sept. 1861, C.O. 234/5; Bowen to C.O., 10 Jan. 1862, C.O. 234/6.
61. Derby to Officer Administering Qd. Government, 18 July 1883, *Qd. V. & P.* 1883-1884, p. 1421.

Behind the proposals to introduce Indians in 1883 were northern sugar planters like J. E. Davidson and J. B. Lawes. Following closely on the rejection of their plans came Griffith's bill in 1885 by which the indenture of Pacific islanders was to cease in 1890. These threats to their labor supply led such planters to lend strong support to the movement for creating a new colony in North Queensland, independent of the Brisbane government and free to introduce colored labor if it desired. The period from 1885 to 1887 was one of the most active of the northern separation movement.[62] Conventions were held, petitions circulated, debates initiated in Parliament, deputations sent to the Secretary of State for the Colonies, and meetings arranged in London. Yet for all this activity there was nothing more to show than a motion in favor of separation defeated by thirty-six to nine votes in Parliament in September 1886, and a bill introduced by Griffith in 1887 to divide the colony into three divisions for financial purposes.

The movement in the north came to life again when the indenture of Pacific islanders ceased in 1890. At the same time there was activity at Rockhampton for the separation of central Queensland. Here the sugar planters were less concerned than pastoralists and Rockhampton urban interests, who complained about administrative and financial injustices rather than problems of labor supply. Nevertheless, representatives of the two areas united in October 1890 in support of another motion in Parliament favoring separation, but again they were defeated. Griffith opposed separation because he did not want the north to become a plantation state of wealthy landlords and cheap colored labor, nor did he want a further set of tariff barriers to hinder trade and commerce. Yet he was aware of the genuine administrative, financial, and representational grievances of the north, and in order to meet these he introduced his bill in 1892 to divide

62. See R. G. Neale, "The New State Movement in Queensland," *Historical Studies*, IV, No. 15 (Nov. 1950), 198-213.

Queensland into two provinces with a central government on the Canadian model.[63] This compromise was acceptable in the north, but not to the central separation movement. The bill passed the Assembly but was defeated in the Council. For the planters of the north this setback was mitigated by the fact that the indenture of Pacific islanders was resumed in 1892. As considerable numbers of Japanese were also being indentured at this time for work on sugar plantations, the labor problems of planters were temporarily in abeyance, and their interest in the separation movement waned.

By the mid-nineties it was clear to Queensland planters that there was little prospect of creating a new state as a means of circumventing the Queensland government's decision to exclude Indian and Chinese indentured labor. It must also have been clear that along with them, Pacific island and Japanese laborers would be excluded if Queensland joined an Australian federation. Every person of note who supported federation also spoke in favor of keeping Australia free of Asian and colored labor, and one of the Royal Commissioners on the Sugar Industry in Queensland wrote in 1889 that "if Queensland is to join in a federated Australia . . . the request of planters for the extension of the terms of the 11th section of the Pacific Islanders Labourers Act of 1885 is practically disposed of."[64]

It may therefore seem surprising that after the failure of the separation movement, there was not at least some resistance by the planters to federation. It is true that between 1895 and 1899 Queensland stood aside from the federation movement, but this was for reasons other than the probable immigration policy of a federal government. When the referendum on federation was held in Queensland in September 1899, the northern districts returned more than an 80 per cent majority in favor of federation, one of the highest in the

63. Norman to C.O., 1 Oct. 1892, 14 Oct. 1892, C.O. 234/54. For second reading debate on bill, see *Qd. P.D.* LXVII (1892), 786 ff.

64. *Royal Commission into Condition of Sugar Industry in Queensland* (Brisbane, 1889), p. XLVIII, minority report by W. H. Groom.

state.[65] This seems to support the view that with the failure of the separation movement, sugar growers were resigned to the temporary nature of their colored labor force, and that they would in future be wholly dependent on European labor. They were therefore more interested in the protected market for the whole of Australia that federation would probably secure for them, and the likelihood that the federal government would continue the policy of the Queensland government by assisting them to meet the higher costs incurred by substituting European for colored labor.

When the first Federal Parliament met in 1901 the expected legislation concerning immigration and the sugar industry was soon introduced. Beginning with Victoria in 1855, all the Australian colonies had passed statutes restricting the entry of Chinese by limiting the number of immigrants in relation to the tonnage of the vessels in which they arrived. Some statutes imposed discriminatory entrance and poll taxes, or denied the right of naturalization to Chinese. There was a move at the Premiers' Conference in 1896 to extend this legislation to the Japanese, increasing numbers of whom were entering Queensland in the nineties. No agreement was reached on this, but the whole question was dealt with comprehensively by the Immigration Restriction Act of 1901.[66] This continued the policy implicit in the legislation of the colonial governments, making it uniform for the whole continent and applying it to immigrants from any country, but with the obvious intention of excluding non-European colored immigrants. The act gave the Commonwealth government power to exclude any immigrant who could not pass a prescribed test in any European language,[67] and others who came within the definition of prohibited immigrants. This effectively ended the indenture of Japanese to Queensland,

65. R. S. Parker, "Australian Federation: The Influence of Economic Interests and Political Pressures," *Historical Studies*, IV, No. 13 (Nov. 1949), 1-24.

66. No. 17, 1901, Commonwealth of Australia.

67. Amended to any prescribed language by s. 5 of the Immigration Restriction Amendment Act of 1905 (No. 17, 1905).

although the maximum number of Japanese allowed in Queensland at any one time had been agreed upon by Queensland and Japanese governments in October 1900.

The Pacific Island Labourers Act[68] was also passed by the Commonwealth government in the same year. Sir Edmund Barton, the Prime Minister, in his speech to Parliament on the bill, outlined the Queensland legislation on the subject in order to show that the Commonwealth bill was both consistent with it and its logical completion.[69] The bill provided for the proportionate reduction of the number of Pacific islanders introduced until 31 March 1904, when the immigration would cease, while all Pacific islanders in the colony on 31 December 1906 were to be deported. In the Federal Parliament some members pointed out that the bill discriminated against immigrants according to their place of origin[70]— a principle which had been omitted from the Immigration Restriction Act at the express wish of the Secretary of State.

The Aborigines Protection Society protested against the indiscriminate and compulsory deportation contemplated under the act.[71] The hardships this would entail were enumerated in a petition to His Majesty purporting to be signed by three thousand Pacific islanders in Queensland.[72] In forwarding this petition the Governor-General enclosed a cautionary note from the Commonwealth Department of External Affairs that those who collected these "signatures" may have been more interested in retaining the services of the laborers than concerned about their rights.[73] However, the British Resident in the Solomon Islands confirmed the view that natives returning to their islands after a long absence did suffer real hardship.[74] When this point was made

68. No. 16, 1901, Commonwealth of Australia.
69. *Commonwealth of Australia Parliamentary Debates*, IV, 5496.
70. *Com^th, P.D.*, V, 5828.
71. *A.P.S. to C.O.*, 18 April 1902, *P.P.* 1903, XLIV, cd. 1554.
72. *P.P.* 1902, LXVI, cd. 1285.
73. Tennyson to Chamberlain, 30 Sept. 1902, *P.P.* 1903, XLIV, cd. 1554.
74. Enclosure in Chermside to Chamberlain, 10 Sept. 1902, *P.P.* 1903, XLIV, cd. 1554.

in a question in the House of Commons, the Secretary of State for the Colonies, Joseph Chamberlain, replied that the Commonwealth government had been reminded of the necessity for careful consideration of the rights of Pacific islanders who had become residents of Queensland.[75] Chamberlain refused to interfere in any other way, declining to make His Majesty's Government a court of appeal for the affairs of a self-governing colony.[76]

In view of these representations the Commonwealth government passed an act[77] granting exemptions from deportation in certain cases. The 1901 act recognized only those exemptions under section eleven of the Queensland act of 1884. The new act gave exemptions to those for whom deportation would be a special hardship because of long residence in Queensland, marriage, or certain other reasons. Of the 6,389 Pacific islanders in Queensland in 1906, only 691 were exempt under the Queensland and Commonwealth acts.[78]

There were, of course, protests as late as 1906 that the sugar industry would be ruined by being deprived of its colored labor, alone suitable for work in the tropics. This had been a constant theme of protest against any reform restricting the supply of such labor, and it proved as false on this occasion as it had in the past. As then the Queensland government had assisted the sugar industry to meet the higher costs of employing European labor, so now the Commonwealth government did the same. It imposed a protective duty of six pounds per ton on raw and refined cane sugar, and an excise tax of three pounds per ton on manufactured sugar, with a rebate of two pounds per ton on sugar extracted from cane grown by white labor.[79] This gave sugar produced by

75. Chamberlain in answer to Sir Brampton Gurdon, 22 Oct. 1902, *P.P.* 1903, XLIV, cd. 1554.
76. Chamberlain to Chermside, 30 Aug. 1902, *P.P.* 1902, LXVI, cd. 1285.
77. No. 22, 1906.
78. Royal Commission on Polynesians to be deported, *Qd. V. & P.* 1906, II, 395.
79. Excise (Sugar) Act, 1902.

white labor an advantage of two pounds per ton over home-produced sugar grown by black labor, and five pounds per ton over imported sugar, which in any case would be produced by black labor. In 1903 the rebate was replaced by a bounty,[80] and from 1907 both the excise and the bounty were increased by one pound per ton. The bounty remained in force until 1913 though at a diminishing rate in 1911 and 1912, but by then the sugar industry was well-established as the first where cane sugar was produced entirely by white men.

So it was that federation brought to an end the indenture of Pacific islanders to Queensland. Because the working class and the labor movement consistently opposed the introduction of cheap colored labor it might be concluded that they were mainly responsible for the federal government's policy. This would be to overlook the non-economic grounds for the White Australia policy. At that time it had support from all classes for cultural and racial reasons. The federal government's legislation merely expressed the will of Australians to exclude from their country persons of non-European stock. This attitude was the determining factor in ending the indenture of Pacific islanders to Queensland. In Fiji, on the other hand, Pacific islanders were gradually replaced by Indian coolies because planters found the supply more reliable and the labor more efficient. In both places these local circumstances were decisive; neither in Queensland nor Fiji did the imperial government play any significant part in ending the recruitment and employment of Pacific islanders.

80. Sugar Bounty Act, 1903.

APPENDIX

The tables in these appendixes and the figures in the text refer mainly to the subject matter of Chapter VII. Table 1 shows that throughout the whole period, 61,160 Pacific islanders were brought to Queensland; Table 4 that 39,681 had been returned to the islands by 31 December 1905. The number of recorded deaths throughout the period amounted to 13,301 by the end of 1904.[1] By this reckoning, without allowing for deaths in 1905, there should have been 8,448 Pacific islanders in Queensland at the end of 1905. There were in fact on 10 April 1906 6,389. Allowing for the deaths from the end of 1904, and for those who returned to the islands between January and April 1906, there still remained some 2,000 natives unaccounted for over the whole period. These were probably unrecorded deaths, as since 1884 no Pacific islander could remain in Queensland except under the act, and the number of exemptions amount to only 350.[2] This means that the mortality figures in Table 3 are lower than the true death rate. Figure 3 shows those returned, the deaths, and those awaiting return as a proportion of the number recruited throughout the whole period.

The number of Pacific island laborers in Queensland may seem a small proportion of the total European population, and the immigration of islanders small in relation to the number of European immigrants. Indeed the largest number of Pacific islanders in Queensland at any one time was a little over 11,000 between 1883 and 1886 (Table 2) when the European population was rising from 287,475 to 342,614.[3] The largest number of islanders introduced in any one year was 4,004 in 1883 (Table 1), when the European immigration was 22,823.[4] Yet Figure 2 shows that in the areas where the laborers were concentrated, they formed a considerable proportion of the population, e.g., 36 per cent in the Mackay area. This helps to explain the strength of working-class opposition to Pacific island labor, which otherwise would seem out of proportion to the fact that Pacific islanders constituted only 2.9 per cent of the total population of the colony in 1881. Of course the opposition is to be explained mainly by reference to the principle of excluding colored labor, which if

1. 1868-1877, *Qd. V. & P.* 1878, II, 39; 1878-1884, *Qd. V. & P.* 1885, II, 554; 1886-1894, *P.P.* 1895, LXX, 148, p. 371. From 1894 in the Annual Report of the Pacific Island Immigration Department. The figure for 1885 could not be found and an average for the preceding five years was used.

2. Secretary Department of External Affairs to Governor General, 29 Sept. 1902. Enclosure in Tennyson to Chermside, 30 Sept. 1903. *P.P.* 1903, XLIV, cd. 1554.

3. *Qd. V. & P.* 1889, II, 985.

4. *Qd. V. & P.* 1884, II, 607.

abandoned in the case of Pacific islanders, would have made resistance to the immigration of Asian labor more difficult.

Though small in relation to the European population of Queensland, the number of immigrants to Queensland was large in proportion to the population of the islands from which they came. The tables for the place of recruitment and the islands to which the natives were returned are not complete, but for the years given, 25,535 natives came from the New Hebrides alone. Until the end of 1874, 5,912 had been recruited in the New Hebrides. By the end of 1877 these should all have been returned except for those who re-engaged; but only 3,678 had gone back. At this rate over the whole period it would be safe to say that some 8,000 probably did not return to the island group. The total population of the New Hebrides was estimated in 1910 at 60,000, but as considerably higher than that throughout the nineteenth century.[5] The labor trade to Queensland certainly contributed directly to the depopulation of these islands, and probably indirectly as well, though these effects are more difficult to measure.

5. Foreign Office Handbook, No. 147. C. Belshaw, *Changing Melanesia*, Appendix II.

TABLE 1. Place of recruitment of Pacific islanders introduced into Queensland

Year	Loyalty	New Hebrides	Banks	Torres	Santa Cruz	Solomons	Other Islands or Unspecified	Total
1863–1868	578	1347	160				556	2641
1869		168	145					313
1870	27	390	217				9	643
1871	290	824	142			82	14	1352
1872	44	313	104					461
1873	7	704	241	42				994
1874	47	1166	151	15		124		1503
1875	5	1806	135	6		710	19	2681
1876		1307	260	8		74	39	1688
1877		1714	156	86			30	1986
1878							1463	1463
1879							2182	2182
1880		1499	409	26		61		1995
1881		1789	163	24	5	655	7	2643
1882		2161	415	123[1]		440		3139
1883		2542	327	8	99	1028		4004[2]
1884							3289	3289
1885							1916	1916
1886								1595
1887							1988	1988
1888							2291	2291
1889		1114	178	120		620		2032
1890		1104	175	15		1165		2459
1891		456	58	20		516		1050
1892		172	49	8		235		464
1893		605	59	50		416		1130
1894		631	95	80		108	945	1859
1895		430	70	24	13	577	191[3]	1305
1896		286	73			423		782
1897		158	43			733		934
1898		425	32			721		1178
1899		637	37			848		1522
1900		713	73	73		884		1743
1901		462	55	13		1151		1681
1902		240	21	3		875		1139
1903		345	21	8		663		1037
1904		17	2			59		78
								61,160

1. This figure includes 37 from Low Island.
2. This figure does not include 1,269 recruited from New Britain, New Ireland, Duke of York Island, and other islands to the east of these.
3. These were recruited in the Gilbert and Ellice Islands.

Sources: Returns published in *Qd. V. and P.* From 1889 onward these appear in the *Annual Reports* of the Pacific Island Immigration Department.

TABLE 2. The numbers of Pacific island laborers employed in Queensland

Date	Numbers	Source
1868 2 March	1543	Census. *Qd. V. and P.* 1882, I, 1179
1868 31 Dec.	2127	*P.P.* 1871, XLVIII, 208
1869 31 Dec.	2135	*Ibid.*
1870 18 June	2033	*Ibid.*
1871 1 Sept.	4336	Census. *Qd. V. and P.* 1882, I, 1179
1875	4441	Estimated Mean Population. *PP.* 1883, XLVII [C. 3641], 423
1876 1 May	5108	Census. *Qd. V. and P.* 1877, II, 410
1877	5874	Estimated Mean Population. *P.P.* 1883, XLVII [C. 3641], 423
1878	5869	*Ibid.*
1881 3 April	6348	Census. *Qd. V. and P.* 1882, I, 1179
1883	11,443	Musgrove to Derby, 13 March 1884. C.O. 234/44
1886 1 May	10,037	Census. *Qd. V. and P.* 1887, II, 1303
1887 1 Jan.	8723	*P.P.* 1895, LXX, 148, p. 371
1888 1 Jan.	8200	*Ibid.*
1889 1 Jan.	7580	*Ibid.*
1890 1 Jan.	8115	*Ibid.*
1891 5 April	9428	Census. Commonwealth *P.P.* 1901-1902, I, 835
1892 1 Jan.	8627	*P.P.* 1895, LXX, 148, p. 371
1893 1 Jan.	7979	*Qd. Legislative Council Journal* 1893, I, 1194
1894 1 Jan.	7489	*Qd. Legislative Council Journal* 1893, I, 1194
1895 1 Jan.	7853	*Qd. V. and P.* 1897, II, 1086
1895 31 Dec.	8163	*Ibid.*
1896 31 Dec.	8444	*Ibid.*
1897 31 Dec.	8224	*Qd. V. and P.* 1898, II, 728
1898 31 Dec.	8485	*Qd. V. and P.* 1899, 1st Sess., p. 1296
1899 31 Dec.	8795	*Qd. V. and P.* 1900, V, 680
1900 31 Dec.	9324	*Qd. V. and P.* 1902, I, 1116
1901 31 March	9327	Census. Commonwealth *P.P.* 1901-1902, I, 835
1902 31 Dec.	8878	*Qd. V. and P.* 1903, II, 444
1903 31 Dec.	8614	*Qd. V. and P.* 1904, 2nd Sess., II, 62
1904 31 Dec.	7879	*Qd. V. and P.* 1905, 2nd Sess., I, 742
1906 10 April	6389[1]	*Qd. V. and P.* 1906, II, 395

1. Of this number 691 held exemption tickets under 47 Vict., No. 12, and under the Commonwealth Act, No. 22, 1906. Commonwealth Act, No. 16, 1901, required that the remainder be returned to the islands.

TABLE 3. Mortality rate of Pacific island laborers employed
in Queensland

Year	Rate per 1000	Year	Rate per 1000
1868	47.90	1888	52.00
1869	21.50	1889	57.00
1870	18.20	1890	46.44
1871	43.10	1891	61.74
1875	85.11	1892	42.74
1876	63.60	1893	52.57
1877	51.39	1894	43.93
1878	85.87	1895	35.99
1879	55.78	1896	36.55
1880	62.89	1897	33.87
1881	64.74	1898	28.70
1882	82.64	1899	39.75
1883	75.31	1900	31.28
1884	147.74	1901	37.13
1885	98.84	1902	38.22
1886	58.20	1903	35.49
1887	59.00	1904	26.49

Sources: 1868-1871, 1886—The rate is calculated from the number of deaths per year given in *Qd. V. and P.* 1878, II, 39, and *P.P.* 1895, LXX, 148, p. 371, in relation to the number of laborers in the colony given in Table 2. The rate is therefore only approximate. 1887-1889—Return enclosed in Norman to Knutsford, 23 Aug. 1892. C.O. 234/53. 1875-1885, 1890-1900—Reports of the Registrar General in *Qd. V. and P.* 1872-1874—No figures available.

TABLE 4. Numbers returned and islands to which returned

Year	Loyalty	New Hebrides	Banks	Torres	Cruz Santa	Solomons	Other Islands or Unspecified	Total
1864							70	70
1865							30	30[1]
1866							7	7
1867							166	166
1868							34	34
1869	51	189						240
1870	83	466	16				32	597
1871	219	443	88					750
1872	32	270	142				3	447
1873	5	176	72					253
1874	122	697	206			30	5	1060
1875	27	279	82			40		428
1876		423	220			2		645
1877		735	86	26		59		906
1878							1602	1602[2]
1879							1354	1354
1880							1564	1564[3]
1881							1048	1048
1882							1200	1200
1883							1112	1112
1884							2033	2033
1885							1857	1857
1886							2611	2611
1887							1981	1981
1888							1292	1292
1889		665	115	70		334		1184
1890		623	153	58	74	446	19	1373
1891		524	112	34		306		976
1892		440	44	41		304		829
1893		551	115	43		492		1201
1894		371	89	1		341	1	803
1895		317	32	5		385	4	743
1896		308	22	35		243		608
1897		256	55	50	47	476		884
1898		224	34	17	29	257	132	693
1899		352	73	2	36	459	1	923
1900		273	75	4		588		940
1901		266	20		1	542		829
1902		826	66	10		872	1	1775
1903		385	59	55		566		1065
1904		92	36	1		506		635
1905							933	933
								39,681[4]

1. These islanders, said to be returned, left Queensland, not for their native islands, but for the *bêche de mer* fisheries in Torres Strait.

2. A later return (*Qd. V. and P.* 1880, I, 1138) gives 1,628 as the number returned.

3. Nine deaths were reported between sailing from Queensland and arrival in the islands.

4. On 30 June 1906 there were 5,280 Pacific islanders awaiting return under the Commonwealth Act No. 16, 1901 (*Qd. V. and P.* 1906, II, 454).

Sources: Qd. V. and P. and *Annual Reports* of the Pacific Island Immigration Department.

BIBLIOGRAPHY

MANUSCRIPT SOURCES

OFFICIAL

The most valuable files at the Record Office for the study of the labor trade in the Pacific before the annexation of Fiji are C.O. 201 (New South Wales) and F.O. 58 (Pacific). The governors of New South Wales were charged with general surveillance over the affairs of British subjects in the Pacific, and the consuls and naval commanders often reported directly to them as well as to the Foreign Office and the Admiralty. One therefore finds in the New South Wales file reports from consuls and naval commanders in the Pacific, interdepartmental correspondence relating to these, as well as correspondence concerning legal matters in the Pacific which were the responsibility of the Colonial Office as the colonial courts had jurisdiction over crimes committed in the Pacific.

All matters relating to kidnaping in the Pacific between 1869 and 1871 are gathered together in F.O. 58/125-130.

After the annexation of Fiji much of the material relating to the recruiting and the employment of Pacific island labor which formerly appeared in C.O. 201 and F.O. 58 is to be found in C.O. 83 (Fiji) and C.O. 225 (Western Pacific), although some of it has been transferred to C.O. 384 (Emigration, Eastern and Australian) which appears to be a file for matters referred to the Land and Emigration Commissioners and which continued to be used after those offices became defunct in 1878.

All matters relating to the labor trade to Queensland are in C.O. 234 (Queensland).

The deficiency in the C.O. files is that after 1873, when the Entry Books cease, there is no complete record of outgoing correspondence. The Entry Books were replaced by Indexes to Correspondence (for Queensland, C.O. 450), which are a record of outgoing correspondence with a statement of its subject. For the detailed contents of outgoing correspondence after 1873, one has to rely on the draft replies attached to the incoming correspondence. Where these are missing one can often find them in the incoming file of the relevant department; but if no draft reply is attached to a despatch from a governor, then there is no record of its detailed content except perhaps in the archives of the colony to whose governor it was addressed.

Most of the relevant correspondence from the Admiralty,

Treasury, and Foreign Office appears in the Public Offices and Miscellaneous sections of the C.O. files. Full reports of many of the special voyages through the islands by Her Majesty's ships were printed for Parliament, e.g., Report of Proceedings of H.M.S. *Rosario*, 1872 (*P.P.* 1872, XXXIX [C. 542]), or appeared in the C.O. files, e.g. Report of Voyage of H.M.S. *Pearl*, 1874, C.O. 83/7.

A. PUBLIC RECORD OFFICE

i. Colonial Office Files

Fiji

C.O. 83. Original Correspondence, Secretary of State, Vols. 1-42, 61-67 (1872-1885, 1895-1897).

C.O. 537. Supplementary, Vol. 115 (1874-1897).

New South Wales

C.O. 201. Original Correspondence, Secretary of State, Vols. 513-573 (1860-1873) and selected volumes from 1874-1900.

Queensland

C.O. 234. Original Correspondence, Secretary of State, Vols. 1-71 (1859/1860-1900).

Victoria

C.O. 309. Original Correspondence, Secretary of State, Vols. 109-113 (1873-1875) and selected volumes from 1876-1900.

Western Pacific

C.O. 225. Original Correspondence, Secretary of State, Vols. 1-68 (1878-1904).

C.O. 537. Supplementary, Vol. 136 (1876-1897).

Colonies General

C.O. 380. Drafts of legal instruments, governors' commissions, instructions, etc., Vols. 112, 114, 127.

Emigration

C.O. 384. Original correspondence. Despatches, Eastern and Australian, dealing with emigration matters including Indian and Pacific island laborers, Vols. 108-154 (1876-1885).

ii. Foreign Office Files

Pacific Islands

F.O. 58. Fiji, Vols. 115 (1869), 118 (1870), 120 (1871): consular jurisdiction in Fiji with reference to kidnapping, Vol. 124: kidnapping of South Sea Islanders, Vols. 125-130: despatches from Sir Arthur Gordon, Vol. 155.

iii. Admiralty Files

Adm. 1. In letters C.O. and Australian Station, Vols. 6026, 6151, 6166-7, 6192 and 6197 (1871-1876).

Adm. 13. Standing Orders and Instructions to Commanders-in-Chief, Vols. 4-6.

Adm. 50. Admirals' Journals, Australian Station, Vols. 324-326 (1855-1884).

B. INDIA OFFICE

Public despatches to India. Original correspondence, Vols. 3-7 (1860-1864).

UNOFFICIAL

There is much valuable material in the Gladstone, Carnarvon, and Kimberley papers, on the labor trade as it relates to the problems of administration in the Pacific. Perhaps the most valuable is the correspondence of Sir Arthur Gordon; the Stanmore Papers in the British Museum contain much material relating to Fiji and the Western Pacific between 1875 and 1884, as do the larger part of two of the four volumes of his letters to Gladstone. The greater proportion of one volume of the Carnarvon Papers consists of letters from Gordon between 1875 and 1878. Some of these letters are reprinted in four volumes of correspondence which Gordon printed privately. Together these constitute a most important source for British policy and administration in the Pacific.

Gladstone's private notes of cabinet meetings he attended place in perspective the concern of the imperial government with the labor trade in the Pacific. It was on the agenda of only one cabinet meeting attended by Gladstone.

There are copies in the Gladstone Letter Books of Gladstone's letters to Kimberley, the originals of which are in the Kimberley Papers. The Kimberley Papers contain correspondence between Kimberley and the second Marquis of Normanby from 1871-1874, when the latter was governor of Queensland. The Kimberley Papers also contain some useful Admiralty memoranda of 1871-1872 relating to the role of Her Majesty's ships on the Australian station in the suppression of kidnaping.

The Disraeli Papers at Hughenden were consulted for some correspondence from Carnarvon on the annexation of Fiji which does not appear in Hardinge's *Life of Carnarvon*.

A. PUBLIC RECORD OFFICE

   i. Carnarvon Papers. P R O 30/6

     Vol. 21. Lord Stanley of Alderley.

     Vol. 25. Correspondence. Colonial Governors, Australia, March 1874–Feb. 1878.

     Vol. 39. Correspondence. Colonial Governors, New Zealand and Fiji, March 1874–Feb. 1878.

     Vols. 42-47. Colonies, Miscellaneous, 1874-1878.

     Vol. 48. Colonies Various, Correspondence, Memoranda, Confidential Prints, etc., 1874-1877.

     Vol. 51. Miscellaneous Memoranda—Political, 1874-1877.

     Vol. 93. Australia, New Guinea, and the Pacific, 1873-1876.

  ii. Granville Papers. P R O 30/29

     321. Pacific Islands, 1875-1885.

     258. Slave Trade, 1819-1873.

     367-370. Slave Trade, 1878-1883.

B. BRITISH MUSEUM

Stanmore Papers
Additional Manuscripts 49199-49285.

Gladstone Papers

     44107. Vol. XXII. Correspondence with Sir Frederic Rogers, 8th Bart., 1851; 1st Baron Blachford, 1871; 1840-1889.

     44111. Vol. XXVI. Correspondence with E. H. Knatchbull-Hugessen, 1st Baron Brabourne, 1880; 1864-1885.

     44224-29. Vols. CXXXIX-CXLIV. Correspondence with John Wodehouse, 3rd Baron Wodehouse, 1st Earl of Kimberley, 1866; 1859-1896.

     44230. Vol. CXLV. Correspondence with A. Kinnaird, 10th Baron Kinnaird; 1838-1882.

     44287. Vol. CCII. Correspondence with George Frederick Samuel Robinson, Viscount Goderich, 2nd Earl of

Ripon and 3rd Earl de Grey of Wrest, 1859, 1st Marquis of Ripon; 1883-1897.

44299. Vol. CCXIV. Correspondence with G. A. Selwyn, Bishop of Lichfield; 1828-1875.

44319-22. Vols. CCXXXIV-CCXXXVII, Correspondence with Hon. Sir Arthur Hamilton Gordon, G.C.M.G., 1st Baron Stanmore, 1893; 1851-1896.

Letter Books
44538-43. November 1869–March 1874.

Official Papers including memoranda prepared for the use of the cabinet.
44617-9. Vols. DXXXII-DXXXIV, June 1871–Dec. 1872.
44627-8. Vols. DXLII-DXLIII, April 1881–Dec. 1882.

Cabinet minutes attended as Chancellor of the Exchequer and as Prime Minister, 1853-1894, including minutes by other members of the cabinet.
44638-41. Vols. DLIII-DLVI, 1870-1874.
44642-47. Vols. DLVII-DLXII, 1880-1886.
44648. Vol. DLXIII, 1893-1894.

C. NATIONAL REGISTER OF ARCHIVES

 i. Hicks Beach Papers, Williamstrip Park, Fairford, Glos.

 ii. Kimberley Papers, Kimberley Park, Kimberley, Norfolk.

D. NATIONAL TRUST

Disraeli Papers, Hughenden, Bucks.

E. MISSIONARY SOCIETIES

The letters, journals, and reports in the archives of the London Missionary Society are, with the reports of the commanders of Her Majesty's ships, the most valuable source of information about the Pacific islands and the native communities.

The society, however, had no resident missionaries in the New Hebrides and the Solomons, where most of the recruiting was done. An unsuccessful attempt was made to locate the records of the Presbyterian missionaries in the New Hebrides. These missionaries were sponsored by a number of different branches of the Presbyterian Church in Scotland, Nova Scotia, Victoria, and New

Zealand. The records do not appear to have survived. Fortunately there is much correspondence from the missionaries and their societies in the Colonial Office files, and a considerable amount of printed material in the *Parliamentary Papers* and in pamphlet form.

The archives of the society for the Propagation of the Gospel contain some manuscript records of the Melanesian Mission, but these are mainly letters from the Bishop of Melanesia on administrative matters. The headquarters of the Melanesian Mission in London has no manuscript records.

The records of the Anti-Slavery Society are in the Bodleian Library, Rhodes House, Oxford, and contain material from their correspondents in Australia and the Pacific on the labor trade.

London Missionary Society, Livingstone House, 42 Broadway, S.W.1.

> *South Seas*
> Letters from missionaries
> > Boxes 31-35   1869-1880
> > Box 38   1884-1885
> > Box 42   1892-1893
> Journals
> > Boxes 10-12   1845-1889
> Reports
> > Boxes 1-3   1866-1892
> *Australia*
> Letters from Representatives
> > Boxes 7-9   1864-1880
> Journals
> > 1 Box   1800-
> *Papua*
> Letters from missionaries
> > Boxes 1-4   1872-1889
> *Outletters*
> > Boxes 8-10   1866-1875

The Society for the Propagation of the Gospel, 15 Tufton St. Westminster, S.W.1.
Letters received, Australia and New Zealand 1865-1874
Letters received, New Zealand 1865-1871

Anti-Slavery Society and Aborigines Protection Society, Archives in Bodleian Library, Rhodes House, Oxford.

CONTEMPORARY PRINTED SOURCES

OFFICIAL

A. PUBLIC RECORD OFFICE

Colonial Office. Confidential Prints.

Some of the material in these papers was later printed for Parliament, e.g. much of C.O. 808/45 is contained in C. 3863. But among them there are memoranda which give useful résumés, such as C.O. 808/54 on the supply of arms to Polynesians. Such memoranda are often a useful guide to manuscript sources.

B. PARLIAMENTARY PAPERS

i. British

Papers relative to the affairs of the colony of Queensland, 1861, XL [2890].

Correspondence relating to the Fiji Islands, 1862, XXXVI, 701.

Correspondence respecting the removal of the inhabitants of Polynesian Islands to Peru, 1864, LXVI, 607.

Correspondence relating to the importation of South Sea Islanders into Queensland, 1867-1868, XLVIII, 391 and 496; 1868-1869, XLIII, 408.

Correspondence respecting the deportation of South Sea Islanders, 1868-1869, XLIII [4222].

Report of Commission appointed to enquire into treatment of immigrants into British Guiana, 1871, XX [C. 393].

Correspondence and documents relating to the Fiji Islands, 1871, XLVII, 435.

Correspondence in regard to the deportation of South Sea Islanders, 1871, XLVIII, 79 and [C. 399].

Further correspondence relating to the importation of South Sea Islanders into Queensland, 1871, XLVIII, 468.

Pacific Islanders' Protection Bill, 1872, III, 497; Lords' Amendments, 503.

Report of proceedings of H.M. Ship, *Rosario*, during cruise among the South Sea Islands, Nov. 1871–Feb. 1872. 1872, XXXIX [C. 542].

Correspondence relating to the Fiji Islands, 1872, XLIII [C. 509].

Correspondence between the Governor of New South Wales and Earl of Kimberley respecting certain statements made by Captain Palmer in his book *Kidnapping in the South Seas,* 1872, XLIII [C. 479].

Further Correspondence respecting deportation of South Sea Islanders, 1872, XLIII [C. 496].

Communications respecting outrages committed upon natives of the South Sea Islands, 1873, L, 244.

Correspondence relative to the introduction of Polynesian labourers into Queensland, 1873, L. [C. 793].

Correspondence respecting outrages committed upon natives of the South Sea Islands, 1874, XLV, 232.

Instructions to Commodore Goodenough and Mr. Consul Layard to report on the Fiji Islands, 1874, XLV [C. 893].

Report of Commodore Goodenough and Mr. Consul Layard on the offer of cession of the Fiji Islands to the British Crown, 1874, XLV [C. 1011].

Report of Mr. Geohegan on Coolie Emigration from India, 1874, XLVII, 314.

Pacific Islanders' Protection Bill, 1875, IV, 455, and House of Lords' Amendment to Commons Amendments, 465.

Correspondence respecting cession of Fiji, 1875, LII [C. 1114] and [C. 1337].

Correspondence respecting Royal Commission to enquire into the treatment of immigrants into Mauritius. 1875, LIII [C. 1118].

Correspondence respecting affairs in New Guinea, 1876, LIV [C. 1566].

Further Correspondence as to the colony of Fiji, 1876, LIV [C. 1404] and [C. 1624].

A Return of South Sea Islanders introduced into Queensland, 1877, LXI, 29.

Further Correspondence as to the colony of Fiji, 1877, LXI [C. 1826].

Ordinances introduced by Sir Arthur Gordon to regulate the treatment of Polynesian labourers, and the introduction of coolies into Fiji, with correspondence, 1878, LV, 241.

Further Correspondence respecting New Guinea, 1883, XLVII [C. 3617 and [C. 3691].

Correspondence respecting the natives of the Western Pacific and the Labour Traffic, 1883, XLVII [C. 3641].

Correspondence respecting the natives of New Guinea, the New Hebrides and other Islands in the Pacific, 1883, XLVII [C. 3814].

Correspondence respecting New Guinea and other Islands of the Western Pacific, and the Convention at Sydney of Representatives of the Australasian Colonies, 1884, LV [C. 3839].

Correspondence respecting the Convention at Sydney, 1884, LV [C. 3863].

Report of Commissioners appointed to enquire into the working of the Western Pacific Order in Council, 1884, LV [C. 3905].

Reports concerning the state of affairs in the Western Pacific, 1884, LV [C. 4126].

Correspondence relating to the native population of Fiji, 1884-1885, LIII [C. 4434].

Memoranda of Conversations at Berlin on colonial matters between Mr. Meade and Prince Bismarck and Dr. Busch, 1884-1885, LIV [C. 4290].

Arrangement between Great Britain and Germany relative to their respective spheres of action in portions of New Guinea, 1884-1885, LIV [C. 4441].

Proceedings of the Colonial Conference, 1887, LVI [C. 5091].

Correspondence relating to the native population of Fiji, 1887, LVIII [C. 5039].

Correspondence relating to proposals for an International Agreement regulating the supply of Arms, Ammunition, Alcohol and Dynamite to natives of the Western Pacific, 1887, LVIII [C. 5240].

Return regarding the Sugar trade, 1888, XCIII, 353.

Correspondence relative to Conference on Sugar Bounties, London 1887, 1888, XCIV [C. 5259].

Proceedings and Papers laid before the Conference on Sugar Bounties, London 1887, 1888, XCIV [C. 5260].

Correspondence relating to Polynesian Labour in Queensland, 1892, LVI [C. 6686] and [C. 6808]; 1893-1894, LXI [C. 7000]; 1895, LXX [C. 7912].

Further Correspondence relating to the native population of Fiji, 1895, LXX [C. 7679].

Correspondence relating to the West Indies' Sugar Industry, 1897, LXI [C. 8359].

Report of the West Indies Royal Commission, 1898, L [C. 8655-57].

A Return of Colonial Bills to which the Royal Veto has been applied, 1901, XLVI, 363 (House of Lords Paper).

Papers relating to the Commonwealth Pacific Island Labour Act, 1901, LXVI [Cd. 1285].

Correspondence relating to the Commonwealth Pacific Island Labour Act, 1903, XLIV [Cd. 1554].

Report of Permanent Sugar Commissions established under the Sugar Convention, 1903, LXXV, 91.

A Return to Order relating to Sugar, 1887-1906, 1907, LXXXI, 334.

Report of Committee on Emigration from India to Crown Colonies and Protectorates, 1910, XXVII [Cd. 5192].

ii. Queensland. Votes and Proceedings of Legislative Assembly.

These were used exhaustively. Some of the papers printed for the British Parliament were also printed by the Queensland government, e.g., the Report of the Royal Commission appointed to enquire into the working of the Western Pacific Order in Council.

C. PARLIAMENTARY DEBATES

i. British

The recruitment and employment of Pacific Island laborers was the subject of question and/or debate in each session of the imperial Parliament from 1869 to 1875.

After 1875 the question of the labor trade was raised in 1877 by Belmore in the Lords (CCXXXII, 1197-1203), in 1882 in the Commons (CCLXXI, 30-31), in 1887 by Sir George Campbell and W. A. McArthur in the Commons (CCCXIII, 1405; CCCXVI, 1600; CCCXX, 1410).

In May and June 1892, at the time of the resumption of the labor trade to Queensland, many questions were asked by S. Smith, E. Ellis, and J. F. Hogan in the Commons. Smith initiated a debate in the Commons, 26 May 1892 (4th Series, IV, 1961). Questions were later asked in the Commons on a number of occasions in 1893 and 1895.

ii. Queensland Parliamentary Debates, 1860-1900

D. GENERAL

> *Instructions for the Guidance of Commanders of Her Majesty's ships employed in the suppression of the Slave Trade.*
> This was first issued in 1844, re-issued in 1865, 1882 and 1892, and contains the texts of all treaties, conventions, Acts of Parliament, Orders-in-Council, etc. relating to the Slave Trade.
> The Navy List.
> The Colonial Office List.

UNOFFICIAL

A. MISSIONARY AND ANTI-SLAVERY SOCIETY JOURNALS

> *The Chronicle of the London Missionary Society,* published monthly, consulted from 1861.
> *The First Voyage of the new* Southern Cross, *1874.* Melanesian Mission, 1874.
> *The Island Voyage.* Published annually by the Melanesian Mission. Consulted from 1877 to 1882, 1884 to 1887.
> *The Free Church Monthly and Missionary Record,* New Series, Edinburgh, 1882-1886.
> *The Colonial Intelligencer or Aborigines' Friend. The Journal of the Aborigines' Protection Society.* Consulted from 1858 to 1871, 1874 to 1882.
> *The Anti-Slavery Reporter, the Journal of the British and Foreign Anti-Slavery Society.* Consulted from 1856 to 1900.

B. NEWSPAPERS

> Much material relating to the labor trade appeared in the colonial newspapers, particularly the *Brisbane Courier* and the *Sydney Morning Herald.*
> Of English newspapers, *The Times* printed regular reports, and between December 1892 and February 1893 printed a series of articles by its special correspondent, Flora Shaw, on the Queensland Sugar Industry and the employment of colored labor.
> From time to time reports, usually from humanitarian or missionary sources, appeared in other English papers, particularly the Liberal organ, the *Daily News,* and the *Leeds Mercury,* whose proprietors and editors, members of the Baines family, were prominent Liberals.

C. Printed Books and Pamphlets

Most of the contemporary printed material was written by naval officers, consular or colonial service officers, missionaries or adventurers. The most authentic account by those actually engaged in the labor trade is probably Wawn's *The South Sea Islanders and the Queensland Labour Trade*. Wawn was the captain of a number of Queensland recruiting vessels, including the *Fanny* and the *Lizzie*, which were accused of kidnaping in the New Guinea area in 1883.

There is no contemporary record of the labor trade from the Pacific islanders' point of view; Fussell's *A Kanaka Slave*, the nearest approach, is a missionary account in story form, and is inaccurate in some details.

Anon. *Aborigines' Protection Society: Chapters in Its History*. London, 1899.
Anon. Article on Pacific Islanders' Protection Bill, *Westminster Review*, N.S. XLVIII (1875).
Bowen, Sir George. *Thirty Years of Colonial Government*. London, 1889.
Bramston, Sir John. "The Colonial Office from Within," *Empire Review*, April 1901.
Britton, H. *Fiji in 1870*. Melbourne, 1870.
Chesson, F. W. *Coloured Labour in the British Colonies*. London, 1872.
———. *How to Influence Members of Parliament*. London, 1870.
Churchward, W. B. *"Blackbirding" in the South Pacific*. London, 1888.
Codrington, R. H. *The Melanesians*. Oxford, 1891.
Des Voeux, G. W. *My Colonial Service*. 2 vols. London, 1903.
Fletcher, P. *The Sugar Industry of Queensland*. London, 1886.
Fussell, J. *A Kanaka Slave*. London n.d.
Goodenough, J. G. *Journal of Commodore Goodenough, during His Command as Senior Officer on the Australian Station, 1873-1875*. Edited, with a Memoir, by his widow. London, 1876.
Gordon, Sir Arthur. *Fiji: Records of Private and Public Life 1875-1880 (Private and Confidential)*. 4 Vols. Edinburgh, 1897-1910.
Guppy, H. B. *The Solomon Islands and Their Natives*. London, 1887.
Hope, J. L. A. *In Quest of Coolies*. London, 1872.
Kay, Rev. J. *Slave Trade in the New Hebrides*. Edinburgh, 1872.

Marindin, G. E. (ed.). *Letters of Frederic, Lord Blachford.* London, 1896.

Markham, Sir A. H. *Cruise of the* Rosario *amongst the New Hebrides and Santa Cruz Island, Exposing the Recent Atrocities connected with the Kidnapping of Natives in the South Seas.* London, 1873.

Moresby, J. *Two Admirals.* London, 1909.

Palmer, G. *Kidnapping in the South Seas. A Narrative of Three Months Voyage on H.M.S.* Rosario. Edinburgh, 1871.

Paton, J. G. *J. G. Paton, Missionary in the New Hebrides.* Autobiography edited by his brother. London, 1899.

———. 'The Kanaka Labour Trade' 1894. Pamphlet, Enclosure 14 July 1894. *P.P.* 1895, LXX [C. 7912].

Rannie, D. *My Adventures among South Sea Cannibals.* London, 1912.

Romilly, H. H. *Letters from the Western Pacific and Mashonaland,* 1893.

———. *The Western Pacific and New Guinea.* London, 1887.

Rose, Kinnaird. *Polynesian Labour and the New Trade Unionism.* Brisbane, 1892.

Shaw, Flora. *Letters from Queensland, by* The Times *Special Correspondent.* Reproduced from the *Times* of Dec. 1892, Jan. and Feb. 1893. London, 1893.

Smith, A. C. *Kanaka Labour Question, with Special Reference to Missionary Efforts in Plantations of Queensland.* Brisbane, 1892.

Speiser, Felix. *Two years with the Natives, in the Western Pacific,* 1913.

Steel, R. *The New Hebrides and Christian Missions, with a Sketch of the Labour Traffic.* London, 1880.

Teall, J. E. *Slavery and the Slave Trade. Facts and Memoranda compiled from Slave Trade Papers, the Statutes at Large and other sources.* London, 1889.

Wawn, W. T. *The South Sea Islanders and the Queensland Labour Trade.* London, 1893.

Wisker, J. "Trouble in the Pacific Islands," *Fortnightly Review,* XXXVII (1882).

LATER PRINTED WORKS

A. BIBLIOGRAPHIES FOR THE PACIFIC

Allen, P. S. *Stewart's Handbook of the Pacific Islands.* Sydney, 1920.

Conover, Helen F. *Islands of the Pacific: A Selected List of References.* Library of Congress: Division of Bibliography, Washington, 1943.

Davidson, J. W. "The Literature of the Pacific Islands," *Australian Outlook,* I, no. 1, March 1947, pp. 63-79.

Edwards, F. *Catalogue of Books, Maps and Prints Relating to New Zealand, the South Sea Islands and the Pacific Ocean.* London, 1932.

Leeson, Ida E. *A Bibliography of Bibliographies on the South Pacific.* Sydney, 1951.

Lewin, P. E. *The Pacific Region: A Bibliography of the Pacific and East Indian Islands, Exclusive of Japan.* London, 1944.

Taylor, C. R. H. *A Pacific Bibliography.* Wellington, 1951.

B. Books and Pamphlets

The labor trade in the Pacific has received very little attention from historians. The Australian aspect of it has been treated in its legislative setting by Myra Willard in *The White Australia Policy,* and in its relation to the sugar industry by Shann in his *Economic History of Australia.* In the context of imperial policy the first years of the labor trade have been briefly treated by Brookes, *International Rivalry in the Pacific,* and in more detail by Ward, *British Policy in the South Pacific,* and Morrell, *Britain in the Pacific Islands.*

Another serious gap in the secondary sources for the subject of this book is the lack of any history of Queensland or any biographies of her leading statesmen. All the Australian colonies suffer similarly in this respect, but Queensland most of all. Graham's *Life of Sir Samuel Griffith* is nothing more than a short essay.

There is a similar lack of histories of the island groups of the Pacific, particularly of those groups most affected by the labor trade.

Armstrong, E. S. *The History of the Melanesian Mission.* London, 1900.

Barton, E. J. T. (ed.). *Jubilee History of Queensland, 1859-1909.* Brisbane, 1909.

Bell, E. M. *Flora Shaw.* London, 1947.

Bell, K. N., and W. P. Morrell (eds.). *Select Documents of British Colonial Policy, 1830-1860.* Oxford, 1928.

Belshaw, C. S. *Changing Melanesia.* Oxford, 1954.

Bernays, C. A. *Queensland Politics during Sixty Years, 1859-1919.* Brisbane, 1920.

———. *The Roll of the Queensland Parliament. 1860-1926.* Brisbane, 1926

Bodelsen, C. A. *Studies in Mid-Victorian Imperialism.* Kjob, 1924.

Brookes, Jean I. *International Rivalry in the Pacific Islands, 1800-1875.* Berkeley, 1941.

Buell, R. L. *The Native Problem in Africa.* 2 vols. New York, 1928.

Campbell, P. C. *Chinese Coolie Emigration.* London, 1923.

Clark, C. M. H. *Select Documents in Australian History, 1851-1900.* Sydney, 1955.

Clowes, Laird. *The Royal Navy: A History from the Earliest Times to the Present.* London, 1897-1903. Vol. VII: 1857-1900.

Coghlan, T. A. *Labour and Industry in Australia.* Oxford, 1918.

Coupland, R. *The Exploitation of East Africa.* London, 1938.

Cumpston, Mary. *Indians Overseas in British Territories, 1834-1854.* London, 1953.

Deacon, A. B. *Malekula.* London, 1934.

Deerr, N. *Cane Sugar.* London, 1921.

Derrick, R. A. *History of Fiji.* Vol. I to 1872. Suva, 1946.

Dicey, A. V. *Law and Public Opinion in England.* London, 1914.

Drus, E. *The Colonial Office and the Annexation of Fiji.* Transactions of the Royal Historical Society. 4th Series, XXXII, 1950.

Dunbabin, T. *Slavers of the South Seas.* Sydney, 1935.

Ensor, R. C. K. *England, 1870-1914.* Oxford, 1936.

Fitzmaurice, E. G. *The Second Earl Granville.* 2 vols. London, 1905.

Foxcroft, E. J. B. *Australian Native Policy: Its History, Especially in Victoria.* Melbourne, 1941.

Garvin, J. L. *Life of Joseph Chamberlain.* Vols. I-III, London, 1932. Vol. IV by Julian Amery, 1951.

Gillion, K. L. *Fiji's Indian Migrants.* Melbourne, 1962.

Graham, A. D. *Life of Rt. Hon. Sir Samuel Griffith.* Brisbane, 1939.

Halévy, E. *History of the English People in the Nineteenth Century.* Vols. I-VI, London, 1949-1952.

Hall, H. L. *The Colonial Office.* London, 1937.

Hardinge, Sir A. H. *The Fourth Earl of Carnarvon.* 3 vols. London, 1925.

Harris, J. *A Century of Emancipation.* London, 1933.

Harrisson, T. *Savage Civilisation.* London, 1937.

Hicks-Beach, Lady V. *Sir Michael Hicks-Beach*. 2 vols. London, 1932.

Hitchins, F. H. *The Colonial Land and Emigration Commissioners*. Philadelphia, 1931.

Hogbin, H. I. *Experiments in Civilisation*. London, 1939.

Jacobs, M. G. *The Colonial Office and New Guinea, 1874-84*. Historical Studies, Vol. V, no. 18. Melbourne, May 1952.

Keith, A. B. *Responsible Government in the Dominions*. Oxford, 1938.

Knaplund, Paul. *The British Empire, 1815-1939*. London, 1942.

———. *Sir Arthur Gordon and Fiji*. Historical Studies, Vol. 8, no. 31., Nov. 1958.

Knibbs, G. H. *Prices, Price Indexes and Cost of Living in Australia*. Labour Report 1, Commonwealth Bureau of Census and Statistics, 1912.

Knorr, K. E. *British Colonial Theories, 1570-1850*. Toronto, 1944.

Koskinen, A. *Missionary Influence as a Political Factor in the Pacific Islands*. Helsinki, 1953.

Legge, J. D. *Australia's Colonial Policy*. Sydney, 1956.

———. *Britain in Fiji*. London, 1958.

Lilley, W. O. *Life of W. Brookes*. Brisbane, 1902.

Lloyd, C. *The British Navy and the Slave Trade*. London, 1949.

Lovett, R. *History of London Missionary Society*. 2 vols. London, 1899.

Lyng, J. S. *Non-Britishers in Australia*. Melborne, 1935.

McIntyre, W. D. *Disraeli's Colonial Policy: The Creation of the Western Pacific High Commission*. Historical Studies, Vol. IX, no. 35, Nov. 1960.

Mair, L. P. *Native Policies in Africa*. London, 1936.

———. *Australia in New Guinea*. London, 1948.

Martin, K. L. P. *Missionaries and Annexation in the Pacific*. Oxford, 1924.

Matheson, W. L. *Great Britain and the Slave Trade, 1839-65*. London, 1929.

Melbourne, A. C. V. "The Relations of Australia and New Guinea up to the Establishment of British Rule in 1888," *Journal of Royal Australian Historical Society*, XII, 1926-1927, Part v, pp. 288-314; XIII, 1927, Part iii, pp. 145-172.

Mellor, G. R. *British Imperial Trusteeship 1783-1850*. London, 1951.

Morley, John. *Life of William Ewart Gladstone*. 3 vols. London and New York, 1903.

Morrell, W. P. *Britain in the Pacific Islands.* Oxford, 1960.

Oliver, D. L. *The Pacific Islands.* Cambridge, Mass., 1951.

Pitt-Rivers, G. *The Clash of Culture and the Contact of Races.* London, 1927.

Prothero, G. W. (ed.). *Foreign Office Handbooks.* Historical Section: Nos. 42, 144-147.

Rivers, W. H. R. *The History of Melanesian Society.* Vol. II. Cambridge, 1914.

—— (ed.). *Essays in Depopulation of Melanesia.* Cambridge, 1922.

Roberts, S. H. *Population Problems in the Pacific.* London, 1927.

Scholefield, G. H. *The Pacific: Its Past and Future and the Policy of the Great Powers from the Eighteenth Century.* London, 1919.

Shann, E. O. G. *Economic History of Australia.* Cambridge, 1930.

Stanner, W. E. H. *The South Seas in Transition.* Sydney, 1953.

Wadham, S. M. and G. L. Wood. *Land Utilization in Australia.* Melbourne, 1939.

Ward, J. M. *British Policy in the South West Pacific.* Sydney, 1948.

Willard, M. *History of the White Australia Policy.* Melbourne, 1923.

Wilson, C. *The Wake of the Southern Cross.* London, 1932.

Yonge, C. M. *Life of John Coleridge Patteson.* London, 1874.

Young, G. M. *Portrait of an Age.* Oxford, 1936.

Young, W. A. *Christianity and Civilisation in the South Pacific.* London, 1922.

INDEX